BOOKS BY THALASSA CRUSO

Making Things Grow
A PRACTICAL GUIDE FOR THE INDOOR GARDENER

Making Things Grow Outdoors

To Everything There Is A Season
THE GARDENING YEAR

This is a Borzoi Book, published in New York by Alfred A. Knopf

Making Things Grow Outdoors

Making Things Grow Outdoors

*Photographs by
the author and
Ellen McNeilly*

Thalassa
Cruso

New York | Alfred A. Knopf | 1974

THIS IS A BORZOI BOOK
PUBLISHED BY ALFRED A. KNOPF, INC.

Copyright © 1971 by Thalassa Cruso
All rights reserved under International and
Pan-American Copyright Conventions. Published in
the United States by Alfred A. Knopf, Inc., New
York, and simultaneously in Canada by Random
House of Canada Limited, Toronto. Distributed
by Random House, Inc., New York.
ISBN: 0–394–46009–X
Library of Congress Catalog Card Number: 70–154903
Manufactured in the United States of America

Published October 25, 1971
Reprinted Three Times
Fifth Printing, July 1974

To *Rik Wheeler*

who first taught me to work hard

and to *Rick Hauser*

who compelled me to rediscover the process

Contents

Acknowledgments

Gardening knowledge is a complicated business: you gain it through experience, you acquire it through tradition, and you absorb it from all kinds of publications. As a result it is extremely hard to sort out and pinpoint where and how you learned about a process, a plant, or a material. Writing a gardening book based entirely upon personal experience makes giving proper credit even more difficult, for it is the rare gardener who does not adapt horticultural advice to his own particular situation.

I am the fortunate owner of a large horticultural library, some of it new, but much of it inherited from the former owner of our country garden who was an avid collector of gardening literature. I read gardening advice in books, magazines, and newspaper articles as other people read novels or detective stories, for sheer pleasure, and there is no one particular writer whose works have meant more to me than any other. They are all grist to my mill no matter how recent, or out of date, or inappropriate they may be for the climate in which I grow things. The accumulation of knowledge that has built up in my subconscious about garden matters by this jackdaw method makes it impossible to be certain of the source of some of my skills. If anywhere in this account I have appropriated ideas without due acknowledgment, I can only apologize.

For exact information concerning the names of the plants, I have used *The Royal Horticultural Society Dictionary of Gardening* and the invaluable new *Supplement,* and also the now hard-to-find *Hortus Second* by L. H. Bailey and Ethel Zoe Bailey, and Donald Wyman's new *Gardening Encyclo-*

pedia, but it has not always been possible to identify exactly the old varieties of plants we found established in our yards.

The imperial "we" that is used constantly in the text refers of course to my husband. It is his methodical, painstaking care that makes our gardens possible. I am all ideas and dash—and sloppiness. It is he who carries the projects through. He refuses to describe himself as a gardener; chore-man is the word he prefers. But there has never been such a choreman as he, and as the relatively unacknowledged backbone of our gardening activities I do not think he has had his due and I want to blazon it out.

There are others who deserve warm thanks: Jane Garrett, the most kind and patient of editors, who has had to contend with English spelling, a matter of unregenerate stubbornness on my part, last-minute changes of organization, and dis-graceful typing—let alone an illegible handwriting which, miraculously, she and her secretary, Ann Thorne, have learned to decipher; Ellen McNeilly, who so ably translated vague arm wavings and my own washed-out negatives into crisp authoritative photographs, and Rafael Palacios for his excellent maps. Also innumerable members of the personnel of Station WGBH Boston, very particularly my producer Rick Hauser, director Douglas Smith, and my assistants Nancy Ewell and Jane Goodrich, whose combined efforts brought about this horticultural Indian summer by putting across a TV series on Indoor Gardening.

In this connection, and in many other matters, particu-larly emphatic thanks are due to Catherine Codman Ep-pinger for her unselfish help and ungrudging effort in more ways than can be enumerated—and for her friendship.

Appreciative thanks should also be given to Joseph Hudak of Olmsted Associates, Inc., who designed the ground-cover bed and new patio in the suburban garden, and Mrs. Julian Underwood, whose sensitive perception made possible the transformation of the courtyard in the country.

I am not a stoical writer; when chapters won't take form or when physical processes fail to translate into succinct, readable prose, someone has to listen to my wails of misery.

To exclude my agent, Ellen Neuwald Sherman, from the list of those who deserve the utmost thanks would be the deepest ingratitude, for it was to her that I always turned in such crises.

To all these, and to the writers of garden books past and present, I owe a great debt, of which I am deeply aware. My mistakes are never theirs, only my own.

To my gardens I owe even more. They have given me pleasure for years, taught me skills, trained me in patience, and rewarded me in enormous measure. Gardens are not inanimate things, pieces of property fashioned by the gardener. They are entities in their own right, with personalities, preferences, and marked individuality.

Our gardens were inherited from people who loved them, and I felt this influence when I took over. When we cease to work our gardens, I hope our affection for them will still be there to encourage whoever comes next.

THALASSA CRUSO

Boston 1971

Introduction

This is the story of the gardens we have owned in New England for many years. I have no intention of setting myself up as an authority on outdoor gardening, for my gardens have never been showplaces; I do, however, want to explain what was and is done in our gardens and why. I work them without professional help except for hedge and grass cutting, so my problems are identical to those that confront every do-it-yourself gardener in these laborless days. And since I have gardens in two places, I also have all the problems that plague those who try to keep an absentee garden in good condition.

Over the years some of the tricks I use in handling plants and saving labor have turned out very well. But I also have made a great many mistakes and had my full share of failures. Gardening is always an up-and-down affair, and everyone who gardens has to learn to be an optimist. No single season produces triumphs in every department, and gardeners soon learn that success, when it occurs, always incorporates a certain element of luck, no matter how much work may have gone into it. And disappointments must be tossed off in the same spirit. For if everything always went according to schedule, a good deal of that marvelous hopeful expectancy, which is the hallmark of the interested gardener, might be lost. There is nothing really reliable in my gardens except my pleasure in them. When something does unexpectedly or exceptionally well I feel more than average delight, for it comes as a kind of bonus. I write off failures as part of the same game, and as a wonderful way to learn what not to do another time.

If this account helps others by giving them new ideas, or forewarning them of possible disasters, so much the better. But providing specific advice is not my main objective. The continental climate of the United States is so tremendously varied that no one book can be considered as a text for the entire country. My aim is to get across the idea that there is a great deal of fun as well as some concrete advantages to be had from working outdoors in a garden. One reaps these benefits without necessarily being an expert or becoming a slave to a demanding and exhausting hobby. A garden does not have to be perfect and in impeccable, prizewinning condition to give a family a lot of pleasure, and, since my gardens are not outstanding but are a great solace to us, I do feel reasonably well qualified to stress this fact.

The rewards of gardening are far greater than just magnificent horticultural achievement—though a little of that commodity is admittedly very heartening! What we can all enjoy is working outdoors in the open air and doing the best we can with what we own according to the use we want to make of it. Learning just enough about horticulture to keep a garden looking reasonably respectable can bring great satisfaction to those who can get up the courage to start—and as you work in your garden you inevitably learn more. By getting involved, even the most timid gardener gains self-confidence, and self-confidence is the first giant step to success, for it leads to inventiveness.

I have been fortunate in having cared for the same gardens for over thirty years, and this has given continuity to my efforts. But it is not essential to stay in the same place for years to enjoy gardening. The first garden I owned after I was married was in London. I planned it myself with a good deal of labor over graph paper, and I made innumerable journeys to country nurseries to find exactly suitable growing stock. It was a small, walled garden with no outside entrance; all the brick, soil, and plants had to be carried through the house. The time and effort involved in making that garden were very great, and I was highly perfectionist in my approach to it. I finished the job the same week that England declared war in 1939, and I never saw the garden again. We spent the war years in this country, and the garden fell victim to the bombing. But I still think of all the effort that went into it with pleasure. I learned a great deal during the preliminary planning, and I got a lot of practical experience chasing down the appropriate plants and getting them into the ground. All I lost was the long-term reward, and that I still feel was a relatively small part of the whole.

As far as I am concerned, physical involvement with open space and the pleasure of working outdoors are just as important as the final results. My experience with the London garden is only one example. When the war and my husband's work confined us permanently to this country, we lived at first in town and rented a country house for a couple of summer months. Just as soon as we were unpacked I used to rush out into those rented gardens to pull weeds and scratch around in the flowerbeds. That these were not my gardens and that I should see no return for my efforts did not matter. What I found so refreshing and delightful was to get my hands in the soil, to feel earth rather than pavement underfoot, and to be tuned in again to the growing cycle. Today people need this release more than ever before. Working in a garden, no matter how minimally, gives us the chance to get back into some kind of contact with nature. It is also a positive activity, a way of releasing frustrations and tension. Today not nearly so many people tire themselves out with physical labor as in the past; instead we exhaust ourselves with frustrating traffic jams and concentrated mental effort. Sometimes we work off those tensions in various sporting activities. Indeed for many people there are no other alternatives. But those who own a garden or have access to any plot of land are neglecting one of the best possible therapeutic rechargers of their physical and spiritual energies by ignoring the pleasure that comes from doing a little gardening. No matter where you live, this pleasure is available, for gardens can be made in every kind of climate if you have the will to try.

Plants and gardens have always been important to me. I

can't remember a time when I wasn't aware of them, for the house was always full of flowers and my family greatly concerned with their garden. Some of my most vivid childhood memories are connected with plants. As a very little girl I can remember taking a long walk with my father down an unpaved country lane where the whole hedgerow, as well as the grass verges alongside, were completely covered with thick white dust. The sight so upset me that I burst into tears, and my father, thinking I was tired, hoisted me onto his shoulders to ride me home. I remember struggling to get down and trying to explain that I wasn't crying because I was tired but because all the "poor flowers were so dirty."

When I first came to this country, it was the plants and the natural landscape that made the most impression on me. We arrived on Christmas Eve during a bitterly cold spell. The boat docked in New York in the early afternoon when the skyline was at its most spectacular. I was impressed but not overwhelmed, for I had heard a lot about this particular phenomenon. What did startle me, and what no one had thought to warn me about, was the desolation of the frozen country we drove through. To my English eyes, the brown grass and secondary scrub growth looked bewilderingly unknown and totally dead, as though it could never revive. It might have been another planet in comparison with the winter landscape I had just left. During the next few days I must have been exposed to many new experiences. But other than the intense discomfort I felt at the heat of the houses, for I, of course, was still snugly encased in the traditional winter woolies of all those who live in unheated houses, I don't have many sharp impressions except my astonishment at finding the church decorated with poinsettias, then entirely unknown to me, rather than the familiar holly. And, among all the new relatives I dutifully visited, the house I recall the best was the one in which there was a Christmas cactus in full bloom, a sight I had also not seen before. I recently had a chance to reread some of the very first letters I wrote to my own family after this initial plunge into the New World. I am afraid I must have caused my parents considerable frustration. For in them I say very little about all the new people and the strange way of life to which I was suddenly exposed; instead I wrote at length about the extraordinary landscape, something which I doubt interested my mother at that exact moment nearly as much as my reaction to the very different life-style.

This interest and affection for growing things has never left me. Obviously there have been periods in my life when other activities have had to have first priority, but the spark has always been there. Horticulturally speaking, it has never gone entirely dormant. And this is, I think, because no matter how busy or concerned with other matters I may have been, ever since we got our own house, I have spent a short time every day in the garden: sometimes working and sometimes just walking around enjoying it.

Enjoying a garden is beginning to become something of a lost art. People who own property are working it less and less themselves, often turning the complete care over to a gardening service. This practice can produce a neat, attractive effect, but it is not what I mean by gardening or enjoying a garden. Enjoyment comes from seeing the fulfillment of something you set in motion. It can be as simple as the spring bloom from some tulips you planted in the fall, or the slow maturing of a tree you chose yourself. This type of enjoyment does not automatically have to be associated with actual physical activity, but it can only follow deep personal involvement with what is being done—at the very least in the form of interested supervision.

As a young man, my father-in-law bought a large piece of property which was laid out in the conventional manner popular at that period. The place was run by gardeners, and during her lifetime my mother-in-law was actively interested in all the formal areas which, I am told, were then unusually imaginative. When I first saw that garden the formal areas were uniformly dull. After his wife's death, my father-in-law supervised the upkeep of this part of the property in an automatic and rather critical fashion. These gardens did not really interest him and his only requirement was that they were kept tidy. In comparison with rather similar formal gardens I had known in England, they looked well-cared-for —and unloved—like an institutionalized child who is properly housed and clothed yet fails to thrive because of lack of affection. Behind the house there was a piece of parkland in which grew a large number of young specimen trees. In this area my father-in-law was a completely different kind of gardener. The house had been built on open meadowland, and these lovely groves of trees and fine orchard had been his special project from the very first. He knew the history of each tree, when it was bought, how large it had been, the year and almost the day of the week it had been planted. I nearly froze to death, despite my British underwear, while being taken on the first of many tours of those trees. But I recognized real enthusiasm and involvement. This part of the garden was cherished and appreciated even though its owner did none of the actual physical work.

When you recognize and watch for the after-effects of a special effort on your part, you ally yourself with nature and become an activist in the present urgent fight to save the environment. Those who give their gardens over entirely to the care of others have not yet made this commitment, and they are, I think, the losers. This should not be taken in any way as a criticism of gardens that have been designed by a landscape architect. On the contrary, I only wish more people would understand the importance of getting professional advice about the layout of their grounds at the earliest opportunity, and from properly qualified people.

But even the best-designed garden has to be kept in order and the planting up-to-date and weed-free. This is the kind of owner involvement that can exist even when professional help has been obtained for the basic plan. Unfortunately, we are still a long way from the day when every houseowner uses a landscape architect as a matter of course. Each year finds still more people owning a piece of land for the first time, or confronted with an ever-growing encroaching wilderness, without having any idea how best to manipulate it to serve their interests before it becomes a Frankenstein devouring all their free time and a great deal of money. And this worry is not confined to people taking on gardens in new developments, it is often an even greater problem to those who have bought an old house with a run-down garden.

In this respect the story of our gardens may be some help. Both were old when we acquired them, and since I was entirely new to this climate with all its vagaries, I had, as it were, to recut my gardening teeth on them. And it is this slow process of learning by doing—without getting completely overwhelmed—that I shall try to describe.

Today the gardens are fairly respectable, though I do not favor anyone critical looking too closely around the perimeters; they are manageable and they fit our needs. They are used for exercise and experiment; they give pleasure to the eye and to the senses; and we use them as places in which to relax. For me at any rate they exude a comfortable, rather easygoing atmosphere, and I hope they give other people the same impression. Gardening has to be a willing activity not a chore, or it will not give you or anyone else pleasure. Perhaps I am rationalizing the defects of our gardens when I say I don't even want perfection in them, but I don't think so. A meticulously groomed garden would mean that every weed or unmown blade of grass shouts for immediate action, and I would soon be frazzled and harried trying to keep up. Even worse I should soon dislike a place that put such a burden on me. I love our gardens, and I don't want to be lured into making them such a burden that I come to dislike them. They are cherished for themselves and for the memories associated with them. There is an easygoing relationship between us that allows me to not fret overly about some of the obvious weaknesses while still finding a place for exciting experiments. Can there be a better way to enjoy a plot of land?

Making Things Grow Outdoors

A Note on Terminology

Before starting this account I should explain the sense in which I shall be using certain terms. In America the land belonging to a house is normally described as a lot, a plot, a place, or a yard, the term garden being reserved for that part of it planted with flowers or vegetables. In England, on the other hand, the whole property around the house, unless it is large enough to be called an estate, is described as the garden.

I have tried to keep to the American terms when referring to American conditions in general. But mainly I have kept to the English tradition in describing our own property. The important thing to remember is that whatever term I use, I shall always be referring to the same thing—land that goes with a house.

I | Three Gardens

Our first American house with a yard of its own was a suburban plot a little more than half an acre in extent, and we still live there. When we bought it, we expected to live in it the year round, and our plans for using the grounds were based on that presumption. The house had been built in the nineties of the last century in an old apple orchard, and a few gnarled survivors of this much earlier time still existed both in our yard and in those of our neighbors. The area had been farmland from the seventeenth century until the nineteenth-century development; our house was among a number all laid out at the same time. The rather busy street on which the house now fronted had been an important road from early colonial times, and the farmhouse to which the orchard belonged is still standing. A huge old elm that once must have shaded the pasture was incorporated into the wall that divided our land from the road.

The orchard had been planted on uneven hilly ground, and it sloped southward down to a shallow "greate ponde" of colonial times which now marks the limits of a shopping plaza. The topsoil runs very deep, which in New England, with its underlying rock formation, is rather unusual. More frequently a thin layer of soil exists—topsoil being the technical name for the fertile layer of earth that provides the roots of all plants and trees with food. The orchard may possibly have been planted on this particular slope because there was such a depth of soil.

The house is set in a hollow some distance from the street, and the yard, when we first saw it, was laid out in an old-fashioned manner with grass lawns and a rather thin boundary planting all around it. This consisted of rather uninteresting deciduous shrubs, which, during their long leafless periods, left the garden rather open to public view, with a few evergreens mixed in among them. The drive runs the entire length of one side of the lot, sloping downhill from the road to a path that leads to the front door, and then rising up behind the house to a detached garage. The double slope must have made the driveway extremely hard for horses in icy weather, and it remains a menace even with modern snow tires. But without expensive earth-moving equipment, there has never been any way to change this arrangement, and though we once contemplated making a circular sweep for a new drive through the front lawn, the presence of the gigantic, ancient elm made this impossible. Apart from the drive, the front yard of the house consisted only of a rectangular piece of grass.

The house stands on high foundations, so there was a three-step rise from the drive and from the lawn to a grass terrace that led to the front door. The rising land between the lawn and the entry terrace was planted with an overrun combination of early flowering lemon daylilies and white iris. Behind the house, again on rising ground, there were two lawns, one above the other—also separated by three steps. Two old apple trees grew on the upper back lawn, one on the front lawn, and one on the boundary planting along the road. There is a local ordinance that forbids any building from abutting right up to a property line, so there was a tangled wilderness about twelve feet in depth behind the garage, and a moderately thick shrub border along the rest of the back line protecting us from an extremely run-down, boarded-up house that eventually was pulled down.

The stretch of grass close to the house at the back contained two large circular flowerbeds. This lawn was smaller than the one above it, because there was a laundry yard on the far side, with an entry from it into the cellar, and stoop steps leading to the kitchen door. This service entrance was partly hidden by a rather battered length of painted trellis over which scrambled a rampant orange trumpetvine. Here

*Suburban house
from road.*

*Suburban driveway
uphill to road.*

perhaps it is proper to pay a rather wry tribute to the tenacity of that particular plant. For though it was, as we thought, dug out thirty years ago, I still have to ferret out greedy new suckers every fall!

The house as it stood was not suitable, but the location and the yard were so close to what we wanted that we decided to alter the house in order to get the land. The changes we made had a double purpose. The foremost was to give us enough room, but we also gave high priority to working out a plan that would move the service entrance so that it could be reached on foot from the road and not through the back yard. We wanted this to give ourselves more privacy but also to make the rear part of the yard safe for children. As long as every service truck had to come down the driveway to make a delivery, small children could not play outside unwatched. We also made the yard safer by putting an unobtrusive link fence inside the rather shabby shrub border, and we added a gate at the top of the drive, which was kept closed. That gate was a pest to open and it made a skidding winter exit onto the road even more of a challenge, but we left it

Suburban front lawn through shrub border.

there until the children were more sensible, at which time we thankfully took it down. But it still stands tall and forbidding in the cellar, and during recent visitations by small grandchildren I realized how right we had been to have this protection. Gates are not common in American yards, and they are a bother. But bother or not, they are commonplace in European countries, and, since it is impossible for children to be watched all the time, we might do well to think of making some arrangements of the same sort here.

The need to have a safe place for the family had been an important aspect of our house-hunting, but it had not been our only essential requirement. I also held rather strong views about the kind of yard I wanted, particularly as I expected to live in it for the rest of my life. I had been brought up in English gardens, which are closed, personal domains. To the English, a garden is a private place, totally separate from those of the neighbors. It is not automatically open to other people's children, or other people's animals. Like most Europeans, I had been much struck by the open, unfenced yards that I had seen in so many American residential areas, but, though I admired the general sense of friendliness they produced, these almost communal lawns were not for me. I wanted something far more enclosed that would serve as an open-air extension of one of the rooms of the house. No matter how neighborly you want to be, who needs all the local dogs tracking through their outdoor living room? I had also been struck by the sameness of those open front yards and their lack of individuality. I thought them dull, and I was not prepared to have my own gardening ideas subject to the taste of my neighbors.

The fact that this suburban place was already enclosed and to a certain degree shielded from the houses on either side was, therefore, a great attraction. We were also delighted by the reasonably compact size of the yard; there was plenty of scope for the children and their friends, yet it was not too large for us to run. We expected to do all the garden work ourselves, and I did not want to take on too much. Too large a garden is a great deflater of owner enjoyment! Above all, the grounds were in pretty good shape, which had become a matter of increasing importance to me. I wanted a yard that had not been allowed to run down, because of the experiences we had had during the rather protracted search for a house. While we looked, we had rented temporary perching places, all with quite large yards, all of which, oddly enough, were in a neglected condition—the result, I imagine, of too many temporary tenants. I had been startled to discover how fast everything deteriorated here. In England, a garden declines more gradually and far less dramatically. In those rented gardens, I had made an attempt to grow a few flowers, but clearing and keeping open space had proved to be a tremendous task wherever the virile weeds and rampant trash vines of New England had taken hold. Because I had very little free time and did not expect to be any less busy in the immediate future, I was determined to find a yard that had not already slid downhill.

I had also been appalled by the huge variety of pests and diseases that infested those overgrown gardens. Some of this came from physical neglect; nothing will thrive if it is so crowded that there is no free circulation of air. Broken branches left hanging from trees and shrubs are an open invitation to insect attack, as well as a natural breeding ground for all the molds and mildews. Withered foliage of frost-killed plants also serves as the wintering-over area for all these same pests. But to my eyes, there was another reason for those fearful infestations. I had been raised in a gardening tradition that put great emphasis on the need to keep the soil fertile and in good condition—that is to say, rich and crumbly, not hard and barren. I had also been brought up to believe that strong plants were far less susceptible to every kind of ailment, and that the way to raise tough, healthy plants was to grow them in good soil which was kept constantly enriched.

In the rented gardens, I had been depressed at the wretched condition of the soil and my inability to improve its physical structure. I am not going to shirk facing up to the lively problem of chemical versus natural fertilizers, but that discussion will come later. Here it is enough to say that since in those rented gardens there was no possible way of improving the texture of the soil by long-term care, I had to rely on chemical fertilizers. Under the existing deplorable soil conditions, these chemical fertilizers did not bring strong plants; they merely gave the plants a lift, a kind of temporary high. But continued applications made the plants soft, with a flabby growth that was even more susceptible to pests. When we found a suitable house, I intended to get right to work making my own fertile soil by a process known as composting. But to make enough compost for even a small place, an out-of-sight working area is needed; just such a hidden area existed in that overgrown tangle behind the garage of the house we were contemplating.

Getting the alterations made took time, and I seethed with impatience. It had been too long since I had had my own place, and I wanted to get going. With the self-assured optimism of the young, I was sure I knew exactly what I wanted and how to achieve it. In fact I moved too fast and too soon, and I have been paying for some of my misjudgments ever since. And though I enjoyed every moment of those long-deferred labors, part of the purpose of this chapter is to prevent other enthusiasts from making these same mistakes.

For the time being we left the front of the yard alone; it needed far more work and thought than I was prepared to give it at that moment. We concentrated our efforts on the back and more private part of the yard. To protect this even more from the openness of the drive, a long hedge of arborvitae, each over six feet high, was set out alongside the two back lawns with an opening through it to get to the garden door. This was done the spring we moved in, for I wanted instant, complete privacy, and during that first summer the new hedge worked beautifully.

The upper lawn with its two apple trees was set aside for a children's playground, with its manifold grass-ruining equipment. The trees themselves, after some rather drastic cleaning out of dead wood, were ideal for shade in hot weather as well as the place for tree houses, swings, rope ladders, and so on. The original laundry yard, which had become pointless after we moved the service entrance, was dug up, the trellis removed, the trumpetvine extracted, we thought, and a place made available for growing-on seeds and cuttings and carrying out small plant experiments. This was divided from the original lower lawn by a dwarf hedge of deutzia. The existing circular beds in the lower lawn that looked like oversized soup plates were grassed over. Stupidly I did not take enough trouble with this job; I wanted results too soon. Some loam was bought, for as yet none of our new soil was available, and we filled in the beds and seeded them to grass as soon as we passed the papers for the house, seven long months before we moved in. The grass germinated well, but the final result was a failure. The filled-in beds sank, and produced saucerlike depressions that never entirely vanished. These filled with ice in the winter, so the grass in them was always sparse. A mistake of this sort is extraordinarily hard to rectify. Twice subsequently those pits were dug up, fresh soil added, and the whole weary process of reseeding undertaken. But some trace of those old beds stayed to haunt us until we changed the design of that part of the yard. It would have been far wiser to have mounded up the earth over those beds and waited for it to settle over the winter. In the spring the beds could then have been topped up level with the lawn surface with yet more soil and then seeded down. Settling of this sort invariably happens with new soil unless you own or rent a special compacting tool, which is not worthwhile for a small job. But, because I was impatient, that lawn never looked or did well.

To replace the two round beds, the lower lawn was cut back on both sides to make a pair of flanking flowerbeds. The kind of garden I knew best was one in which flowers were the main feature. I wanted to reproduce something of the same sort, but to do so I had to go through what now might be described as a mild identity crisis. I knew I wanted to grow flowers and I was fairly sure I was capable of doing so, but I was not entirely sure how I meant to go about it.

Improperly filled in flowerbeds with ice sheets.

My ambivalence stemmed from the fact that I am the descendant of entirely different kinds of horticulturists, both of whom grew excellent flowers but from a very different basic concept. The family garden of my youth was, like Gaul, divided into three parts. My father's domain consisted of the area around the house. Here in the most prominent place, where every visitor saw them immediately, were neat, orderly flowerbeds without a weed in sight, with every plant staked into a straitjacket of prim rigidity. Nothing sprawled, but nothing grew gracefully either, and every dead leaf and flower was meticulously removed. The effect was good, for the flowers were well grown, and the show was made even more effective by the excellent lawns that set off the display —but it was not very exciting horticulturally.

My mother ruled over a far more casual area, which in deference to my father's feelings, had to be visited, rather than thrusting itself upon the general notice. It included a large perennial bed that lapped up to a meadow. The border itself had huge interlocking groups of flowers with contrasting steeple points of tall plants in the background. What little staking was done was always of natural brush or bark-covered bean poles that stood out like sore thumbs, and, though this bed could look lovely, it also had excessively untidy periods.

The utilitarian area of the garden—hedges, paths, vegetables, greenhouses, and the like—was handled by the gardener, who didn't hold with new ways and did everything at a snail's pace. But he understood plants and their needs, and what had been good enough for his forefathers certainly suited the plants he grew. The only point of agreement, horticulturally speaking, between my mother and father was that they both liked roses. But even here their approach differed. My father liked rose beds neatly edged, with weed-free soil nourishing heavily pruned bushes. My mother loved climbing roses which she grew up pillars or trained on wire on the walls along the front of the house. If a branch fell away from its restraints, she left it, for she enjoyed a naturalistic feeling. There was an occasion when one of those trailing branches scratched my father's head. For once he said nothing; it must have been about the only time he did restrain himself about my mother's style of gardening. But that night he went out after dark and cut the offending branch down to the ground. It was a *gloire de Dijon* rose that reached my bedroom window, and in the morning I noticed that a large section was missing. To my, and I am sure my father's, secret amusement my mother never noticed.

I had, therefore, been exposed to very different styles of successful gardening, and in the large family garden there was room for all this individuality. But I was now about to start a flower garden in a rather limited area, and I had to make a choice (or I thought I had) as to which style I would follow. I wasted a lot of time and energy worrying about this, when I should have known better. The main consideration was not what I wanted, but what I was going to be able to grow in the very different climate to which I was now exposed.

Preconceived attitudes and ideas should never take precedence in outdoor gardening. It is nice to have a scheme, but you must always keep your options open for fear your ideas won't work. In my case, I ended up with compromises that took something from the style of both parents but had local modifications. Confronted with a similar situation today, I would handle things differently. By now I feel that the most constructive attitude to take when one first acquires title to a piece of land is to sit tight and do nothing, and I often wish I had enforced this bit of discipline upon myself. For though some of my early ideas worked, I made some bad mistakes. In any new place, by which I mean somewhere that is new to the gardener, it pays to wait through an entire growing season before undertaking drastic changes. No matter how much advice is given you, let your key words be "not yet," whether you are a beginner or an experienced gardener. This applies equally to a raw new development or an established yard.

Obviously there has to be some action, if only to get you into good standing with the neighbors. In existing yards grass should be cut and flowerbeds planted to annuals—a few boxes of these bought at the local garden center won't break anyone financially, and they are a token of good intentions. Undeveloped land can be made to look a little better by potted plants. And if you can only will yourself to buy the same kind and in the same color, these can look extremely effective grouped at the front door. Anything more is a mistake, for unless you are a landscape architect trained to sum up and evaluate the full potential of a place after a short inspection, you will need a full growing season in which to study your land and find out its virtues and its weaknesses.

Long before you start physical activities, it is extremely important to know where water stands after heavy rain or where ice sheets and snowdrifts can be expected. If rain and snow cascade heavily from the roof at one place, making it impossible to plant anything underneath, you need time to discover this. You ought to see where the sun bakes the ground and where the long shadows fall. You need to know where the wind blows the hardest and where the air is still, hot, and stagnant. These are all essential pieces of information that you cannot get by studying the points of the compass, and none of them is immediately obvious on taking possession of a house.

But though I am against zealous overactivity, there are plenty of things a new owner can do during this waiting period. To give maximum pleasure a piece of land must fit easily, like a well-worn glove, into the family's way of life. The first thought, therefore, should be given to how best to organize the lot so as to include all the outdoor activities that you and your family like. If you can rough out your ideas on a piece of paper so much the better, but a carefully kept notebook can be just as useful and almost as effective.

In a brand-new development, you may have to cope with the so-called landscaping that the builder has put in. This is usually a mass production job, and done without much imagination, though there are notable exceptions to this rule. But you need not live with these plantings forever. Recently set-out shrubs will not yet be strongly established, and, if they are kept well watered while you are rearranging the yard in your mind, they can probably be moved at the appropriate season.

In an old yard the situation is a little different, but the waiting period is even more important, for it gives the new owner a chance to discover how well the existing design works for his family. The sort of terrace that suited a rather formal way of life may not suit a more relaxed, do-it-yourself family. A new cookout area may be needed even though a terrace already exists, and this you won't find out until you try to use the old one. The effectiveness of paths is something that can change completely from family to family. You may all go outside by a different exit from the other owners, which will call for a change of design.

Old gardens are sometimes overgrown, and new owners cut back fiercely, for they feel smothered. If shrubs and vines are tapping at your windowpanes, some trimming is in order, but at first keep it light. Big shrubs, even when overgrown, represent a plus on any piece of property. Before grubbing out a bush or cutting down a tree, wait and see how selective you can be, and whether professional pruning may not do the trick.

Forest trees that were misguidedly planted as foundation material are a pest in old gardens. They look out of place and block out light and air. Often they can't be cut back without mutilation, so a new homeowner grubs them out. We inherited just such a clutch of overgrown foundation plantings, including arborvitae, false cypress, hemlocks, and old-fashioned rhododendrons. I was all for taking them down then and there, before we made any changes to the house. But my husband objected, he can't bear cutting anything down—ever. So we waited until the alterations to the house were finished. By the time some windows had been enlarged and the interior lightened with fresh paint, those shrubs did not look so bad. Some still had to go, but our interior changes had made such a difference that it was possible to leave big bushes at the corner of the house, where they have since been pruned into large, distinctive specimens that I now would be sorry to lose.

The same is true for trees; always take your time. A large tree, close to the house, may first seem overwhelming and out of place. We have just such a tree in the country. Though it was a fine copper beech, at first I was sure that I had no option but to take it down, for it blocked all light from the kitchen. After a couple of summers in that house, we realized that the previous owner had known exactly what she was about when she positioned that tree. It shades not only the kitchen but the entire back of the house from the western sun, and without it the rooms would be ovens. Precipitous destruction of mature plantings can cause grief later; so if you are fortunate enough to have old trees and shrubs on your land, do move slowly. What you destroy cannot be replaced in your lifetime.

The other side of the coin is the barren new development in which the nakedness seems intolerable, and the owner rushes trees and shrubs into the ground. But hurried planting of this sort can spoil a later, better conceived plan. Plant material is expensive, exhausting to get into the ground, and troublesome to carry through the first few seasons, so most people are unwilling to go through the whole process a second time—even when they know the first idea was a mistake. I understand this all too well, because I made a serious error with the large arborvitae hedge I rushed into the ground. It did the trick, but the material was poorly chosen. Arborvitae is brittle and does not regenerate satisfactorily if the branches get broken. Had I waited for the first winter in that house, I would have found out how fiercely the wind howls along the drive, carrying huge, shattering drifts of snow exactly where I put those bushes. It would have been wiser to set them much farther back and to use a slower-growing, more resilient material, like tall-growing Japanese hybrid yew, which comes back satisfactorily if it gets broken. As it is, I still have the arborvitae hedge, now tied up to something like a redwood gallows to prevent the snow smashing what little is left of it. And in spite of its tattered look, I shall never replace it, the cost of the labor alone would make the change impracticable.

A season's wait in an old place also gives new owners a chance to find out what already exists that can change their plans. We originally intended to enlarge the turn-around in the back yard, but with so much else to do, the project was put off until spring. Then we found that we were going to black-top a place that was full of bulbs and a rather rare trout-lily, so we changed our minds. There was a stage in our lives in that house when we could have done with more room for cars to maneuver. But it was a short period, and now, with the family grown up, that need is gone. And we would never have been able to reestablish the trout-lilies, for they are shy movers.

And there are other important reasons for taking your time. No one should start outdoor garden work on an intensive scale until they can decide, without any sense of pressure, the sort of yard they want. There can be as many variations on this basic theme as in a Bach fugue. A garden can be thought of only as a neat setting for the all-important house; a slaphappy playground for children; an enclosure where dogs are kept confined; or something in between these

Copper beech that shades the country house. The flood now comes each winter, since the water table was shifted by the weight of a tidal wave.

extremes. There are so-called easy-care gardens, and there are gardens that can become engrossing hobbies. But no matter what you want, you have to be realistic about the possibility of actually producing your ideal. Many of the worst frustrations of outdoor gardening follow attempts to force land to conform to a style for which it is not suited by nature. A small plot full of big trees will always be too shady for flowers or vegetables and, if that was your ambition, you will have to settle for something more naturalistic. It is no good planning on a wide sweep of velvety lawn if your ground is rocky and hilly. A spot that stays wet and cold late into the growing season, and floods with standing water after heavy rains, will never make a good playground for children. All this may sound absurdly obvious, but often people do try to force their plans on pieces of land where they simply won't work; the results are always unsatisfactory. In outdoor gardening all the flexibility has to come from the gardener; it is he who has to make the compromises. The land and the climate will not alter their essential characteristics.

An investigation of nearby gardens is very useful during an initial waiting period. Anyone starting to garden in a new neighborhood would be wise to look around carefully and see what grows well in other people's yards. I did a great deal of this peering around while pushing baby carriages to and fro. I am a firm believer in first putting out materials that have already proved hardy in a district. You don't need to buy the same dull, old-fashioned types; you can ask for better and more interesting varieties at the local garden centers. But if, for example, you notice that rhododendrons are well established in the local gardens, then you can be sure that you too can grow them. You can win your spurs acclimatizing rare and unusual plants after you have the basic planting of your yard in place.

Another point on which you should be equally hardheaded is the kind of person you are and the amount of time you expect to put into the place. If you are a perfectionist and cannot afford (or find) regular professional help, keep the part under active cultivation quite small, or you will never get any rest. Obsessively tidy gardeners are better off with something informal; otherwise every weed or unswept leaf will seem like a personal affront needing immediate action. I react like that in formal areas, so I speak with feeling. Clipped hedges please me only after they have had a hard trim, but the huge, slightly untidy informal shrub border that we also possess does not bother me nearly so much. In it weeds and intrusive vines are part of the scene, while they are anathema to a clipped hedge. Paradoxically, casual gardeners are the best fitted to run rather formal areas. They can enjoy the design of the regular planting without having that compulsive urge to get everything immaculate. People know themselves better in these days than they did in my youth, or if they don't it is not for lack of urging! But in case your temperament outdoors is a mystery to you, think of it in terms of your reaction as a housekeeper. If you empty the ashtrays while your friends are still smoking, you will be equally bothered by weeds in the yard, and you will be better off with a style of garden that doesn't show them up. Don't try to fool yourself into thinking that your nature will be any different outdoors than inside. If you are a casual housekeeper, go right ahead and lay out brick terraces and clipped walks, for you will still enjoy them even when you know full well that you ought to do something about their appearance. Fortunately there is a place for both temperaments in outdoor gardening, but you must match your attitudes to the sort of place you want to have.

It is also important to realize that a garden never stands still. It changes in use as the family life-style alters. It changes in outline as the trees and shrubs mature, or it can be deliberately redesigned because of a change in the gardener's taste. Our gardens have passed through several phases which have been set in motion for varying reasons, and I hope that the end of change is not in sight. One of my delights in gardening comes from this sense of freedom to experiment. If a new idea fails—and they will—don't worry too much; try something different. A good gardener should never be afraid of turning ideas upside down, sometimes that can be the unexpected road to success!

One of the major changes of direction in my gardening life was brought about by the acquisition of a second garden. For a considerable number of years we had a great deal of enjoyment from year-round occupation of the suburban garden. Slowly, by trial and error, it had turned into an all-purpose, well-kept, and reasonably well-organized yard, with room for many different activities. Then, unexpectedly, a change occurred in our way of life, and we decided to look for a house by the water where we could spend the summers. In theory we knew exactly what we wanted: a sound roof over our heads in a small community where the children could roam safely. I also wanted the surrounding property to be in a natural unimproved condition so there would be no garden care. At the back of my mind I had vague plans for an eventual modern garden of my own design, but this was all to be in the very distant future when the family took less time. For the

Country garden. Summer view of the waterfront.

moment, if I had to leave the suburban garden, over which I had worked hard, for the entire summer, I wanted to be free of additional hot-weather gardening.

With this in view, we set out on a house-hunt that took several years, and anyone who has gone through the process knows what follows. Everything we saw was too expensive, in the wrong place, or totally unsuitable. While we searched we rented summer houses, which stiffened my resolve to have nothing to do with summer gardening on a part-time basis. Then one cold, bright day in April we were taken to see a house available for rental in a small seaside community. This house was the complete antithesis of all our requirements. It was a perfectly enormous peeling old ark, surrounded by a tangled, impenetrable wilderness that could easily have contained the bower of Sleeping Beauty without anyone noticing. There was a big, neglected lawn in which ankle-high dead grass rustled in the cold wind off the sea, and an overwhelming air of neglect hung over the place like a shroud. The agent told us that the house had been built and occupied during the summer months by the same family for over fifty years, and that, after the widow of the original owner became elderly and less active, the place had been devastated by two hurricanes. Some attempt apparently had been made to tidy up after the first disaster, but almost nothing had been done after the second, more destructive hurricane, which had taken place three years previously. Since the death of the owner, the house had been rented to summer tenants.

We looked it over with the utmost gloom. For though we were anxious to find some place for the coming summer, we had grave doubts about spending even a single temporary season in such a house. The rooms were dark; the furniture was creaking wicker; and the beds were iron, with mattresses that defied the possibility of sleep. Some of the floors tilted menacingly where the foundations had been undermined by the sea, and the front porch was so splintered and broken that a chart was needed to make safe passage across it.

But if the house was in bad shape, it shone by comparison with the garden. This covered a huge acreage, most of which was still a litter of broken tree branches at the foot of dead trees all entangled in a confusion of brambles. The front of the yard seemed originally to have been surrounded by a large shrub hedge, but, even in the leafless state of early spring, it was obvious that this was completely smothered by a strangling growth of Japanese honeysuckle and bittersweet. Bittersweet had also been allowed to scramble up one side of the house, where it had reached a jack-in-the-beanstalk height of twisted stems climbing up over each other to form a haven for abandoned birds' nests, the paper lanterns of hornets' nests, and heaven knows what else.

On the other side of the house, a rank, unpruned wisteria had pulled away most of the old-fashioned wooden gutters. This had also penetrated inside a screen porch and was adventuring under the shingles into the house itself. To one side, there was a large unpruned privet hedge enclosing what appeared to be the remains of a rose garden. The rose bushes stood tall, stark, and half dead in the cold April light. And it was all too obvious that the soil in which they were planted had been totally neglected. Behind the overgrown lawn, there were remains of a large vegetable garden enclosed by what once had been a cordon of espaliered apple trees. These were a mass of unpruned growth with only a rusty wire framework to show where once the branches had been trained. On the far side of the big lawn there was a small, freestanding wilderness into which I was advised not to go because it was full of poison ivy. In it, the agent assured me, there was a pond. Leading up to the front door from the road was a straight walk with two large flowerbeds on each side— both knee-high with the uncut stalks of years of inattention. The whole desolate scene was topped off with a derelict little greenhouse full of broken panes of glass.

Nothing less promising could be imagined, except for one thing. Along the side of the property line there was a ditch almost completely obliterated with litter and overgrown, un-pruned bushes. Pushing their way through the encompassing jungle were hundreds of daffodils; I could just see them as a yellow streak, but, even under such unpromising conditions, the clumps looked bigger and healthier than any naturalized daffodils I had seen since I left England. The lack of any al-ternative choice and those daffodils—for the agent cagily plunged into the thicket and picked me an armful—com-bined to force our hand. Reluctantly we signed a summer lease, stipulating firmly that we would do nothing about the garden except mow the lawn.

During the early part of the summer, I spent most of the time at the beach and paid very little attention to my sur-roundings. But old habits die hard, and, since I had to pass that area daily, I did cut the privet hedge and prune the roses. Their miserable appearance got on my nerves. The hot weather brought on a fearful infestation of Japanese beetles to add to the garden woes, and I remember my mother, who was staying with us, remarking that she did not envy whoever eventually took on the job of trying to pull this wilderness into shape.

But as the summer wore on, something about that battered old garden began to speak to us. Even in decay it had great dignity, and the more I poked around, for by now my curiosity was getting the better of my intentions, the more evidence I found of an earlier careful plan. There were, for example, a few unusual trees that had survived the hurricanes, including the superb copper beech. I found some good varieties of climbing roses fighting for their lives on a trellis among the invading bittersweet. And late in the summer, in spite of the beetles, the pruned rose garden rewarded me with a few flowers. When I gingerly poked my way in among the poison ivy, I discovered the carved stone head of a lion which once had served as a fountain. In yet another tangle of honeysuckle there was a sundial.

Though I was interested, I was far from ready to become involved. And even though we had by now discovered that the place was for sale, I did not want to take on a ruined house as well as a desolate garden. Our sights were still set on a small place with a naturalistic area around it. Then one wet day, poking around among the rented furniture, I came across an old blanket box in which books had been stored to get them out of the way of summer tenants. One of these looked familiar and turned out to be an English horticultural treatise which had been the mainstay of one of my gardening aunts. The rest were also gardening books, and the collection added up to a considerable number of old-fashioned but well-considered gardening manuals all marked with the date when they had been bought. Leafing through them, I noticed that there were plans and penciled notes in many of the margins. Since rented houses are not noted for the interest of the books they contain, I took them all downstairs to read.

After I had got the years when the books had been purchased into chronological order, I discovered that I had stumbled onto a sort of horticultural treasure trove, for they told the story of the stages in which the ruined garden had been constructed. The house itself had been built in 1898, very much the same time as our suburban house, and the owners had immediately set to work laying out a garden, buying these books to help them with their ideas. The various pencil sketches that appeared in some of the margins showed how the ideas evolved. The first plans were rather simple—the work of youngish people. The increasing sophistication of the garden design showed up clearly as they became more experienced—and also as they bought more complicated gardening books! It made fascinating reading, and it also cleared up a lot of questions that I had not been able to solve from my own investigation of the overgrown areas. Apart from the plans, which were rough and faint, the penciled notes included lists of plants that had been tried, and some rather brisk comments on them: "Nonsense, grows well here" beside a warning that a special plant was hard to handle; "Hideous color, do not recommend" against another overenthusiastic description. The record of over forty years of gardening in one place was there for the searching, and the sense of rediscovery made it all great fun. There was one note to which I felt I must add a postscript. The original entry

Country garden. Vegetable-growing and play areas.

Country garden.
Dying and still
healthy elms.

read "Spring 1905, planted wisteria against the house, hope it grows." I felt compelled to add, "Spring, 1946, it did."

This cache of books increased the influence that the old garden was slowly exerting on me. Another wet day I went down to the far end of the lot to investigate an old shed that I was told had been the tool shed in the days of plentiful garden help. Now that the tenants were the gardeners, it was no longer used, and the hand mower we unwillingly pushed across all that grass was kept much closer to hand. In that rather desolate building I found a great variety of excellent gardening tools and equipment, far better than any I had seen since I started gardening in the United States. Much of it was rusty but it had obviously seen hard use.

The personality of the writer of those penciled notes now became much clearer. These were not the tools of a casual gardener but the equipment of an accomplished horticulturist; indeed, I later discovered that the old garden had been a well-known showplace in its prime. Standing there among the dust and cobwebs, I could imagine all too vividly how the creator of the garden must have felt in her later inactive years, watching her well-ordered garden going to ruin because there was no manpower available, owing to the war, to clear away the wreckage of hurricanes or to do the work she could no longer undertake.

By now I was getting more emotionally involved with this aged white elephant than seemed sensible, and since the summer was coming to an end, it seemed better to put it out of our minds. At the end of the tenancy, I put the gardening books back in the blanket box, picked myself some roses, to which I felt entitled, for there would have been none without that pruning, and firmly shut the door forever on that desolation.

Back in town we set off on another round of house-hunting, but something had gone out of the search and we both knew it. No matter what we saw, we now found we were comparing it with that preposterous derelict old house and garden. Eventually we decided to look it over a final time, telling ourselves that seeing it cold and empty, with the lawn again unmown, would get it finally out of our systems. We went down on Columbus Day, which was fine and hot, and had a picnic lunch on the swaying porch. The bittersweet rampaging everywhere was a mass of red and orange berries; flaming vermilion strands of Virginia creeper were tangled among the dead trees; the sea showed Mediterranean blue across the unmown lawn, and the house was as impossible as ever.

As we sat there debating what to do, the old garden played its trump card. Unexpectedly, we suddenly noticed big clumps of autumn crocus thrusting up among the verges of the overgrown hedges and shining out in the neglected flowerbeds. These indomitable little bulbs have always meant a great deal to me, for in them, more than any other plant, I see the forgiving promise of spring. It was impossible not to be moved to see them still there, in spite of all that had happened to the rest of that yard, carrying on the tradition of the garden that once had been.

We bought the house, and it has been a headache and a haven ever since. We were not able to afford all the land, and I still regret the espaliered trees which went with the piece we did not take. In later chapters, the details of how the garden was restored, and has subsequently been changed, are described. Here it is enough to say that the work, which continues to this day, would never have been possible if I had not first had the chance to learn the basics of gardening in this climate in the suburban yard. Without that experience, the job confronting us in the country garden might have seemed so overwhelming that we would not have bought the house in spite of the autumn crocus.

But it took a lot of effort, for with a growing family there were strict limits on the amount of time available for gardening. Our work in this garden was also confined to the summer months, for at first there was no heat in the house. So for years I felt as though the jungle was only just being held at bay. Then about the period that I was at last getting the upper hand, we took on another immense problem. While I struggled to bring back the country garden, I occasionally rested from my labors and walked across a little bridge that connected our yard to the one next door, in order to enjoy an immaculate garden. This was a house identical in vintage to our own, with a huge piece of lawn and many flowerbeds all beautifully kept up by a resident gardener. After many years of invalidism the owner died, and the very extensive land and woods belonging to the house then fell vacant. I watched with dismay the speed with which a beautiful garden and lawn collapsed during the long drawn-out job of settling a complicated estate. Eventually the heir to the property put the land up for sale for subdivision, and for self-protection we bought the large portion that adjoined our land. In so doing, we reopened a Pandora's box of garden problems that I hoped had been settled forever, for once again I had a decayed garden on my hands crying out for help.

By this time, I had regular garden help, and together we converted this extra piece of land into an integral part of the country place. The house there eventually had to be pulled down; we could find no one to take it away, and we had no use for it. Slowly the land that had belonged to it was transformed to fit into our style of gardening rather than the immaculate but very old-fashioned way in which plants had been grown there previously.

This piece of land brought us plenty of new problems, including one of the few still healthy elms in the entire village, with which we have struggled ever since. It also doubled the amount of land to be cared for. But in compensation it brought us new delight, a small piece of woodland that proved to be a flyway for migrating birds. As will appear in later chapters, this third garden was also the source of many new gardening ideas and produced some fundamental changes in my approach to gardening. Rather curiously it still retains a rather different personality. It was never the garden of a horticulturist, as ours had been; rather, it had been a "well-kept-up place," which is something very different. But it has added enormously to our pleasure, and a garage on the property has provided us with a guest house where we now can spend weekends all year round.

By now I am finished with taking neglected gardens under my wing. There was a frightening period when we found ourselves the owners of yet a fourth enormous piece of land. But by then we had at last learned to say "no more," and we sold this off, though I must, in truth, report that we did keep a small stretch of its waterfront. We are still wrestling with it, and there is a long way to go before that is finally cleaned out! I would not willingly give up an inch of our gardens and there is not an inch that I don't know as well as my own hand. This is how it should be with gardens and gardeners. They should love what they own, and own what they love; but their gardens must never own them, for there will be no pleasure in them if they do.

II | Outdoor Living Areas

Gardens must be more than places to admire the successful cultivation of grass, flowers, hedges, and trees. They should be places where things are done and where things happen. The entire family should be encouraged to have some kind of stake in the garden, even if it is only providing a place for a golfing husband to practice approach shots! Unless there is a way for nongardeners to make use of the yard, it becomes sterile and uninteresting to them, an artificial area in which they have no part. A lovely well-kept garden can be a delight to the eye, but to be really beautiful, in my estimation, it must also look lived in and loved, or else it is lifeless. Gardens can easily become like beautiful rooms so full of fine furniture that they give far more the impression of a museum than a house.

Gardens are ideal for summer entertainment, and they should be used for that purpose. There should be places for cookouts, particularly in these days of overcrowded camp sites. The rage for home swimming pools has added a new dimension to a great many gardens, and the horticulturist in the family should adjust designs and ideas to fit this new concept. Gardens should also serve as meeting places for children, where they have space and are encouraged to do what they like. Above all they should include an area in which adults can relax.

It is quite an undertaking to incorporate multipurpose use into the design of one small lot; obviously everything cannot always be included. New gardeners, however, should bear all these possible functions in mind when making their first tentative plans, while those with established gardens should try to see how best to modify the existing design so as to include some of these modern necessities.

It is especially important to be realistic about the activities of children after they have passed the toddler stage. If there is any available space, children are going to throw balls, scratch around in the flowerbeds to find lost ones, or make shortcuts through the hedges to get to the houses of their friends. No matter how much you may urge care upon them, that is not in the nature of active children. If you want them to play in your yard and enjoy having their friends over—not just vanish every day to someone else's yard—you must provide a place where they feel free. What it amounts to is simple. Once basic privacy is assured, every garden should have somewhere specially designed for outdoor living. In a household with active children, the second requirement is that there is space set aside where they can roughhouse at will. Much as I love flowers, blossoming shrub borders, and the like, these I feel come third in the list of priorities.

Dividing a garden into areas planned for specific purposes is not at all new, though it has fallen a little into disuse. The gardens of my youth had terraces for walking dryshod in bad weather, croquet and tennis lawns, areas set aside for great sweeps of herbaceous beds, as well as separate rose gardens, pools, kitchen gardens, and what have you. And it was not only huge estates that were laid out that way. Small gardens were and often still are compartmentalized in England, with the functions of each such area strongly defined. As children we never felt the least restricted, because, although there were certain parts of the garden where we could not do anything we liked, there was other space where we were free to follow our own devices. People do not resent restrictions if some provision is made for their personal interests. You will get more pleasure out of your yard, and it will also look better, if it can be broken up into a few component parts. To do this, some kind of visual barrier or line of demarcation is needed, and these are most simply and inexpensively achieved by artificial flooring to form a patio, sundeck, or terrace. It is also easy to define particular areas of a yard with dividers such as hedges, lattice, or some of the newer ornamental fences which, alas, are not cheap. The principle is exactly the same as the old one of using a lattice fence to hide the laundry yard.

Since I had not been exposed in my youth to space deliberately contrived for outdoor living, it took me some time to appreciate the desirability of this type of area in a garden. And it may well be that I was even slower discovering their pleasures because both our houses, being old, came equipped with wooden porches. My ideas began to change through a combination of circumstances. The first was the acquisition of the third piece of land and the small guest house. When this came into our hands, we started to spend many more winter and spring weekends in the country. But the guest house had no wooden porch attached, and for the first time since I had had a garden in America, I suddenly found myself without anywhere to sit outside on those lovely balmy days that occur even in midwinter. To deal with this problem, and also to provide a place to stand decorative container plants in the summer, we put down a small paved area made of square concrete blocks, sixteen inches a side and two inches thick, on the sunny, sheltered side of the guest house. This was set between the wall of the house and a venerable, freestanding grape arbor that ran the entire length of the building on that same sunny side. This position had a great many advantages: the nearby grape arbor provided shade for summer guests, while the little terrace was a place where I could sit dryshod in winter and where sun-lovers could bake to their heart's content in the summer. Green blocks were used in order to blend with the lawn and not produce a sudden change of pace in the overall impression of simplicity that we wanted to create in this area.

The paved floor was put down primarily because I always prefer having a solid surface underfoot when I sit outdoors in anything except the hottest summer weather. But an artificial floor is in fact a good idea for any area that is to be used regularly as an outdoor living room. It solves the problem of having the grass ruined by chairs and the feet of partying people. It also saves it from an even worse hazard, the ashes from a cookout grill. A paved area of some sort, whether it is of brick, paving slabs, concrete, or any combination also dries off far faster after a shower than does grass. It also sets the special area apart from the rest of the garden and, if you so wish, can be individually landscaped to form a room within a garden or make an unobtrusive, practical addition to the usefulness of a house.

For anyone starting to build an outdoor living area, cement blocks are the simplest and the cheapest of the home-laid floors. The disadvantage is the uncompromisingly square shape that you will have to follow. Patios made from these blocks are strong and long-lasting, and even in New England do not have to be set in cement. Our flooring was very easy to put down. We laid the concrete blocks straight onto the surface of the ground after stripping off the sod. The terrace, which is eight feet wide, was produced by putting down four blocks tightly butted together. It was extended into a simple rectangular area twenty-four feet long in exactly the same way. Our main concern was laying the blocks so that they were entirely level with the existing surface of the lawn that ran alongside. This is very important; an uneven artificial floor can collect pools of rain that turn into dangerous ice slides when winter sets in. It was also important to keep the blocks entirely level so that the tractor wheel could ride easily over them when the lawn was mowed. To achieve this I used a carpenter's level, and there was a certain amount of lifting and putting in more earth, or raking some out before we got it right—but on the whole the job was child's play. If I were to do it again, I would put a layer of black plastic on the soil surface under the blocks. This would serve as an additional preventative against weeds growing up through the cracks where the blocks are pressed together. But weeding has been very little trouble in this patio. I put down very heavy weed-killer on the soil surface before the blocks were laid, and there has been almost no trouble. Instead a pleasant moss has slowly formed where the blocks join, and this we leave alone.

Once down, this terrace proved an instant success. I used it in the winter not only for sunning but also for gardening. I had a cold frame built next to it where I could work in relative comfort with dry feet and deal with such matters as the early seeding of vegetables and hardy plants. Prior to building the little terrace, the cold frame, which I will discuss in greater detail further on, had been farther away from the house, where it was often inaccessible because of snow or mud; in consequence I hardly used it.

Fired with success, we then laid a brick terrace in front of the main entrance to the guest house and linked this to the terrace with concrete stepping-stones. Another set of stepping-stones, made of the same blocks that formed the terrace, were put down on the far side to take us dryshod onto the drive the other way.

This very simple piece of construction changed the whole complexion of the guest house for winter use. It was now possible to walk right around it in wet or muddy weather without ruining the grass or getting soaked. Also we now had a little complex on the warm, sheltered side that fitted every possible requirement for sitting outdoors in the fall, winter, or early spring. For midsummer use it was connected to a delightful shady area underneath the grape arbor. I found the site extremely restful when the guest house was empty in

Brick terrace of guest house with iron band, in foreground, to prevent spread of brick.

The old grape arbor beside guest house.

the summer. Partly, of course, it was the novelty I enjoyed, but there was also a sense of serenity and relaxation in this area that did not exist anywhere else in either garden, and that came from the fact that all I could see from this spot were woods, grass, and trees.

By this time, the children were all grown and married. They, their friends, and their families found the guest house extremely pleasant, and periodic descents were made upon it. The children had hardly begun to establish themselves as regular, independent occupants of the guest house before demands arose for a place where they could hold cookouts and have parties. For this, the little sitting-out patio beside the house would not do. It was too small and so placed that cooking smells drifted indoors; somewhere else suitable for these functions had to be found.

When we pulled down the old house, we had left the original flagstone terrace at the back of that house untouched. I had seen no point in painfully breaking up a cement area even though it served no particular purpose. As it was, the old terrace was too small for the kind of use the young people had in mind, but it had many advantages. It faced an open area and could therefore be enlarged; it had the additional advantage of being extremely private, for the en-

Junction of old terrace and new extension.

circling shrub border had grown very fast. It proved quite easy to extend the existing terrace to something far more usable, simply by adding more rows of those same concrete paving blocks that had served us so well for the first small patio; this time, however, we used gray blocks to match the existing flagstones.

All these changes took place at a time when fairly extensive reorganization was going on in both country gardens. With the acquisition of the extra piece of land, we had to avoid too much duplication of growing areas in order to make the extra acreage manageable. An early decision had been to get rid of all the flowerbeds in the third garden and confine flower growing in that manner only to our original country garden. At the same time we decided to transfer the growing of vegetables, which had taken place rather untidily in what once had been my predecessor's rose garden, to the new piece of land. The problem was where to put this new vegetable plot. We didn't want it too near the guest house. It would be hard on visitors to have me constantly tiptoeing by to pull carrots! On the other hand there was no sense in putting a vegetable plot so far from the main house that there would be no water available, and it would be a long walk to get there. Enlarging the old terrace solved this problem for us. The piece of grass that faced the new cookout area was, even by my rather relaxed standards, a complete disgrace. This had been the place where all the trucks and heavy machinery used in demolishing the old house had been parked, and the ground had never recovered. Adding onto the terrace covered some of this poor land and we decided to use the rest for the vegetable plot instead of opening up a brand-new site; for this would make it part of an active area of the yard. The method by which we improved the soil is discussed in Chapter XI. When the regeneration of the soil was successfully completed, the vegetable plot-to-be was laid out as two rectangular areas, each enclosed by railway ties, with a cement block path between them leading from the cookout area to the better grass beyond.

The enlarged terrace was immediately put to work, and

has proved its usefulness for parties and cookouts ever since. But the new vegetable garden was not a success. For one thing it looked a little odd sticking into the lawn, for there was no visible connection between it and the tall, freestanding shrubbery that sheltered the cookout area. Worse still, it was continuously battered by the high winds that screeched across from the sea. It proved impossible to grow anything like corn or even dahlias for cutting; everything was flattened. To filter out the wind an almost evergreen variety of privet was set around the outer sides and the back of the new growing area, leaving it open only where it faced onto the terrace and where the path came through. The bushes were rather small when they went in, and for some time did not break the wind. In fact we have never let them grow tall, for that would spoil the open expanse of the back meadow, which is one of our pleasures. The hedge, however, has been allowed to thicken into a dense mass that is kept clipped back around three feet in height, and this now serves as enough of a windbreak to make all the difference.

But though the hedge may not have done much to protect the vegetables from the wind while it was small, the fact that we planted it made all the difference to the overall appearance of the area; it added the final touch. Even better, the privet hedge visually linked the vegetable-growing area with the nearby shrub border that encircled the old terrace. Though it was rectangular in shape, enclosing this piece of land gave it something of the feeling of one of those sweeping bays which are in themselves a feature of the shrub border, and thus made it fit into the overall design. To prevent the privet from stealing all the goodness of the soil away from the vegetables, the bushes were planted in a trench that had a metal strip sunk into the side of the growing area to keep back the foraging roots of the hedge.

In new and in small gardens, patios, terraces, cookout areas, and pools may easily be the most obvious and the most important part of the yard. But judging from this experience, they will always look better and give the owners far more sense of privacy if they are surrounded by living green walls of shrubs, trimmed hedges, or even vine-covered fences. Happily, these outdoor walls can be flexible and curved at will, and they can be any height the owner prefers. But invariably they add a sense of security as well as a look of distinction to the place they surround. They also soften the hard effect of artificial flooring. Wherever paving of any sort is used, glare should be taken into consideration. Artificial floors outdoors radiate heat in hot weather, and provision should always be made for some kind of shade. The use of hedges around the area, with ground covers at ground level, will absorb some of the heat, but these cannot provide enough shade to make it pleasant to sit outside on brick, concrete, or flagstone patios in brilliant sunshine.

Any outdoor living area will be a great deal more useful and attractive if it can be laid down near a shadow-casting tree. If no such tree already exists, it is a good idea to leave an open area in the paving, into which a quick-growing tree can be planted. In spite of the attraction of crab apples and other spring-flowering trees, it is as well to avoid any that berry or fruit heavily. Fruiting trees are messy and they also attract birds, which are even messier. If you are setting out a tree to shade your patio, choose one with a light, feathery foliage that does not flower too obviously or have fleshy

Privet hedge around new vegetable-cutting garden at early stage and recent stage.

fruit. The area beneath a courtyard tree should be softened with a ground cover. I am not too fond of seeing paving run right up to the base of a tree; I think it produces a hard look. A soft encirclement of green is easy on the eye, not hard to grow, and cuts down the reflected heat of summer.

If it is impossible to build a terrace near an existing tree, or to plant a tree while the terrace is being laid down, then some kind of lathe house or shaded pergola can be constructed. This is not at all a complicated job. All that is needed is to have the posts professionally set in the ground, having first treated the lower levels with a wood preservative. A simple roof of laths nailed to frames can then be set on top to give the desirable shade. If you do not want to be quite so complicated, acceptable roofing can be made from lengths of snow fence. Basically all that is needed is something to throw moving shadows over the paved area. We made a very simple arbor of this sort at the entrance to our flower-growing area, after I had come to appreciate the pleasures of the grape arbor at the guest house and realized that there was no equivalent place in our own immediate garden. We used the back of the old privet hedge that surrounds the flower garden to provide shelter from the wind, and shade was produced by a removable lath roof. The whole structure was deliberately set so that this arbor faced only grass and the huge old hedges—to imitate, as far as possible, the restful feeling of the grape arbor, where garden jobs left undone do not come into the line of vision.

But, unlike the grape arbor, which is covered not only with vines but also with climbing roses that have worked their way in, the new arbor is very austere and plain. Nothing is allowed to grow on it except clematis, and this is cut to the ground each spring so that the growth is under strict control. The reason why we can treat the clematis vines in this manner and still enjoy their flowers without having to allow them to scramble up all over the pergola is the fact that clematis come in two blood lines: those that will flower even if the vines are cut back each spring (which are the kind we grow), and those that will flower only if the old and untidy stems are left intact. The variety of clematis that can take rough treatment includes all the descendants of the jackmanii clematis, and these are the easiest for beginners to handle. They flower later in the growing season, with us after the Fourth of July. If you want early clematis bloom, most of those have to have the old stems left for flowers. For best results, clematis likes a cool root run with shade at the base of the stems and its head in the sun. Sometimes clematis will do well growing where other plants provide this essential shade; the trick is to get it established in such a position.

Don't send away for clematis, no matter how glowing the catalogue descriptions. It is much better to grow locally bought clematis that comes to you in pots. Clematis that has traveled with the roots wrapped in wet sphagnum moss takes far longer to recover. Dig a big hole, choosing a position where baking sun will not fall all day long on the base of the stems. Put drainage material in the bottom; clematis does

not like sodden soil. I use an inch of sand before adding the bottom layer of soil. If your soil is naturally acid, that is, if you can grow azaleas out-of-doors, add some horticultural lime to the soil you are putting back around the clematis roots. This is a plant that likes sweet soil, and the lime corrects the acidity. Firm down the material in the hole; knock out the plant, being extremely careful not to injure the stem of the plant where it rises out of the soil surface. This is a critical area; stem injury here will open the door to a dangerous disease known as "wilt." Set the plant in with as little disturbance to the root ball as possible, and bury the emerging stem at least an inch below ground level, and then fill in the soil around it. Don't tread the soil down—press it in firmly with your hand; clematis roots are extremely delicate. If the only place to plant your vine is in full sun, put a heavy mulch over the planting area to keep the ground cool. We set paving blocks on top of the mulched area for additional protection, and the roots seek out the cool area they like by traveling back under the pergola. Since our soil is acid, we lift the blocks each spring and sprinkle a little lime over the top

Austere pergola with clematis.

of the ground. Don't try and scratch this in, you will damage the roots; water it in instead. We repeat this program in June when the buds appear. If it is not possible to shade the bottom of the stems with other plants, an upturned clay flowerpot with the whole base broken out can be used for vines that are regularly cut back. In the early spring when the vines are pruned to within six inches of the ground (and this is work that should be done early, before the sap starts to rise), I chip out the bottoms of large clay pots or reuse the old ones. All that is needed is to set the big pot over the amputated stumps of the clematis; new growth will work through the opening and the pot will both shade this critical stem area and also protect the stems from casual injury through mowing. But don't try and pull vines that have already started growing through opened-up pots; the pots must be set out at pruning time or not at all.

If you want to let your vines grow vigorously, just don't prune. You will get fine flowers—but almost out of sight. Clematis looks absolutely delightful allowed to scramble, unpruned, up trees. The problem here is getting them established, and for that I would suggest the plant-in-a-box method described on page 226.

Our clematis is not spectacular, half the time I forget about the flowerpots or break them when I cut down the vines, but we do have some flowers all through the summer— and I am not afraid that the plain effect of the pergola in general will be spoiled by the overexuberance of clematis. The reason for the almost bare appearance of the arbor is the fact that it had to be constructed alongside one of the huge, unmanageable boundary hedges that I have already described. This was the only place in the country garden where I could get shelter from the wind, be near the house for party-giving, and also face onto a restful scene. But with so much rampaging virility of growth in the adjoining hedges, the arbor is infinitely more attractive by being kept bare. If bittersweet or honeysuckle ever invade, it will, I think, lose much of its charm, which is its contrast to those exuberant hedges.

Bricks make delightful patios and terraces, but they cost

more than concrete paving blocks and are far harder to lay well. For good results, the ground underneath the bricks should be dug out and a fill of sand put in its place. There are innumerable books that give very detailed instructions about laying brick walks and patios, and they also show the various delightful patterns that can be made with brick. But even the best-laid brick tends to have an irregular surface unless it has been set in cement. This, I think, ruins the charm of the material. There is often a problem with brick tying, or holding in the final layer so the bricks won't spread outward. Here some cement work may be needed, and the home handyman should read up the subject carefully before he goes to work. Nothing looks worse than mislaid brick—I have every reason to know. The first time I handled bricks I did the work so badly that eventually it had to be torn up.

Brick does, however, blend beautifully with the landscape, and it fits well into almost every type of house; it also lends itself to far more flexible designs than do the rectangular cement blocks. New brick is usually rather raw and red; old brick, if it can be tracked down, looks far better, being a more weathered color. But apart from being rather rare, old brick is also more expensive and somewhat less reliable for flooring, for it has an unfortunate inclination to crumble. If you have used new brick, the effect can be softened by sweeping a thin coat of whitewash over it. This will wear off unevenly and soften the hard effect; it can also be redone inexpensively and as often as you wish. Wherever a new brick wall is built, a coat of whitewash or even thin white paint will be a great improvement. This should not be intended to hide the bricks but just to soften the rather hard look of new brick.

Outdoor living areas can also be constructed of flagstones, other materials laid in cement, or partitioned cement which is given texture by being brushed with a wire brush before the cement is completely hardened or by having small pebbles set in as a contrast. The variations of artificial flooring available are many, and the elaboration of the work depends only on the amount the homeowner is prepared to spend.

The Country Garden

Present Garden with Acquired Guest House and Garden

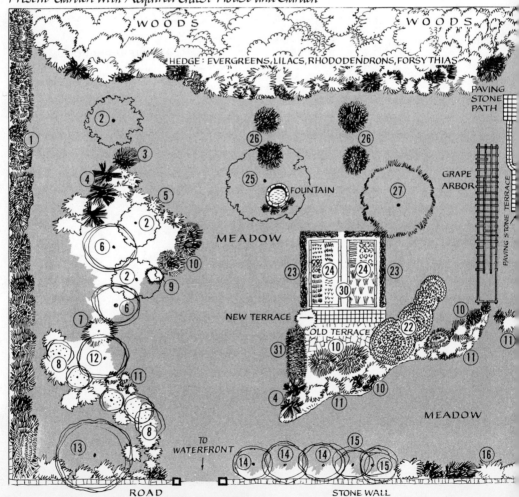

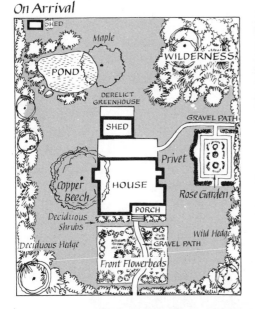

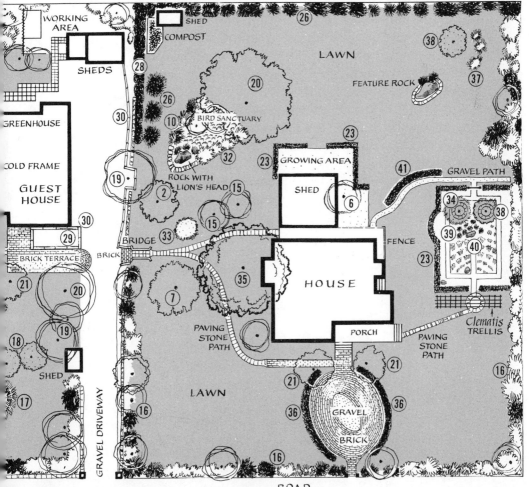

The Suburban Garden

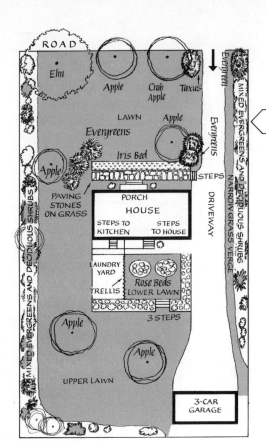

On Arrival

The Present Garden

(23) Clipped Yew Hedge
(24) Pieris Japonica
(25) Bulbs
(26) Pachysandra
(27) Arborvitae
(28) Arborvitae Hedge
(29) Mountain Ash
(30) Fern Garden
(31) Lilies of the Valley, Peonies, Oriental Poppies

(32) Deutzia Hedge
(33) Trumpet Vine and Cotoneaster
(34) Ilex Crenata
(35) Weigela
(36) Vinca
(37) Mixed Evergreens and Deciduous Shrubs and Trees

The Year-Round Garden

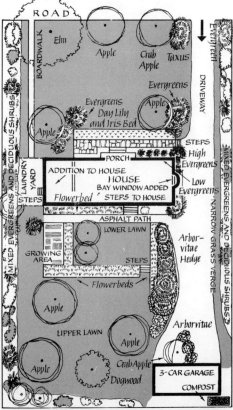

(1) Tall Yew
(2) Low Yew
(3) Viburnum
(4) Azalea
(5) Dogwood
(6) Ilex Crenata, Forsythia Quince
(7) Large Evergreen
(8) Tall Juniper
(9) Crab Apple
(10) English Yew
(11) Taxus

(12) Low Yew Hedge
(13) Magnolia
(14) Apple
(15) Evergreen
(16) Ground Cover
(17) Euonymus
(18) Shrubs
(19) Dwarf Pine
(20) Flowers
(21) Low Evergreen
(22) Rhododendron

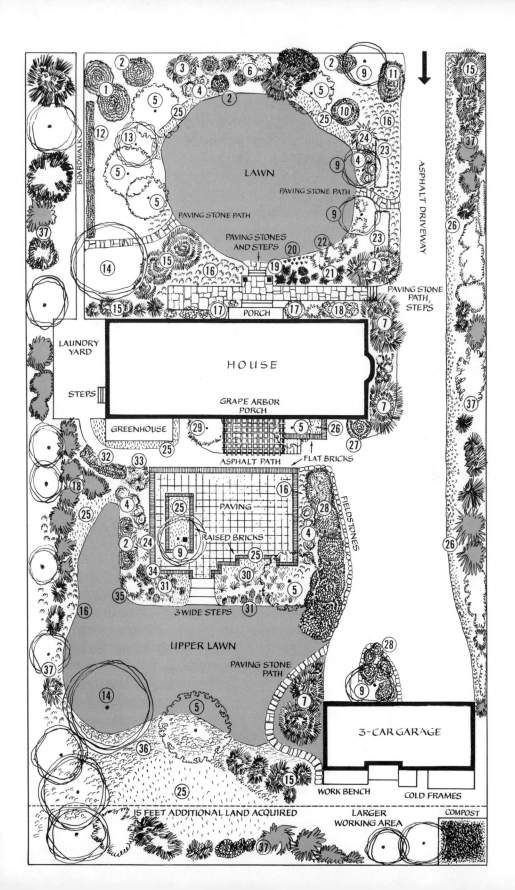

BOARDWALK

② ① ③ ④ ⑥ ② ⑨ ⑪
⑤ ⑫ ⑬ ⑤ ④ ② ⑤ ⑩ ⑯ ⑮
② ⑤ ⑤ ⑤ ⑤ ⑤ ㉔ ㉓
⑨ ④ ⑨

LAWN

PAVING STONE PATH

⑨

㉖

PAVING STONE PATH

PAVING STONES AND STEPS ⑳ ㉒ ㉓
⑭ ⑮ ⑯ ⑲ ㉑ ⑦

PAVING STONE PATH, STEPS

⑮ ⑰ PORCH ⑰ ⑱ ⑦

LAUNDRY YARD

HOUSE ⑦

STEPS

GRAPE ARBOR PORCH

GREENHOUSE ㉙ ⑤ ㉖ ⑦
㉗ ⑦

㉜ ㉝ ⑤ ASPHALT PATH FLAT BRICKS
⑱ ④ ⑯ ㉚
㉕ ② ㉔ ㉕ PAVING ㉘ FIELDSTONES
⑨ RAISED BRICKS ④
㉞ ㉕ ㉖
㉟ ㉛ ㉚ ⑤
⑯ ㉛
3 WIDE STEPS

UPPER LAWN

PAVING STONE PATH ㉘
⑨
⑦

⑭ ⑤ 3-CAR GARAGE
㊱

⑮
㉕ WORK BENCH COLD FRAMES

15 FEET ADDITIONAL LAND ACQUIRED LARGER WORKING AREA COMPOST
㊲

ASPHALT DRIVEWAY

However, large-scale cement work is a professional job and one that should not be undertaken lightly by the novice!

If the homeowner intends to spend money having an artificial floor laid in paving or in brick, with or without a pool, it is extremely important to set aside from the very beginning a proportion of the amount you can afford to spend for the landscaping. This should be planned at the same time the floor is planned, and it should go into the ground as part of the project. It is better to build a smaller patio and have it properly planted. A large, bare, outdoor living area looks all too like a parking lot, no matter how elegant the material underfoot, if it has not been integrated and incorporated into the existing garden with careful landscaping in the form of the largest bushes and the best ground covers you can afford. If you are employing a contractor to lay the terrace but expect to do all the subsequent planting yourself, have an exact outline drawn on paper of the projected floor. It will be far simpler for you to work out the planting that you intend to add if you have this plan in front of you. Also watch carefully that the rubble from the job is not buried below the surface of the soil along the edge of the patio. To grow well, the planting that is to go in will need the best soil you can provide. Debris below the soil surface will make the digging harder for you and may be extremely bad for the plant material. Make sure before signing the contract that the rubble and debris are all to be taken away by the contractor when the job is over; otherwise you may well find yourself paying someone else to remove the rubbish left around by those who laid your patio floor. If you are contracting out both the construction work and the subsequent landscaping, find out before you sign the contract whether the quoted price for the plant material includes the cost of getting it into the ground as well as the cost of the extra loam and peat moss that may be required.

These are small matters that are often overlooked by new or inexperienced gardeners when they are paying for outside work. Getting all this information settled in advance makes the difference between a smooth job well carried out with no ill feelings or disagreements and a bothersome job in which everyone feels vaguely ill-treated. Those who contract to do these jobs are not trying to cheat you, they may simply be working in an accepted framework which you have not fully taken in. It is far better to have in advance a complete understanding of what and how much responsibility is involved for the quoted price.

Absurd as it may seem to stress the fact, it is also extremely important to have a faucet and hose readily available alongside the area where the work has to be done. The responsibility for the aftercare of the planting is always the home-owners'. You may lose valuable plants waiting for the plumber to come. It is far better to have all such outside facilities installed before the first spadeful of soil is turned!

If you are not a do-it-yourselfer, and can't meet the price of getting someone else to put down an elaborate patio, there is a possible compromise in the form of a wooden deck. They are modernized descendants of the old wooden porches, and they have a great many of their advantages. Decks clean very easily with a hose, and weeds do not grow on them. Made of redwood, they are extremely long-lasting, and they do not splinter easily. It is also perfectly possible to use a modern well-built grill on them. Decks can, of course, be custom-made, but this is by far the most expensive way and seldom necessary, for decks exist in a large variety of prefabricated styles ready to be set up freestanding or cantilevered to the house. One of their great advantages is the ease with which benches for extra seating can be contrived along their outer edges. Similar low benches made of brick or stone are extremely expensive additions to a paved patio. Wooden decks are particularly useful for outdoor living in areas where the ground slopes sharply. They are also excellent wherever the ground is inclined to be wet, for they can be installed at whatever height seems most appropriate. Decks are also easier on the feet around swimming pools in very warm climates, for they radiate much less heat than stone or brick.

So far, all the outdoor living arrangements I have described have been on a rather small scale, something the owner-gardeners can add or at least plan for themselves. But if the outdoor living area is going to be one of the most important features of the entire yard, then it is wise to consider the advantages gained from calling in the professional help of a landscape architect.

Gardeners are often a little hesitant about employing trained landscape architects; they feel it to be an unnecessary luxury and also something of a reflection on their own capabilities as a gardener. This is a mistaken point of view. Trained assistance is never cheap; you are, after all, paying for highly specialized knowledge. But in every other profession we take this cost for granted when we have need of specialized help in jobs for which we are not qualified. We use architects to design our houses or to redesign and update our kitchens and bathrooms. We pay professionals to teach us how to ski or play golf without turning a hair, for we know we shall never learn all the tricks of the trade on our own. Gardening is very much the same. No matter how well we may learn to grow plants or how excellent our horticultural knowledge, unless we have been trained in design or construction work, we do not have the skill to carry out the more elaborate operations that may be called for in reorganizing a garden. I do not know any first-class horticulturist who has not taken some professional advice about the layout of his land. The design of a landscape architect can transform an average yard from a hard-to-work, unsuccessful garden into a convenient, easily maintained area. To employ such help is an extremely important aspect in maintaining the value of the property. We are all swayed by small and sometimes irrelevant things when looking at houses or when trying to buy property, and there is no question that a well-designed garden has a very positive effect on all who look at it.

Good landscape architects do not attempt to impose their ideas upon you, or try to change everything about your garden. Rather, they want to carry out, to the best of their ability, your ideas. If, however, the homeowner's mind is a complete blank about the best way to utilize the surrounding lot, a landscape architect is far the most sensible person to go to for long-range planning. And the job does not have to be a large one to make it worthwhile calling for professional help. I used a landscape architect to plan and plant a small ground-cover bed that lies alongside the drive in the suburban garden. I didn't know what plant material would stand up best to the everlasting salt splash from the road, and since this was a highly important position, I wanted the job correct from the first. I also used the same professional later to re-design one of the curves of a boundary shrub border, that, in spite of much effort, looked out of proportion. Both were small jobs, and both were brought to a successful longterm conclusion by the landscape architect in a matter of weeks.

Not everyone knows how to find a landscape architect. To the average small gardener they seem rather remote, frightening people. One of the most common ways is through word of mouth. Ask who your friends have used when you see a new and highly successful patio-pool complex being put down. If you don't know anyone who has ever used a landscape architect, look the term up in the yellow pages of the telephone book. Call several and name the maximum price you are prepared to spend. And make that price a little lower than the amount you can in fact afford: gardening costs are extremely difficult to figure to the last penny. The firms that do not do small jobs will tell you so when you name your price—I am assuming that you do not have a bottomless purse. Go on telephoning until you have lined up several firms that sound interested. Arrange for them to send a representative to look over the land and draw up a very rough guide and cost plan. I would arrange to have the representatives come on different days—there might be a little embarrassment if two showed up at the same time—but there is no reason in the world why you should not shop around to find the firm that suits you the best, in fact, you would be foolish not to do so.

When the representative arrives, explain exactly what you want, particularly if you have strong preconceived ideas about the use of certain material, shade, or even your al-lergies; these are all-important. Also restate the amount you are prepared to spend. Nobody can be expected to draw up even the roughest guide unless they have a clue as to what you will pay. If you are setting too low a minimum for the work you have in mind, this is the time to find it out. During the course of all this, you will find that your own ideas begin to consolidate, and that one of the projected plans appeals to you more than the others. At that stage, settle for that particular firm and dismiss the others. Then ask for a detailed blueprint and as close an estimate as possible of the cost of the plants. Again, as with a contractor, make sure that the cost of planting the plants is specified, as well as their cost unplanted. Make sure that hidden charges, like peat moss and loam, are also figured in. When the plan arrives, go over it with the landscape architect so that he can explain it to you, and then keep it on hand for a week or two, going over it again and again by yourself. The plan is not Holy Writ; it can and should be altered where you don't like it or if you think the material overcrowded or inappropriate. But don't demand enormous changes without making sure that these will not go far over the projected budget. The first plan was probably drawn with your figure in mind, and structural changes will send the price up.

Landscape architects vary in the way in which they handle jobs. Some will draw up a blueprint and a planting plan which you can then buy from them and finish off yourself either with another contractor or by doing your own planting. Other firms will not sell plans and will only undertake a job when it is handed over to them entirely. This is something to find out at the preliminary stage.

For most gardeners with large-scale problems, I am in favor of getting blueprint and planting plans, and having the firm itself oversee putting in the first essentials—essentials to me being privacy, a place for outdoor living, and somewhere for children to play. I then prefer to contract to have the same firm slowly finish off the work in subsequent years. This way I think you get better service and a continued interest in your garden. If you can afford to have the whole job done at one time, well and good. But do get a guarantee written into the contract that they will be responsible for the replacement of any valuable or costly material that dies within a year of being planted.

Other than a few small jobs, I did not use a landscape architect in either garden for a great many years, largely because there was nothing projected that I couldn't handle myself. But as time went on, an important area of the country garden became an increasing problem: a piece of ground that lay in front between the house and the road. Since there is no driveway at the country house the main and only path to the front door went through this particular piece of land. My horticultural predecessor in the country garden had turned this small lot into an important flower-growing area. In it she had constructed two large herbaceous beds divided by the path that led from the road to the house. For a long time I kept the same ground plan and used the flowerbeds for perennial and annual plants. And as mentioned elsewhere, I defined and sheltered the area from the prevailing wind by planting a large yew hedge around the outer sides. The various problems that gradually arose in connection with these beds will be discussed in Chapter XI. In a nutshell, the beds had become too worn out and too shady to grow flowering plants well any more. They also demanded a steadily increasing amount of regular attention to look even as well as they could—more than I was willing or indeed able to give them.

Each spring I found myself dreading the huge job of weeding and replanting these beds—a necessity if there was to be any kind of summer show. During the summer months, after the initial effort was over, the work was still hard and demanding, because the flowers were arranged in such a free-form style that no one but myself could work among them without damaging valuable plants. This meant that I could get no help even with routine jobs like mulching. Worst of all, since these beds were the first thing every visitor to the house saw and walked past, I could not just allow them to deteriorate in peace. One of the most fundamental views I hold to as a gardener is that there must be pleasure and fun in gardening. Once working a yard becomes a duty and a chore, I am against it. Those beds were no longer fun, they had become a nuisance that nagged me; the obvious answer was to abolish them. What was not quite so obvious were the probable alternatives that could serve as an introduction to the house and garden.

The first necessity was to replace the flowerbeds with something much simpler that did not call for anything like as much upkeep. A plain stretch of grass would not do, for it was necessary to have a means of getting dryshod from the road to the house. The area was surrounded by yews, which I did not want to change, and there were also a pair of matched kousa dogwoods at the house end of the old flowerbeds that had to be saved. Since the encircling yews suggested an enclosure, we decided to turn the entire area into a small courtyard, framed by the yews and featuring the dogwoods. This idea combined many of our requirements. An artificial floor of some sort would deal with the necessity

Kousa dogwood with old front beds and with new courtyard.

of getting to the house without tracking in mud. It would also serve as an interesting visual feature in itself. The quiet austerity which I now planned for this entrance court—for I was determined to have only ground-cover plants and no more flowers in this area—would provide a fine contrast to the increasingly lavish display of flowering plants in containers which I now grew on the nearby porch.

The ideas were fine, but the job itself was far too com-

plicated for me either to design or to have a general contractor undertake. Someone was needed who could plan
not only all the details of the visual effects, but who would
also possess enough technical training to make them work.
The land sloped and there were difficulties of pitch and
level. I was anxious to use brick for the floor since these
blend well with a shingled house. But there was quite a
large area to be bricked over, and I knew that I did not have
the training to break this up in an interesting way so that
the large expanse would not just look dull. The design also
had to be fitted into the asymmetrical layout of the old
flowerbeds. This could not be changed because the yew
hedge had been planted around their original crooked outline. The obvious answer was to employ a landscape architect. It took time to track down the right person. A good
many rough plans were produced and rejected before someone was found whose ideas and schemes meshed with mine—
and just as importantly with my purse. Once I had agreed to
her ideas, and accepted the various modification of my
schemes that she insisted upon in order to make the whole
courtyard idea work at all, I stepped out of the picture with
great relief and left all the details of installation to her. It
was a great pleasure to have no further responsibility, and to
watch someone else deal with sensitive skill with a garden
problem. It was luxury beyond words to watch the design
take shape from the comforts of a chair, and I relished every
moment of it. My only part in the entire project, once the
plan and the price had been agreed upon, was to choose
from the various samples of brick and stone that were offered
me. I did undertake the afterplanting of the ground covers
that soften the edge of the bricks. To that small extent I
was involved. For the rest, it was like adopting a child rather
than bearing one—the result was just as lovable and delightful as though I had done all the work myself.

A garden that is laid out to suit the needs of a young family, full of energy and ambition, is unlikely to be as well designed for those at a more mature stage of life. As you get
older, and more experienced, your horticultural interests of-

New courtyard in early summer and in midwinter. High pruning and strong design holds winter interest without statues and succulents.

ten change. An out-of-date layout can be frustrating to your ambitions as a gardener, as well as being too much for you to keep up. Whenever a major change takes place in your way of life, whether it is the children getting married and leaving home, the acquisition of a much-longed-for boat, or even the chance at last to travel, you should take time out to give your garden a long, cold appraisal. Gardens need updating as much as bathrooms and kitchens, and like these rooms, they can be greatly improved by all the modern conveniences!

Look at your garden as though you had never seen it before. Study the layout as you would if you were contemplating buying the place. Is it easy to look after? What about snow removal? How much of that lawn is really necessary? Do you really want to go on struggling with that huge, untidy old flowerbed? If you are a little startled by the results of such a dispassionate inspection, the time may be at hand for a consultation with a landscape architect, a consultation, incidentally, that should turn on how best to simplify and reorganize the grounds without eliminating your cherished trees and shrubs, and how to incorporate into the existing design new ideas that may save you hours of previous labor.

Unfortunately many older people leave a house they love because the upkeep of the garden seems too much. This I think a pity. As long as the house remains suitable, no one should allow themselves to be driven out because of the yard, even in these laborless days. Gardens can be radically redesigned so that most of the upkeep is eliminated. The price of such changes is nothing to the upheavals and cost that accompany a move. The trick is to act before your garden runs downhill, and to have it reorganized long before you reach the point where it all seems too much trouble. If more of us would call in professional help before we are unwilling to stoop, bend, or kneel, we would not have that defeated, depressed feeling that follows when changes are forced upon us. Every landscape architect has numerous tricks up his sleeve which can make gardening simpler for the less active. I am all for taking advantage of these tricks while I am still highly mobile—in order to give me more time to do other things!

Suburban garden. Concrete block patio with brick edges and a piece of garden statuary on trial.

The success of converting the old flowerbeds into the tranquil entrance court led to a long overdue decision to get rid of the lower back lawn in the suburban garden. This was the piece of land where I had filled in the original flowerbeds incompetently when we first bought the house, and the grass in the area had always been a problem. The same small lawn was also the place where, in a moment of madness, I had planted two crab apples in a space that could only just accommodate one, as it developed. One, therefore, had to be cut out, and the survivor stood pointlessly to one side of the area. Around the edge of this lawn we had added other flowering trees and shrubs, and the ground below them was full of small bulbs which had spread tremendously. Each fall I planted new daffodils in the side beds. The area should have

been an attractive place: enough work went into it to make
it a paradise. But, in fact, it never looked well, for each
spring the overall appearance was ruined by the wretched
grass. The small terraces in the third garden had proved such
a pleasant place for winter sunning that we decided to provide some place for the same activities in the suburban garden. The obvious answer was to build a small patio in place
of the lower lawn and get rid of that miserable grass forever.

We ended up with a dark concrete-block terrace that
matched the asphalt path and drive that ran nearby. The
outer limits are marked by a line of flat bricks and two small
flowerbeds were included, each edged with upright brick.
These break the stark simplicity of the terrace and take away
any lingering feeling that all that was needed were the white

*Looking toward
suburban house
from patio.*

lines for parked cars! One of the flowerbeds was created around the crab apple, which suddenly came into its own as an off-center shade tree that produced delightful moving shadows on the patio. Both small beds were planted to bulbs and are now being softened with ground covers. Since this is not a summer garden, the side beds are kept heavily mulched, and ground covers are also being trained over them for a general softening effect. The terrace itself is kept entirely weed-free by using a strong concentration of weed-killer, which is watered in twice a year, once in the early spring and again just before we leave for the country.

Adding this little patio to the existing garden has updated the yard to an astonishing degree, as well as cutting out an eyesore and diminishing the general upkeep of that garden. For year-round use it would be a perfect outdoor living area. It is private, near the house, shaded and sunny, and dry underfoot. If at any time someone wants to put a swimming pool into the yard, there is only one possible position—the upper back lawn. The new patio would fit into any such complex without need for further construction work. This is a very clear example of the way in which new schemes can successfully be incorporated into old gardens without ruining the basic design. To date, it is the most recent of my innovations, and I now cannot imagine why I took so long to make the change.

Apart from our pleasure in the success of these two new areas, we gained a most unexpected bonus from them. They proved the ideal solution for a very long-term problem, what to do with the garden statuary. In general, I am more than lukewarm about all forms of garden adornments. I verge on positively disliking them. Suitable, satisfactory outdoor ornaments are extremely rare, most of them are lamentable. And good or bad, they are always hard to incorporate attractively and suitably into a garden setting. Gnomes perched on mushrooms, rows of plastic ducks waddling across a lawn, petunias in a wheelbarrow, and almost all sundials and birdbaths fill me with the deepest gloom: they look both inappropriate and silly.

Left to myself, I would never buy garden ornaments of any kind and I have only occasionally enjoyed their appearance in other people's gardens. But with the usual perversity of fate, I inherited a considerable amount of garden statuary from my father-in-law, much of it quite good. I was all for selling them when the family property was disposed of, but my husband, who remembered them from the garden of his childhood, insisted that they be given a suitable, happy home somewhere in our gardens. Elaborate lead and stone figures do not fit into our rather casual style of gardening, and for many years I struggled to find appropriate places for these relics of the past. Year after year the statues were moved from spot to spot, only to be banished once again as totally unsuited to that particular place. And stone statues weren't the only problem. Along with them, we inherited an elaborate lead birdbath, complete with toe-dipping cherub, a lead statuette of a small boy who could do with a crash course of strict dieting, some stone benches, and other architectural odds and ends.

The benches came suddenly into their own when we built the rather plain pergola as a quiet sitting-out place for the country house. They fitted perfectly into that context, indeed they improved the overall appearance of the place as well as being highly functional. Once they had been placed on cement blocks to cut down on the problem of hand-trimming the grass around the bases, they became a great success. The reorganization of the flower garden, discussed in Chapter XI, provided a final home for the lead birdbath and the stout small boy. But the real triumph came with the construction of the brick courtyard. This proved to be the final and totally successful resting place of my supreme problem, a pair of grotesque stone dwarfs from Sicily. That courtyard might have been designed with them in mind—though in fact I only thought of them in connection with it after everything was finished. Statuary looks so natural in that setting that we next moved in a pair of Japanese stone lions which had not been happy beside the guest house. I am not quite through with my rather peculiar problem, for I still have a large plaster head of Zeus and an over-ornamental Italian alabaster birdbath to place successfully, but in the main a great difficulty is now solved!

If you love garden ornaments and feel naked without some around, always try and incorporate them into a formal setting —don't just strew them about the lawn. Figures can look well set against the half moon of a clipped hedge, against a wall or even a fence. They will be even more effective in these positions if a matched pair of ornamental shrubs can be set beside them. To be effective, garden ornaments must make an important focal point. The mistake many of us make is to try and incorporate them informally into the garden.

Sundials, to be functional, should of course stand out in the open, and so should birdbaths, so that stalking cats cannot creep up on them. I prefer birdbaths hollowed out of natural rock and set on a pad of gravel or blocks in an open area. This way, birds are just as safe from surprise as they are on those half plates on a stick. Whenever you do set something like a sundial or a birdbath in the center of the lawn, always construct a paved area underneath of closely butted cement blocks. This makes more of a feature of the object, helps with the grass trimming, and gives a stronger impression.

In spite of all that I have just written, garden ornaments have their place. Under certain conditions they can point up a setting and give it a final charm. Oddly enough, we now need an ornament in the new patio in the suburban house. The small central bed that contains the crab apple would be more effective with a low stone ornament. I could hardly believe it, but I found myself putting a request for something of the sort in my most recent Christmas list!

Soil | III

Do you know when your garden has iron-poor blood? Do you send your plants off for a hard day's work fortified by the right kind of breakfast? We have become used to this sort of talk about ourselves and our pets, but most of us don't think of our gardens in these terms, when, in fact, we should. A garden can be only as good as the soil in which the plants grow; if it is poor, nothing will do really well no matter how hard you work at it. Soil is a very complicated subject, and trying to read up on it is more apt to frighten off a new gardener than encourage him. Yet proper manipulation of the soil on any lot is essential for good growth, so, like it or not, the beginning gardener must learn something about it.

The first step in unraveling the soil problem is to try to understand what good soil is and why it is so important to plants. Plants live through a combination of two processes: the effect of light on their leaves and stems, and the nourishment their root systems draw out of the ground. The light falling on the green portion of a plant sets off an energy process which enables it to build plant tissue, that is, grow larger by using the mineral salts and oxygen that the roots have pulled into the plant structure. Moisture is essential to keep the plant stiff, so that the leaves can be exposed to the all-important light. A plant that has wilted through lack of water hangs down drearily, and the energizing light cannot strike the drooping leaf surfaces. Moisture is therefore essential to plant growth, but it is not enough in itself to produce a healthy plant. Plants growing in sterile sand can have all the moisture they need and still not thrive, because water alone does not contain the mineral elements that build plant tissue. These vital minerals come from the soil, and they are not present in infertile substances such as sand. Minerals vary in their basic concentrations from area to area, and their side effects, which change according to the variety and intensity with which they are deposited in the soil, differ accordingly.

Light, moisture, and earth salts are the vital elements needed to make plants thrive, and the success or failure of this triple play depends on the successful activity of the root systems of all growing things. Roots have a double job: they anchor a plant's top structure safely in the earth, and they also conduct most of the essential moisture into the plant system. Plant roots are amazingly complicated pieces of living machinery; they resent light, and, when the living conditions are right, they grow deliberately away from it, thrusting down deep into the ground. But roots are very conscious of the urgency of their life's mission. They are sensitive to dampness in soil, and the tips, through which the moisture is drawn, work well only in damp soil zones. If the lower levels of the soil are very dry because of prolonged drought, the root systems of healthy shrubs and trees and even deeprooted perennial plants will suffer, for roots cannot develop in very dry areas nor can they reach moisture beyond dry patches. But roots, like the rest of us, have a weakness. Searching for water is very hard work and, if the gardener makes the error of just lightly sprinkling the land during dry periods, the plant roots struggling to find enough moisture in the lower levels will sense the dampness in the surface layer and put aside their natural instinct against light to turn upward toward the source of supply. This is the reason why gardeners are cautioned against regular sprinkling of a garden during dry spells. It takes a lot of water to penetrate the ground to any depth, and unless the hose is used over very long periods, this artificial supply will only moisten the very top of the surface soil, causing important roots to rise up after it. This is a great threat to the plants they support. Root tips are extremely fragile, and near the surface they are easily damaged, with grave results. Generally speaking, in times of drought it is better to lose the shallow-rooted plants by doing no watering rather than lure the roots of important long-lasting trees and shrubs to the surface. If the drought is unnaturally prolonged and tree leaves droop, then any water that may be given must run for hours on end in a thin, slow stream so that it reaches the lower levels of the soil.

But though moisture attracts, roots cannot function properly if the soil is sodden, that is, without air. To stay alive and carry out their purpose, roots must have access to oxygen, which they get from the air spaces that exist in healthy soil. It is therefore extremely important for gardeners to understand that the presence of oxygen is essential to the continued good health of the roots of all growing things, and that the only source of this important oxygen is air pockets in the earth. Once this is understood, the constant harping by the experts on the need to keep the ground open so that air can penetrate makes sense.

Air spaces form around the loose, rough material that is part of the texture of rich, coarse earth. Fine powder soils and heavy clay soils have poor air retention, and plant roots are not happy in them; the same holds true for waterlogged soil where water stands continuously. Ground that has been badly compressed by having heavy machinery run over it gets packed down so hard that the vital air pockets are eliminated. For this reason, anyone building a new house should do his best to prevent a constant procession of heavy trucks going to and fro over land intended for use as a garden. If this is impossible, or if in a new development the ground looks and feels extremely hard, it is wise to hire a man with a spiking machine, which punches holes in the ground to let air in. Small versions of these machines are used on golf greens, which tend to be overcompacted by the steady pressure of feet.

But like a soap opera on radio or TV, the story of soil does not end when the gardener has brought together the proper combination of factors that produce good soil and good plants. Any lot that is full of thriving trees or shrubs or lawns or flowers is having its soil steadily depleted by the assorted root systems, and this stealing of nourishment is taking place at every level underground. Trees and annual plants, to take the two most extreme examples, operate at very different levels below the surface. The annual roots rummage around for food just below ground, while the tree roots forage deeply and far afield. So for overall success in a yard, good earth must not only exist to a considerable depth, but its fertility (which is that famous mineral content) must also be renewed regularly. Unfortunately for the enthusiastic gardener, the better a garden grows the more nourishment it takes from the soil, and somehow that goodness has got to be put back in.

Now it's all very well to know this and read about it, but how are gardeners to recognize soil starvation on their own lots, and what can they do about it? Experienced gardeners usually can make a quick judgment by digging up a spadeful of earth, and there's no reason why beginning gardeners can't learn a lot this way too. Rich, fertile soil is always dark in color, and the feel of it is also very significant. It should be rough and slightly gritty to the touch and full of vegetative odds and ends, not sandy and powder-fine, or sticky clay. Soil in good heart, which is one of those technical expressions that can be dropped into a horticultural discussion with a certain amount of aplomb, crumbles when it is squeezed together. It neither sticks like hamburger nor dribbles through the fingers like sea sand. Another clue is worms. If they writhe out from under the spade like small-scale snakes, the soil is very rich and in excellent condition. If none appears after several shovelsful have been spaded up, I would be suspicious. A tremendous crop of stones is also a bad sign. It is easy to judge the depth of the topsoil, or humus as it is often called. Dig down until subsoil, soil that has never been cultivated, is reached. If you have not found it by the time you have gone down into two spits—another technical term meaning the depth of the blade of the spade—the garden has an excellent depth of humus and you can let up on the exhausting digging!

Subsoil varies in different parts of the country, and there

is no hard-and-fast rule for explaining how to recognize it. Generally it is very hard to get the spade into, lifeless-looking, without worms, and poor in quality. Subsoil is usually infertile, and, even if this is not the case, it is usually too hard and airless for feeding roots. In all too many new developments the developer strips off all the topsoil when getting the site ready for construction and sells it elsewhere as loam. When the building is finished, a thin layer of poor loam, in which it is almost impossible to grow anything, is spread over the infertile subsoil. If you are building your own house, it is an excellent idea to have the topsoil removed around the working area before the trucks roll in. In that way the problem of overcompacting the soil is avoided. But make very sure that the contractor piles it up nearby where it can be seen, and that he spreads this pile, not some substitute material, when the job is done. A written contract to this effect is a good idea. There have been many instances in which the original valuable topsoil, which had accumulated for countless years on the house site, was replaced with inferior material brought in from elsewhere.

I would never buy a house in a new development without testing the depth of the topsoil. Carry a small shovel around in the car and turn over a spit near the house. Never mind looking silly—if you are interested in your future garden this is one of the most worthwhile preliminary inspections that can be made. You have no shame about inquiring and demanding proof of interior matters such as insulation, so why not apply the same standards to the soil? If the real estate agent protests vehemently, you can assure him that you are not going to do any damage—but in such a case I should be even more anxious to get a look at the depth of the soil! The all-too-frequent trick of selling houses that have nearly all the topsoil removed from the yard is the cause of many of the difficulties unwary young buyers encounter with pre-purchase landscaping and lawns.

In any new development it is also important to make sure that fill has not been bulldozed up against the trunks of existing trees to change the level at which they originally emerged from the ground. It means slow but certain death for the very trees that may have been part of your reason for buying the property in the first place. When the ground level has to be altered, existing trees must have their original surface left exposed. This can be done by building a small retaining wall around the base of the tree about three to four feet away from the trunk; incidentally, it is important always to keep the resulting well free of debris. If a well has not been constructed and new fill has been pushed up against the bark at a higher level, the tree will suffocate and die. Here again that handy shovel can tell the story instantly. Dig carefully around the base of a tree that stands in an open area. If there is grass, lift the sod (carefully to spare the feelings of the agent), but don't allow yourself to be deflected; sod goes back very easily.

The fact that there seems to be an established lawn against the tree is no guarantee that the lawn is an old one or that the tree has always stood at its present level. There are quick grasses that can make a deceptively good showing for a short time and could fool a new gardener into thinking that it was an established lawn. If the shovel hits hard ground at the base of the trunk, indicating roots nearby, the tree is standing at its original level. But if the shovel goes into soft earth around the tree trunk, the level has been changed. To save the tree, the suffocating fill will have to be taken out and a retaining wall built. This, surely, should affect the price you are expected to pay!

Old run-down gardens frequently have poor, depleted soil, but almost always there is a considerable depth of it—unless the natural terrain is very rocky. In investigating old houses with a view to buying, a shovel is not such a necessary piece of equipment.

I didn't have to do any digging to see that our gardens had poor, starved soil. One look at the pale, powder-fine earth in the flowerbeds told the story. Also I could see in the surroundings of both houses, when they first came into our possession, many of the clear signals of distress that growing things send out when the living is too lean. Warning signals from a tree, shrub, or plant that is in trouble are unmistakable, and a new gardener should learn to recognize them. The signals may not always be due entirely to poor, infertile soil, as I will explain in Chapter VII, but they do occur with great regularity whenever the situation below ground does not suit the feeding roots. Stunted growth and poor leaf color are two danger signals.

In the country garden I planted two small smokebushes in an informal curve that I was laying out. One has grown well, but the other remains a puny misery, no larger than when it went in, now many years ago. I know perfectly well why this has happened. This particular curve of shrubs runs almost down to our waterfront, and near the water there is very little topsoil; the sandy subsoil rises to within a couple of inches of surface level. I was away the day the poor misery was set out, and no one thought to fill the planting hole with rich, homemade soil. Instead, the wretched bush was settled back into place, and the same poor soil that had been taken out of the hole was thrown back around the root ball. In spite of regular top-dressing—that is, spreading good soil around it —the roots cannot find enough congenial nourishment to do more than just keep the bush alive. But I was around when the second smokebush went in. We dug out a large pit, filled it with very rich, homemade soil, and settled the root ball in with a great many shovelsful of the same heady food. This bush basically is growing in the same sandy soil that's around the other unhappy specimen, but the roots can find enough food in the fresh earth we barrowed into the pit to support a large, growing plant.

In the country garden we inherited a fearfully decrepit rose garden in which the soil had been reduced almost to straight sand. Even the weeds that rushed out in the spring in frightening profusion turned a sickly yellow and withered off before midsummer. When weeds fail to flourish, then there is real cause for alarm about the condition of the soil!

The color and size of the leaves of well-established trees and bushes are another clue. Leaves that have a yellowish tinge should always be regarded with suspicion, unless, of course, they are variegated plants. There can be many rea-

Stunted smokebush in unimproved soil and one, originally identical in size, that was properly planted.

sons for a jaundiced look, but poor drainage or inadequate minerals in the soil is sometimes the cause. If the leaves of old plantings seem unnaturally small, that again is a danger signal. Those old apple trees in the suburban garden had such small leaves that they might have been out-of-scale bonsai; the stunted twig ends told a clear story of poor nutrition. The average amount of new growth put out each year by trees and shrubs is another clue to the fertility of the soil. A gardener taking on a new place should study the branches of the bushes and see how much growth has been made in the past year. New growth can be identified because it is lighter in color and has a softer bark that is easily scratched with a fingernail. Once the new growth has been identified, its length should be noted and then compared with new growth in the following season. Very wet years produce abnormally long, new growth on some trees. But if the new growth seems to be steadily decreasing in size each year and if the shrub is not just suffering from faltering old age, then there may not be enough nourishment in the ground.

Another sinister sign is premature leaf drop. We have a quince which is tied, or espaliered, to the side of the house. Espaliering, incidentally, is the process by which a shrub, a vine, or a small tree is kept cut back by selective pruning either into a fan shape or to two or three lateral branches growing from a central trunk. The branches that are allowed to remain are themselves trimmed back and then fastened in an attractive outline to a fence or trained to a wire framework. This produces stark, interesting effects and often stimulates flowering trees to tremendous bloom. It can also be done very successfully with some evergreen shrubs, particularly Japanese yews. But it is a long, slow process that calls for regular upkeep and is not likely to appeal to a harried new gardener. The roots of our espaliered quince are jammed between the house foundation and the footings of a cement block terrace, and they can only spread sideways in one direction because the greenhouse is in the way. With such limited space in which to operate, the roots have their work cut out to keep the shrub healthy, and I am always extremely grateful for the extravagant amount of bloom that appears. I do my best to help by cutting out greedy lower suckers which don't flower and by pruning the tied-up branches severely so that the roots don't try to take on too much. I also regularly top-dress the base of the plant to add extra food. The quince is one of the new double hybrids and is not subject to the natural leaf drop that afflicts the unimproved varieties of this shrub in midsummer. It usually remains tactfully clothed right down to the base until the end of the growing season. But every so often, by some fluke, the bush sets fruit even though double hybrids are usually infertile. Whenever this happens, we run into problems. Both the plant and I want to save the crop: quinces make delicious jelly which I enjoy

Espaliered quince.

and the plant wants to save the fruit because that is its ultimate mission in life—to perpetuate itself. But the extra effort
called for from the roots to hold the crop until it ripens is
just about the last straw. There is too little food in the confined space to save both the fruit and the leaves, and like any
parent, the plant opts to save its children rather than itself.
So whenever we have a fruit crop, the plant discards most of
its leaves in order to send the available nourishment up to
the ripening fruit.

If a tree or shrub with an undisturbed root run sheds
earlier than usual, look out! Early leaf drop is an indication
that something is wrong with the soil. If the drainage in the
area is good, the rainfall normal, and there are no extraneous
problems of disease or attacks by pests, the difficulty may well
be insufficient food. With conifers the same type of warning
is given by a premature drop of the needles. Every evergreen
tree or conifer eventually loses its oldest leaves or needles,
those that are farthest from the growing tip. There is no need
to be alarmed when the green part of the arborvitae branch
that is nearest to the trunk turns brown in late fall and drops
off; this is a normal process—the equivalent of the leaf drop
of deciduous trees. Yews lose their old needles in the late
spring when new growth is bursting out not only at the growing tip of each branch but also along the branches themselves.
The warning signal is when the needles of a conifer near the
growing tip brown and fall off. Some conifers naturally grow
long and lanky with a tuft of needles at the end of each
branch. But at midsummer the whole tuft should be green.
A conifer that has brown needles showing near the top of the
branches at the height of the summer should be regarded
with suspicion. It may be a pest, but it could be malnu-
trition.

Trees that are growing on land that has been compacted
with heavy machinery take their miserable time dying. At
first nothing particular may seem to be wrong; the first signal is mild die-back at the ends of some of the outer branches.
But each subsequent year there are more dead branches, and
the leaf canopy will steadily get thinner. Maples are particu-

larly vulnerable to this kind of damage, for they have shallow roots. The death throes may be long drawn-out, but, unfortunately, they are inexorable. Eventually the tree will quietly succumb, for there is almost nothing that can be done to save one that has started this downward path. The same route is taken by trees that have had the level of the ground changed around the base. But in this case rapid removal of the suffocating mounded-up earth can sometimes reverse the decline. In both instances the best cure is never to allow the trouble to start in the first place.

In areas with poor drainage, which can happen to what previously was good land as a result of changes from house or road building, the trees and shrubs will also sicken. But their death will be faster than trees in compacted ground because the roots rot off in perpetually wet soil. But here there is hope, for wet ground can often be revivified quickly by proper land drainage. This is a technical job for which most amateur gardeners would be wise to employ professional help. It should be undertaken promptly whenever an area that contains good trees and shrubs, which previously has been normal in its appearance, turns wet and swampy when there has been no unusual spell of rainy weather. Land that is drained soon fills up again with air, and the roots of the material growing in it will regenerate as long as they have not been left too long in waterlogged soil.

With all this misery around, and I agree I am describing a very sad sack of a garden, full of falling leaves and browned-off conifers, what do you do? How can you help? To have a good garden that can support everything you may want to grow, it is essential to put back into the soil the fertility all growing things take out of it each year. And since the feeding roots, searching and working through the soil, also slowly break down the desirable rough texture, it is equally important to restore the coarse roughage that attracts air pockets and has good water-retention. This, by the way, is what is meant when the experts tell us to keep the soil rich and in good tilth, tilth referring to the rough condition.

The old-fashioned method of rebuilding starved soil and

keeping the earth in good condition was to add to it manure and the straw litter that also accumulated in the stables. The organisms that exist in all soil worked on this decaying matter and in so doing released the mineral salts it contained back into the soil. And since straw litter breaks down, or decays, more slowly than manure, that added the necessary roughage. But animal manures and stable litter are no longer available to most of us, so what is the alternative? Here we run head-on into the battle between those who advocate chemical fertilizers to replenish soil and those who wouldn't lay a finger on a bag if it were given away free—which it most certainly is not. I am not about to go on record as being adamantly opposed to chemical fertilizers, providing they are properly used—and that means following the instructions for application to the letter. Unfortunately we are now discovering that even the most careful professional use of chemical fertilizers, when it is done regularly and in quantity, has some serious drawbacks, for these fertilizers have come under grave suspicion as a strong factor in the death of many of our ponds, lakes, and streams. All chemical fertilizers contain nitrogen, which stimulates vegetative green growth. Invariably some of this runs off in the rainwater and is not taken up by the plants it is used upon, no matter how carefully it may have been applied. Nitrogen dissolved in ground water makes its way into the local water-holding areas and stimulates abnormal growth in the plants which border the verges of lakes and streams. This population explosion among verge plants, the rushes and the reeds, often diminishes the area of open water to such a degree that a once large lake can soon degenerate into a swampy area.

An equally abnormal growth of aquatic plants, those which actually thrive in and under the water, is stimulated by the phosphorus that chemical fertilizer also contains. A huge growth of aquatic plants demands the extraction of an equally large amount of oxygen from the water to support them; often, in consequence, not enough is left for fish and other forms of water life. The mysterious fish-kills that we sometimes read about are almost always produced either by a sudden infection or, more frequently, by a combination of circumstances that has sharply reduced the amount of available oxygen already depleted by the underwater plant explosion. This kind of death of open water should not be confused with the pollution spewed into our waterways from cities, factories, and reactors, but the final effect is the same. In all fairness it must be pointed out that the death of inland waters through the overgrowth of the plant life in them does not result solely from the use of chemical fertilizers. The various detergents that are used in washing machines and dishwashers are also very heavily laden with phosphates. We have all read horrible stories of foaming detergent coming out of the faucet rather than clean water, and this eventually also works down into the lakes and streams. Detergents, as they are presently constituted, are one of the prime agents in stimulating the overgrowth of aquatic plants. This is yet another instance of the way our life-style upsets the delicate ecological balance of the world we must share with other living things.

In a small garden around the house overuse of chemical fertilizer may not be destructive to the environment, but it can do a garden considerable harm unless the instructions which come on the bag are followed exactly. The material is sold in a variety of mixtures, usually in granular or powder form—and for that reason it doesn't do anything to improve the physical structure of the soil. Farmers, who must use the chemical or inorganic fertilizers, as they are sometimes called, in order to raise their huge crops, take care of this problem by plowing the material in and bringing fresh, coarse earth to the surface. Plowing also distributes the fertilizer evenly and deeply, so that no dangerous concentration builds up at surface level to burn the tender feeding roots. The home gardener who uses inorganic fertilizers must take particular care to follow very exactly the instructions put out by the manufacturers about the proportions that can be used in any particular area. For proper results the square footage should be measured and the exact amount, no more and no less, applied. If a spreader is used, it is necessary to match the aperture on the spreader to the rate of release of the fertilizer recommended by the manufacturer. Unfortunately, there are spreaders and spreaders, and the aperture markings are not the same on them. It is, therefore, necessary to be particularly careful that money is not wasted by putting down too little, or worse still, too much, chemical fertilizer. I think there is urgent need for some kind of conformity to be instituted about the markings that guide the rate of release of either seed or fertilizer from a spreader. A little consumer resistance, not to mention a little consumer indignation, might help! The home gardener must also understand that inorganic fertilizer is not effective when just spread on the surface of the soil. For good results it must be deeply incorporated into the earth, either through double digging, an exhausting job, which is almost as extinct as the pterodactyl, or by using a rototiller, a plow designed for home use which churns up rough lower soil. When used on grass, chemical fertilizers must always be well watered in.

All this is a good deal to expect of a novice gardener, and that is why I am a little cautious about the success or even the suitability of powerful nonorganic fertilizers in the hands of totally inexperienced gardeners. Far too many people coming new to their land think that a shot of some kind of fertilizer will solve all their problems. Each spring when I see bag after bag of all kinds of high-powered stimulants being carried off in station wagons from garden centers, I always wonder whether the purchasers realize the potential of the horticultural dynamite they are taking home so bravely. But in experienced hands, chemical fertilizers have an important place in gardening, and, though I use them but rarely, I am not prepared to suggest that other people, who may not have the facilities for producing homemade soil that exist in our gardens, should keep away from them entirely. All I want to make clear is the need to understand the importance of proper application.

There's also another problem for the novice who uses nonorganic fertilizers. The material as it is put up by the manufacturers is marketed in formulas in which the ratio of nitrogen, potassium, and phosphorus, the three basic elements, varies, as does the addition of other mineral elements. One danger in using chemical fertilizers is the potential harm to the plants from over-application, but there is also the matter of getting the most for your money by buying the mix that suits your particular soil the best. This can only be done by knowing the basic composition of the soil in your own lot, a technical matter that I shall discuss in a later chapter. It is not hard to learn, but I don't think this kind of specialized information is necessary in the very early stages of owning a garden. Certainly I, for one, was not prepared to get involved in such complicated matters as judging the exact mineral content of my own soil when I first began gardening.

My first concern was the trees. Mature trees are such an important asset to any property that they call for first attention. To help ours we sought professional assistance. It is hard for the amateur gardener to gauge the amount of additional food a tree may need, or the exact place where holes should be bored in the ground and the food inserted. The vital pruning and cabling of trees is also not a business for amateurs. The care of trees on most places is better handed over to accredited specialists—but I hope you will note the word "accredited." Unfortunately, tree work has taken the place of horse trading as a field in which the unscrupulous operate. Make very sure you know the qualifications of people you hire, and also something about their equipment, before you hand over to them the care of valuable trees, and, unluckily, a good deal of your equally valuable money!

But the newest of gardeners can set to work immediately to improve their soil, and this activity should have the other high priority. In our case, in the suburban garden, I incorporated dry cow manure in the flowerbeds to give the first annual flowers something to grow on. In the fall, for slow, long-acting improvement, we turned bales of leaves deeply into the soil. Dry manure was also spread among the shrubs, and we raked the ground lightly to get it into the soil. Heavy raking is never advisable in areas where there are rhododendrons and azaleas, for these are very shallow-rooted plants that can easily be damaged severely. After the manure was down, we outraged the neighborhood by piling armfuls of leaves around the base of all our bushes instead of scratching them all out and leaving tidy, bare earth underneath. The shrubs in the suburban garden were extremely sickly in appearance, and the annual rate of stem growth had, I found, decreased steadily in the previous years. The impoverished ground beneath them made it clear that our predecessors at the house had valued a neat appearance more than soil fertility and had meticulously cleaned up every leaf that fell to the ground. But in so doing, they had taken away the natural material with which land renews its fertility. In the wild, soil maintains its goodness because it is always covered with a slowly decomposing layer of leaves, twigs, and other horticultural debris. When the ground is scraped clean in a misguided attempt at over-neatness, this normal process of renewal is interrupted and the soil depleted. This is particularly true where large bushes are planted, for they are greedy feeders.

In the country garden no attempt ever seemed to have been made to clean up underneath the boundary hedges. Our predecessor in that garden may well have forbidden the practice. In consequence, in spite of their size, which had led the plantings to encroach tremendously on the land, there were absolutely no signs of soil starvation, even though the soil in the country garden is far more sandy and less naturally fertile than in the suburban garden. The difference lay in the self-perpetuating program of soil renewal that had taken place annually for many years, for the leaves had been left to rot where they fell.

After that first crash program, on the suburban boundary hedges, we never had to do any further supplementary feeding, and in a remarkably short time the decrease I had noticed in the yearly growth reversed itself, and the hedges have now become a rather harassing problem, demanding severe pruning in the spring and again in the fall. Here it may be important to stress that knowledge is required about spring and fall pruning, otherwise a new gardener can regularly cut off all the flowering branches and wonder why they do not have the blossoms their neighbors possess. This is a matter I shall discuss in Chapter VIII.

These were the preliminary steps we took toward conserving and improving the quality of our land, a small but important start that can be made by even the most rank beginner. But it is only a start. To have a good garden, one also needs access to plenty of fresh, rich soil to add to depleted flowerbeds, to use for pot plants, and to throw into planting holes when new shrubs are being set out. In most instances a beginning gardener has to buy loam—which is just what I did. But I was not impressed with its quality, and I was horrified by the price. So the second step in renewing the garden was to set about making our own homemade soil.

Compost | IV

One of the many depressing signs of the casual, present-day misuse of our natural resources is the huge plastic bag stuffed chock-full of garden debris put out in ever-increasing numbers on the sidewalks to be carted off as trash. To throw away weeds, hedge trimmings, leaves, cut-down plants, and grass clippings in this reckless manner is wanton waste, and we really cannot afford to squander our heritage in this way. A garden is despoiled of the very materials it needs to rebuild its fertility when these waste products are thrown out. Instead of taking them to the sidewalk, the contents of those plastic bags should be emptied into a pile in an out-of-the-way corner of the garden. If the pile remains moist, all the green material, even as you keep adding to it, will be slowly recycled into an odorless vegetable manure called compost that is as rich in minerals as the garden itself.

The recycling process is a form of fermentation aided by the natural heat that builds up in any decomposing matter. The breaking-down process is also helped by the actions of tens of thousands of minute soil organisms that work through the decaying material to speed up its decomposition. The internal heat builds up during warm weather without any artificial help—anyone who has put his hand into a pile of recently cut grass clippings is aware of the almost instantaneous heat that is being generated.

For the beginning gardener, all one needs to do is constantly replenish the home pile of green garden trash, for as it works, or decomposes, the material shrinks. And since most of us feel overwhelmed with trash that we cannot reuse in any way, it is a positive relief to have this convenient dump-

*Country compost
area in early summer.*

ing place for all the mishmash that comes from keeping a
garden trim—especially when there is nothing more to do
to it except wait. If you are very anxious to get the final soil,
or compost, the decomposing process can be speeded up by
turning the pile. This lets in more air, which fuels the internal fire, and also gets the outer debris into the heated center.
We use a pitchfork to turn our piles, but a garden fork will do
as well. And here I would like to put in a plea for the market-
ing of a small pitchfork. We turn our piles because we are in
constant need of the end product, and we want to get the
material broken down as soon as possible—also my husband
enjoys puttering around the compost piles until they freeze
solid. But I also have a gardening daughter with a golfing
husband who wouldn't consider it an amusement to turn
piles of garden trash. Yet she always has all the compost she
needs, and she gets it by burrowing into the heart of her one

and only pile. My husband's orderly piles of regenerated soil, stacked like pipes of port by the year in which they were made, are easier for me to get at, but the material in them is not necessarily any better than the soil my daughter scratches out when she needs it.

This magic compost—and it is almost magic to see a jumble of old marigold stalks, apple windfalls, and the like turn into clean, sweet-smelling soil—has a great many of the assets of animal manure without some of the obvious drawbacks. It does not, for example, attract flies, and it does a superb job of reviving worn-out soil without all that digging and delving. Anything organic can go in, although I would keep hardwood branches out, for they break down much more slowly. At the seaside garden we add a lot of seaweed, and dedicated organic gardeners often add their garbage, although I am a little against this. There is nothing wrong with the principle—we add peapods, the outer leaves of cabbages, the tops of the carrots, and kitchen wastes of that kind—but table scraps and true garbage must be buried very deeply in the heart of the pile each time they're added, and this is a chore. What's more, there is only a limited amount of space deep in a compost pile where household garbage can be adequately buried. And if this kind of material is not very thickly covered, the local dogs will soon disinter it, and you may even find it attracts rats. Also I don't happen to like the appearance of half-decayed grapefruit rinds scattered around the edge of a pile of garden rubbish—it invites adverse comment! If garbage is to be used, the pile must be covered immediately afterward with a layer of earth. Otherwise the neighbors may complain of the smell, and you may find yourself the local lord of the flies.

All this, is, I think, adding an unnecessary complication to what ought to be a very simple, clean process. But I would be less than honest if I didn't admit that the steady moisture needed to produce good compost does bring mosquitoes. We keep a can of nontoxic insecticide handy in case they get too bad. These are available at any garden center and contain, as the basic ingredient, either rotenone or pyrethrum. Both materials are safe to use and will not adversely affect either you or any bird or beast.

Watch out for thorny material. Barberry, pyracantha, brambles, rose canes, and the like shouldn't go in the family compost pile. The thorns don't break down as fast as the rest of the soft wastes, and they remain ready to attack you in the finished product.

The fiercer the internal heat and the longer it lasts, the sooner the compost will be made. If you prolong the period in which the heat steams away inside like a miniature volcano, you will get speedier results. In the late fall in the seaside garden, we pile seaweed over the garden trash of the current season to form an insulating blanket that holds the warmth in. The seaweed takes a very long time to decompose, so the thick layer does not disintegrate under the weight of snow or ice. In the suburban garden no seaweed is available, and the compost takes markedly longer to "make," that is, to turn into usable soil.

Compost and compost-making has, unfortunately, become something of a cult. Ardent proponents of its use can, by their ardor and overenthusiasm, put off nervous gardeners by making the whole process sound far more complicated than it need be. Composting can be a very elaborate scientific process, and the mineral content of the finished product can be varied by experienced horticulturists to better suit the needs of specialized plants. But all that comes at a far later stage in home horticulture.

There are many advantages connected with this homemade soil. First, it's free and you have it in your power to make as much or as little of it as you want. This is no small blessing. Commercially purchased loam, which is far from cheap, is now hard to get in small quantities. Most home gardeners have no place to store a huge load of soil, yet this is what they are often compelled to buy when, in fact, all they really need is a full bushel basket. Compost is also much richer—that is, much fuller of those vital minerals—than any purchased soil. Commercial loam, alas, is often "stretched" with extra sand to make it go further. Compost may not contain every mineral element needed for superb plant growth, but since it is made from the materials that grew in your own garden, it does at least return to the soil the very same minerals it took out of it to grow the flowers you enjoyed and to make the shrubs and trees leaf out and blossom. Also, since compost is made from the slow decomposition of a whole variety of vegetable waste, everything does not break down at the same speed. Tough materials like plant stems disintegrate less quickly and less completely than soft hedge trimmings. The finished product, therefore, contains a lot of roughage, which is not the case with purchased loam, and this, as we already know, is extremely important to soil because air pockets form around it. The roughage in compost also keeps the soil open, making it easier for the roots to spread out in their search for food.

Compost, or homemade soil, does a superb job of revitalizing worn-out soil, and, because it is not a chemical product, it can be used without any of those cautionary warnings that have to be given to those contemplating the use of inorganic fertilizers. No matter how much compost is applied to a gar-

Country compost in fall. Seaweed insulation blanket already in place on the middle pile and the one on the end nearly ready for use.

den, it will never burn tender roots and, in my experience, unlike its inorganic counterpart, it does not have to be dug in to work. You can just spread it, leave, and love it—and so will your garden.

One of our very first activities after we purchased the suburban house was to dig a deep pit, which is the way I had seen compost made in my childhood, in that out-of-sight area behind the garage and throw the various garden wastes into it. We were anxious to build a reserve of good soil as fast as we could, so at the beginning we used an activator. These are available at any garden shop and consist of powdered chemicals which are sprinkled over a pile and are alleged to speed up the process of decomposition. Our wretched garden soil was crying out for help, and we felt we must do all we could to get fresh, rich earth. But once we'd accumulated enough reserves and my husband had perfected his composting skills, we stopped adding anything except our own garden waste. Activators are expensive, and just one thing more to remember to keep in stock. I am always one for doing everything the simplest possible way; also, I'm not at all sure that

The same area in a midwinter, icy quagmire. End pile still workable owing to insulating seaweed blanket.

Suburban compost area in early spring.

activators really make any difference to the speed at which good soil is made—as long as you keep your compost piles turned. If, like my daughter, you do not turn your piles, then possibly it is a useful addition.

Doing things the easy way also led us to give up the pit. Digging out the compost from it was both time-consuming and unnecessarily exhausting. Instead we began making compost on ground level; the end product is much easier to turn and work, and it is just as rich. The only drawback is that this method is not as tidy.

Compost is in heavy use in our gardens. We add it annually to the flower- and vegetable-growing areas. I use it for all my house and greenhouse plants. I store large bins of it for winter work, and it is piled along the roots of the clipped hedges each year to renew their fertility. On the rare occasions when we have an oversupply, we spread the surplus in the shrubbery on top of the natural accumulation of leaves. There's no soil that will not be improved by a top-dressing of compost. Put through a fine screen, it also is excellent for patching and rebuilding lawns. A disadvantage is the fact that it is invariably full of weed seeds which survive the heat of decomposition, but then so is commercial soil. There is no way out of this particular difficulty unless you're prepared to spend a considerable sum and buy a bag of sterile loam. This I, for one, couldn't possibly afford, in the amount that I need for the garden. We are lucky in having enough room out of sight in our gardens where this rather untidy business can be carried out, and where there is enough space to turn the piles.

If you can't stand the slightly elemental look of that home-made volcano, equally good compost can be made inside a neat enclosure of cement blocks. This can be filled with all the debris and, for the superneat, the pile covered with a sheet of black plastic. This makes the whole process entirely unobtrusive, and the cover keeps the pile working with additional energy by holding in moisture. The cement blocks also conserve some of the heat through the first early frosts. But if you cover your pile, you must remember that no rain or snow will wet the material down; you must add water yourself. And in that case build your compost enclosure near an outdoor faucet.

I've also seen very elegant compost enclosures made just like corn cribs with heavy beams. These containers were almost a decorative feature of the yard, most impressive but beyond the means of most of us. The cinder block arrangement is, however, not expensive and is simple for the average gardener to manage. The blocks should not be set too closely together on one side. Then, when made compost is wanted from the base of the pile, the loose blocks can be pulled out and the available material scooped out. I should find taking off a plastic cover each time I wanted to add debris a bore, but then I'm an impatient person. I've talked to those who do use a cover and they give it glowing recommendations, for by being undercover none of the goodness of the soil is leached away by heavy rains. If a cover is used, it must be fastened down very securely on all sides. If you throw earth on it you defeat your purpose of neatness, so it's better to use heavy stones or cement blocks. Wind easily gets under plastic, and the cover may balloon out one stormy night, sail away, and get tangled in a tree. Plastic sheeting is one of the new and more insidious polluters; it never decays, so bits and pieces can remain an eyesore forever in the back of the shrub border or tangled in the bushes. Future archaeologists digging in the residue of our civilization are going to be enveloped in discarded plastic bags still almost as good as new!

If you have a very small yard and no place even for a cement block enclosure, you can, it seems, still make compost. I recently read—and to my shame I cannot remember where —a fascinating description of using a bottomless plastic garbage pail for this purpose. The instructions suggested cutting out the entire base of the pail, and then setting the open-ended container into a slight depression in the ground. All you then have to do is pile in your leaves and other garden rubbish, add a little water, and shut the lid. Very neat and tidy and nothing for anyone to complain about. The open bottom lets the moisture drain out but still keeps the rubbish wet. It also gives the natural soil organisms that speed up the decomposition process access to the container. If you set the whole contraption in a sunny place, it should heat up and work very fast. As the contents shrink, more garden debris can be added. The account didn't say how long it took to make compost, but obviously it would be no trouble to tip up one side occasionally and see what's happening at the bottom of the pile. I wouldn't pack the contents in too tightly— remember that air is an important factor for speeding up composting—but other than that it seems a most admirable plan.

However you make your homemade soil don't leave it standing around too long. Worms love it. They move in as soon as the material breaks down sufficiently, and they then enrich it by ingesting it. But as worms work through a pile, they slowly reduce all the compost to a rather fine texture. This makes it less valuable for potted plants or even for use in the garden. Also, the feeding roots of every bush and shrub for yards around a pile of compost will work their way into it, and in so doing, not only take the goodness out of it but, again, break down the desirable coarse texture. But even an old, rather powder-fine pile of homemade soil can be richer in minerals and better in texture than much of the commercial loam that is offered for sale.

Above all, don't be frightened off by the rather alarming descriptions of compost-making that are written up by the brotherhood of organic gardeners. Compost can be made very scientifically, and with great precision and skill in the balance of its mineral wealth, but that belongs to quite an advanced stage of gardening. Those descriptions of composting that sound a little like the first chapter of Genesis usually deal with the preparation of specialized soil, or standard com-

*Roots invading
rich compost.*

*Old rose garden
under winter mulch
of seaweed and
half-made compost.*

posts in which the ingredients are stable and constant, and
this isn't the kind of everyday activity that the casual gardener
needs to undertake. New gardeners should be encouraged to
try their hand at the simplest possible form of recycling garden wastes—once they have started doing so, their enthusiasm will carry them into the more complicated aspects of the
process without any further encouragement.

Compost that is richer than plain recycled garden wastes
can be produced by adding a layer of soil to cover each thick
layer of garden trash. Made this way, the compost piles cannot be turned, for the sandwich layer of soil would be displaced. Layered compost is therefore slower to break down,
and it also calls for plenty of spare soil—and room to store it,
which is beyond many gardeners. Our compost piles do contain some soil that comes in on the roots of some of the contents, but we do not add it deliberately. The green volcanoes
of garden trash piled up with an indentation at the top to
catch the rain take about twelve months to break down into
black, half-decomposed material, and another season to turn

into crumbly soil. We use it at the halfway stage as a mulch on the flower garden, which I shall discuss in Chapter VI, and this coarse, unfinished compost is invaluable at the bottom of a pot for a house plant. The final material we use everywhere in the garden.

Once our soil was reasonably rejuvenated, a new problem arose. It now became important to know exactly the type of soil we were constantly rebuilding with its own waste products. The continuous cycle of refertilizing that we had underway meant that we were steadily intensifying the basic soil reaction. Since certain plants won't grow in certain soils, it became important to know exactly what we had underfoot. Soil falls roughly into three categories: acid, or sour soil, of which the extreme example is peat swamp; alkaline, or sweet soil, which has a high lime content; and between the two extremes a rather rare neutral soil that exists mainly in the Mediterranean. The intensity of the variation from sour or acid to sweet or alkaline soil can be measured in two ways: a sample of the soil in a garden can be sent to the local agricultural field station for analysis, or it can be tested with a simple home kit which is available everywhere. The home kits are much less precise than the careful analysis of the agricultural stations, but they serve the purpose for most home gardeners. The method is along the lines of a litmus paper test; a color change is recorded on special testing paper according to the characteristics of the soil. The relative acidity or alkalinity is recorded in what is called a pH unit. Acid soil has a pH reading below 7, alkaline soil a pH greater than 7, and that rare bird, neutral soil, reads exactly 7. In the home-testing kits, the red and orange reactions show high acidity, the blue-green readings mean a strong concentration of lime in the soil. Most plants grow best in a slightly acid soil—yellow-green on the home kit. We were lucky in having that particular reading in our gardens. This meant that, making allowance for our particular climate, there were few plants we couldn't grow.

Plants that prefer an alkaline soil, such as all the clematis, can usually be persuaded to put up with a mildly acid soil as long as horticultural lime is added around the roots each year to sweeten the soil. Had our soil been naturally alkaline we would have had far less choice of what to grow. The acid-loving plants, which includes the huge family of Ericaceae, all the rhododendrons, azaleas, mountain laurel, heathers, heaths, and blueberries, to mention only a few out of a tremendous list, are completely intolerant of any lime in the soil. Highly expert gardeners can sometimes get these plants to grow (though not really to thrive) by building peat beds. This involves extracting all the soil from a chosen position and replacing it with special acid soil or even turfs of peat. This is advanced and complicated gardening, and it doesn't work well for long, for the ground water carries the natural lime deposits back into the specially acidified soil, and the plants ultimately react in misery. My brother lives on chalk or lime soil in England, which cuts him off from growing azaleas and rhododendrons. He is an excellent gardener, but his attempts to grow these plants, using special soil beds, have proved in vain. Beginning gardeners who have not yet reached the stage of worrying about the pH factor in their soil would do well to buy their stock plants from local retailers. Plants that cannot grow in any particular area are not offered for sale, so there is no danger in planting whatever the local garden centers carry. The trouble comes when the new gardener gets carried away by technicolor advertisements in out-of-state catalogues. Plants bought through the mail may well be incompatible with the local soil. Good catalogues usually stress the specific requirements of fussy plants, but this unfortunately is not a universal custom, and many new gardeners have suffered maddening disasters, after spending a great deal of money. By far the best way of stocking a garden is to use locally raised material that is accustomed to the soil and the climate of the area in which it is offered for sale.

Apart from the necessity of finding out the pH factor in order to discover what can be grown, this knowledge is also very important to those gardeners who use chemical fertilizers. Knowledge of the local soil reaction makes it possible to choose very exactly among the many mixes the one that best suits the particular area. In small gardens, the soil reaction can be modified to a limited degree. It can be brought into more even balance, if it is either extremely acid or overwhelmingly alkaline, by a judicious choice of inorganic fertilizer that puts more of the missing element back into the ground. The same is also possible when mixing up a batch of soil for house plants. Composting will not have this effect, for the decaying plant material will only return to the land the original minerals it took out. Altering the soil reaction in a large area is not worth the effort; it can't be done. Bend with the wind and grow plants that like your soil; you and they will be much better off!

The need to understand the basic components of the garden soil comes after the fertility and good tilth of the land have been restored. And the compost pile is the easiest route to this restoration. Soil reaction sounds rather frightening to new gardeners, but composting is a simple matter that can be made to work by anyone anywhere. Everyone should set to work and make compost, even if he owns only a tiny plot of land. It is one small way we can undo some of the damage we are causing the environment through our wasteful habits, and we save ourselves money at the same time. I cannot think of any better reasons for getting started!

Lawns & Grass | V

Recently some English horticulturists were brought to the country garden to see some succulent plants. If I had had my way, they would have arrived by helicopter and been kept confined strictly within the brick courtyard where these plants are grown. The English are renowned for the excellence of their lawns, and I was not particularly proud of the appearance of our grass. But my visitors were prepared to accept the hard realities of the American climate, and they expressed a genuine interest and curiosity about how we obtained as good a lawn as we did. They were, in fact, so understanding that, rather to my astonishment, I found myself showing them some of the more deplorable patches in order to illustrate a few of the outstanding difficulties with which we all have to contend in this country, as well as explaining the efforts that have to be made in order to grow our so-called lawns.

After they had gone, I felt encouraged that here at last were rather rare horticulturists who were prepared to understand that the poor grass many of us have in America is not just the result of incompetence or inadequate effort. Later I was annoyed with myself, for this reaction meant that I had again fallen into the foolish, familiar trap of feeling self-conscious about not being able to produce a lawn as beautiful and weed-free as those which are commonplace in England. This is an absurd feeling and one to which far too many American gardeners are prone, and it is time we got over it once and for all. Those pleasant English visitors had come to see plants in my garden which they cannot grow outdoors because of their weather. They had not come to see lawns which they can grow far better than most Americans, because the climate in the British Isles is particularly well suited to growing excellent turf.

In spite of the fact that so much of the climate in the United States makes the production of fine grass a time-consuming and often unsuccessful occupation, a well-kept lawn in front of a house is still very much a homeowner's status symbol. Uncut, unkempt grass is a rare sight in most American communities, and even the most determined non-gardener feels a moral obligation to keep up the property values by keeping up the lawn—even if he has to pay a gardening service large sums to do it for him.

Considering the fearful problems involved in handling grass in most of America, I find this respectful attitude toward the necessity of having a neat lawn very impressive, but I question whether the results are worth all the effort involved. After we bought the country house, I had to come to terms with what looked like an insurmountable problem of having far too many lawns and far too little time to look after them properly, if they were to be kept weed-free. I solved the matter by lowering my standards about what would count as acceptable grass when not looked at too closely, and I have operated ever since at this rather reduced level. And in all honesty I don't think that the overall appearance of the gardens has suffered very much as a result!

This was a complete about-face for me, for I didn't feel at all casual about grass when we got our first garden. The lawns in the suburban garden were all thin and weak, and I was disgusted by their appearance. I was accustomed to my family's immaculate turf, and I still held to the lofty British tradition that the problems of poor grass can be cured by proper handling and regular attention along English lines. In consequence, I spent a disproportionate amount of gardening energy trying to achieve the impossible, a traditional English lawn in New England, and the result of all my work was not particularly encouraging. But my efforts, though unsuccessful, were not entirely wasted. The experience taught me to be a good deal less sure of my ability to force my own ideas upon the landscape, a lesson that every gardener must absorb sooner or later. It also freed me from the tyranny of the struggle for perfect grass, for, though I did not have sense enough not to start on this venture, I did realize that I was getting nowhere and that some change of plan was in order, even before we acquired the country place.

Surely the time has come to take a new approach to grass in America! Gardening outdoors should involve more than just the lawn. It should be a combination of various horticultural activities, in which grass is a part of the story but not the whole book. I still think that something green sets off flowers, trees, and hedges better than anything else, and when the grass looks particularly bad, the appearance of the rest of the garden suffers. I am, therefore, ready to take a certain amount of trouble to avoid bare patches and try and achieve some kind of pleasant green carpet that can be walked upon. But this is as far as I will go, for I am no longer willing to make a fetish of having grass that is gleaming, weed-free perfection. We keep the lawns mown, seeded, weeded, and fertilized on a regular schedule, and that has to suffice. The most that I expect in return is that the grass looks green and is reasonably smooth, for any other attitude would be totally unrealistic. I do have help with the mowing, and my rather casual attitude about the lawns sometimes upsets my helpers. But I have done with worrying about this aspect of our gardens. If I were to continue along the lines I started in taking care of the grass at the suburban house, I should never have a moment for relaxation, nor, what is perhaps worse, any real certainty of success—and that's not my idea of having fun with a garden.

If, therefore, you are a perfectionist about grass, if a single dandelion ruins your night's rest, this may be the chapter to skip, for we are not on the same wavelength. In point of fact, in these days of scarce labor there are not too many options open to gardeners who will not take a relaxed attitude about grass. One possibility is to give it up entirely and have a grassless garden. If something green that can be walked upon is an absolute requirement, Astroturf may well be the solution for homeowners who don't mind the artificiality. I cannot

The rough-cut lawn of the third garden.

imagine using it in a garden, but then a few years ago I would not have been able to imagine seeing it used for baseball diamonds or tennis courts. And since it seems to suit these activities fairly well, I don't doubt that when the price comes down, it will also turn up as a substitute for the traditional front lawn. For carefree so-called grass, Astroturf has a good deal to recommend it, but it does have two very considerable disadvantages. Unlike grass, Astroturf does not absorb heat and give off oxygen; instead it radiates heat and raises the ground temperature several degrees in its immediate vicinity, which may be a problem in hot climates. It also can easily be fouled by dogs, birds, and wildlife in general, and the job of hosing it down may turn into another housewifely chore.

Another quick but expensive route to instant, perfect grass is to have a sod lawn put down. This has the enormous advantage, as far as I am concerned, of being natural growth, but is, I am afraid, the most expensive solution. Sods are squares of weed-free grass that have been specially grown on sod farms under carefully controlled conditions to produce strong, clean, excellent turf. When the grass is sufficiently mature, it is lifted, with the roots safely enclosed in a block of earth, and the squares can then be relaid like floor tiles in the homeowner's yard. The use of sod either to produce a new lawn or repair an existing one is not a new process; it has always been part of the British method of managing grass. But as a large-scale commercial activity it is fairly recent in this country, although it seems to be gaining in popularity in spite of the cost. Fitting and laying sod is not a job for the home gardener; it must be done professionally and only after the ground has been properly prepared well in advance. The preparation of soil for growing grass is the same whether it is to come from seed or from pre-grown turf; the details will be discussed in relation to making a lawn from seed.

If you are contemplating a new sod lawn, make certain you are dealing with a reputable company, for, as always happens with new, successful ideas, sharp operators have entered the field. It is well worth the money to employ a good neighborhood gardening contractor to undertake the whole operation. The cost will be slightly higher, for he will have to buy the turf from the grower, but the savings to you will be sizable. A local contractor can be held responsible for the proper preparation of the area where the lawn is to go, as well as putting down the sod, and you will then have somewhere to turn for restitution if the grass does not take but dies.

The immediate appearance of a sod lawn is extremely satisfying but, unfortunately, that is not the end of the story. A newly sodded area needs exceptionally careful aftercare. It has to be properly and regularly watered, and the chinks between the sods must be carefully weeded until the turfs blend together. The mowing also has to be done with particular care, for in spite of all the rolling and tamping into place that goes on when the sods are laid, they are at first only a rug of grass put down on your ground. Nothing but gravity holds them to the soil until new roots grow. Careless mowing during the first few months can ruin everything by dragging the turfs slightly upward and thus preventing them from establishing deep new roots in the ground below. If you are going to the expense of a sod lawn in the first place, it would be wise to turn the aftercare of the new lawn over to the contractor who laid it, at least for the first growing season. Otherwise you may not only be deeply disappointed by the results but highly frustrated in your attempts to get remedial action!

Also—and I am sorry to drone on so gloomily but it is better to be prepared—there can be no long-range guarantee from even the finest garden contractor that the lawn will remain forever weed-free. If weed-inhibitor is put into the ground under the sod before it is laid (a rather questionable practice), the natural weeds in your soil will not grow into the new turf for some time. But that will not prevent weeds from appearing in the grass. They will be blown in by the wind, carried in on your feet or by animals and birds. This is not the fault of those who sell you the sod, this is nature at work and there is very little that can be done about it except revert to all the old tiresome procedures of trying to eliminate weeds, which was exactly what you had hoped to avoid!

For those who cannot afford the expense of a sod lawn the alternative is to put down a new lawn by growing it from seed. This is the most usual method all across the country, and it can be done by any novice gardener with a reasonably strong back and a little spare time.

Most people only think about grass in the spring, and at that time of year garden centers are besieged by eager throngs getting themselves equipped to do something about the grass. Unfortunately, spring is not the proper moment to try either to make a new lawn or to reseed an old one. Grass seed is always slow to germinate, and it needs a long period of moist, cool weather during which it will throw deep roots before even a blade of green shows above ground. This early rooting stage is a very critical period; if the ground dries out in a sudden spell of hot weather, which is very frequent in American springs all over the country, you may never even see any result from all your careful seeding. The tender roots will have perished in the heat before they have developed sufficiently to go down deep enough to withstand it. Nor is overhead watering the complete answer to the problem, for a sprinkler often washes the seed out of the ground or to one side. We all have experienced the frustration of finding a newly seeded patch of lawn coming up thick and green in one corner but remaining obstinately bald everywhere else.

If the seed comes safely through these first hazards and the thin green blades appear above ground, the dangers are still far from over. Newly sprouted grass is tender and vulnerable to hot sun and drying wind. Spring-sown grass is also in perpetual danger of being torn out by the mowing machine. It is not deeply rooted enough to withstand the sawing effect of the cutting blade, and yet the warm weather causes it to grow tall, so that it has to be cut in order to thicken up. Skilled professional gardeners do manage to make lawns by seeding them in the spring, but I am not prepared to try and do the same myself. When we have to make a new lawn, and this rather grim prospect has thrust itself upon us several times recently, I find we get far better results by doing the job in the fall.

We get to work around Labor Day, for by then the temperature is on a falling curve and there is much less likelihood of a sudden spell of searing weather. The soil is warm and mellow, which speeds germination of grass faster than the cold earth of spring. The heavy night dews that cover the ground at this season also provide the ground moisture needed both by the seeds and by the emerging grass blades, obviating the need for dangerous overhead watering. The process of establishing a newly seeded lawn calls for quite a lot of rather hard work. Any area in which grass is to be grown needs to be dug over deeply so that there is a considerable depth of rich, good soil. Grass is a perennial plant, and to survive our hot summers it must be able to root thickly and deeply in rich soil. One of the many problems beginners have in making a good lawn stems from the fact that they do not understand the importance of having at least a foot of very rich soil in good tilth as the basis for a lawn. This depth of well-worked soil can be had either by hand-digging, which is an exhausting but inexpensive process, or by hiring a roto-tiller. Do not attempt to skip this stage and make your new lawn on an inch or so of worked soil that you merely raked over. The grass may come up just as well and as thickly on this shallow depth of soil, but it will not withstand drought, for the roots will be too near the surface to find moisture deep in the ground. Furthermore, since constant cutting calls for a great effort on the part of the grass to keep its shorn growth constantly renewed, the roots have to have access to a great deal of good nourishment. A couple of inches of smooth, raked soil will not provide sufficient food. If planted in an inadequate seedbed, a lawn of this type will thin out and be full of weak places into which weeds will move with speed and enthusiasm.

If the place where the grass is to grow has a natural layer of poor soil, even deep digging will not put nourishment back into it, though it will improve the texture. In such a case a thick layer of compost should be incorporated as the ground is turned over. This is far cheaper than buying commercial loam for the same purpose. If you have no spare compost and have gone to the trouble of hiring a rototiller, you can enrich the soil by plowing under green garden debris that has not yet broken down into what we call compost. In that case, before you put the rototiller to work, or before you start digging, you should hire a shredder. A shredder is a noisy little hopper which can run on electricity, gasoline, or can even be exhaustingly worked by hand, according to the model you get. It is a very small relation of those incredibly noisy machines with which tree men grind up branches. A shredder grinds garden trash into small pieces for easier, faster de-composition, and they are used a great deal by organic gardeners to speed up compost-making. Shredders are also ex-cellent for turning waste materials into on-the-spot mulch and thus cutting down on the need to drag everything off to the compost pile. To produce good soil for a lawn, shred the garden wastes and spread them over the ground, then add grass clippings and all the fallen leaves you can find and have this all turned under by the man with the rototiller or, if worst comes to worst, by yourself with your foot on a spade!

If the area you have set aside for lawn is not too big, it is also an excellent idea to incorporate damp peat moss at the same time. The material of which peat moss is composed absorbs and holds a great deal of moisture and is therefore very useful below ground. The one catch to peat moss, which is not always understood, is that it must be damp when it is mixed with soil, either in a pot or in the ground, or it will defeat the very purpose for which it was intended. Dry peat moss repels water just as duck feathers do; the water runs off instantly. Anyone who has left a bale of peat moss standing outdoors through rain and snow can attest to this fact. And just because it is almost waterproof when dry, peat moss is hard to regenerate so that it will absorb water again. Hot water does the trick instantly, but a bale calls for far too many boiling kettles from the kitchen. Very few of us have a hot-water attachment for the hose faucet, though this, in fact, would be a sensible idea for any garden. Without that luxury, what is to be done with a bale of obstinately dry peat moss? I usually solve the problem by boring a hole with a stake into the heart of the bale and forcing in the hose nozzle. Then I allow a steady slow drip to trickle in for hours on end. Don't run the hose hard or the water will just force a passage through the dry material and gush out at the bottom. A very slow drip—the kind that wears down a stone—will be absorbed by the peat moss, and gradually the center of the bale will become sodden. When this happens I scoop out the wet moss and put the dry outer hunks into a plastic garbage pail floating in water. I put on the lid and set the pail in the sun. The water inside soon heats up and the peat moss absorbs it. But after it is wet, I keep it covered in the plastic can so that there is no more of this petrified forest bit.

Once everything has been dug or rototilled, the surface of the ground should be raked smooth with a close-tined iron rake. Tine, by the way, means teeth, and close-tined simply means a rake that has the teeth close enough together to break up the topsoil into a smooth, fine surface that will serve as a seedbed. Raking also gets rid of an astonishing number of small stones that will rise to the surface out of even the best compost. If you have a roller, a piece of equipment I think we make a mistake in not using more on our grass, this is the time to compact the seedbed lightly with it. Don't add water to the roller to make it heavy; you are not, after all, laying the foundation of a building. Grass seed germinates far better on a firm, even surface, and the light rolling does the job. If you have no roller, walk over every inch of the lawn-to-be, compacting it with your feet. Next sow the seed. This should be the very best you can afford, and it will not be cheap. Make certain that it is suitable for the place you are seeding and the use you intend to make of the area. There are, for example, special all-purpose grass seed mixtures for places that are going to have hard use, such as a children's play yard. There is seed for sunny areas, for shady places, and unbelievably costly bent grass seed for those who want to struggle with golf-green grass. The way to find out what grass seed to use is to ask at the best local garden center. Don't buy any old mixture at the local hardware store unless you are extremely knowledgeable about grass and really understand the label of contents.

Apart from the fact that mixtures exist for different types of lawns, there is also a considerable difference in the quality of the seed in the various packages. If you can't get professional help from a garden center and have to make your own decision, avoid any mixture that has a large percentage of rye seed. This is usually the cheapest grass seed offered for sale, and it is not worth any price. Rye is an annual plant, that is, it dies after a single year of growth. A perennial rye grass has just appeared on the market but I have had no experience with it. An area sown with seed that contains a lot of rye will germinate faster and look better at first than any other. This, by the way, is the grass used by the real estate dealers to give the impression of a mature lawn. But after the first season, the rye dies, and after the winter, the new lawn greens up full of dead patches. Look for packaged seed that is labeled "Shady Lawn" mixture. This will be the most expensive around, but it is worth the price. It is called a "Shady" mixture because it contains a high percentage of fescue grass seed, which is the grass that will grow best in shade. But that is not the only advantage. The fescue grasses, and there are many of them, also do beautifully in the sun, and they spread by underground runners, so they are excellent for filling in a new lawn.

One of the great problems for a newcomer confronted with a bare lawn is how much seed to buy. The only way to know—and not undergo the frustration of having to rush out and buy more seed halfway through the job—is to measure the area you are going to put down to lawn. Get a long tapemeasure and write down the length and the width of the area to be covered, then multiply these together for the square footage. I may be insulting you by offering this simple mathematical formula, but it is astonishing how many people shrink at the sight of the words "square feet" on a label. Here in the North, a brand-new lawn needs a minimum of one pound for every two hundred square feet, and a little more won't hurt. Big areas can be seeded with a spreader, another piece of equipment that can usually be hired. Spreaders come with an aperture number that corresponds to the amount of seed that is to be released for each square foot. Make sure you know which aperture number is right for putting down a pound of seed. Unfortunately spreaders come in a variety of styles and with a different aperture release rate, depending on the manufacturer. The number that is correct for seeding a new lawn on one type may be all wrong on another. This is one of those unnecessary gardening irritations that I wish could be abolished. Just as I feel that all car seat belts should open in an identical manner, so also do I feel that spreaders, which are also used for fertilizing, should be standardized.

Once you have the correct aperture, march to and fro across the ground, seeding as you go. But be particularly careful at the turns, otherwise you will put down a wasteful double layer of seed. Each row should overlap the other very slightly; grass seed is expensive, so don't overdo the overlapping. If you still have a lot of seed left after you have traversed the lawn (and you measured correctly), you have

Entry courtyard, country garden— through high-pruned kousa dogwoods.

Kousa dogwood in bloom and with fruit.

Copper beech shading country house.

Country compost piles topped with seaweed and apples.

Flowering shrub border in suburban garden with azaleas, crab apples, and dogwood.

New patio in suburban garden with crab apple and white tulips.

*Azaleas by front door
in suburban garden.*

*Autumn crocuses
among purple ajuga.*

*Bottom right:
Canterbury bells,
country garden.*

Naturalized daffodils

*Old flowerbed
in the early fall,
country garden.*

*New flowerbed,
country garden—
in midsummer
and in fall.*

spread seed too thin. In that case, crisscross the lawn in the reverse direction, using a much smaller aperture until most of the spare seed is gone. But don't use it all up; save half a box. Unfortunately there is inevitably some patching that you will have to do after the grass is up. If you don't want all the bother of a spreader, you can sow a lawn by hand in biblical fashion. In that case, divide the amount of seed you have in half. Walk to and fro in one direction sowing the seed broadcast until you have covered the entire area. Start by seeding lightly; you can soon judge if the seed is going to last, and then, if you have been too meager along the first line or two, thicken those up. Take the second portion of seed and crisscross the same area, seeding as you go. This gives full coverage to the area and is an amazingly satisfactory way of spending a nice fall day. Don't worry about walking over the seed; you will press it into the seedbed as you do so, and this is all to the good.

I don't think it is wise to combine seed and fertilizer at the same time, though I sometimes see this practice advocated. A well-prepared seedbed has all the nourishment in it that the minute feeding roots can take; extra fertilizer will burn them if it is a chemical product, or go to waste if it is organic. Once the seed is down, it should be lightly covered with soil, either with a spreader or by hand. The covering serves a double purpose. It gives the seed the darkness it prefers to germinate, and it also prevents heavy rain from washing it into the small unevennesses that exist in every surface, no matter how carefully the seedbed was prepared. I usually buy sterile soil for this final covering. I am not sure it makes the slightest difference to the future weeds, for they are all lurking in the soil under the grass seed, but psychologically it makes me feel better! Don't put down too much of this final covering or you will suffocate the seed and prevent any chance of good growth. Once it is down, either reroll the area very lightly (this again is no time for water in your roller) or walk over it.

There are compounds on sale which can be used on the soil to kill the weed seed that is lurking in the ground. I am rather wary of all these unless they are used with extreme care. The material, misused, can poison the ground so effectively that it not only inhibits weeds but also prevents your expensive seed from germinating. During my long drawn-out struggle to produce weed-free lawns in the suburban garden, I used an early variety of a preemergent crabgrass-killer, a compound that will prevent crabgrass seed, but not other seed, from germinating. But the material was so powerful that not only did it prevent crabgrass seed from germinating, it also prevented everything else from growing on the areas where I had put it down. Absolutely nothing appeared in that poisoned soil, not even dandelions, for over three years in spite of steady reseeding. In the end we had to dig out all the soil to over a foot in depth and refill the cavities with fresh soil. While I am willing to take the blame for misuse of the material, and while I also understand that the new preemergent crabgrass-killers are far less potent, the experience has left me extremely uneasy about the application of this type of material. On the bag of material that I used, there was not sufficient warning of the almost permanent damage that can follow overuse—and there still is not on the newer products.

All the time you have been laboring over your lawn, freeloading birds will have been keeping a sharp eye on the operation. As soon as you thankfully take off for a well-earned bath, birds will come down in flocks after the seed. It is no good rushing out after them, they'll simply wait until the early morning when you are asleep. I don't think bits of rags or black thread put birds off very much, and I am against worrying too much about them. If you have sown the grass seed thickly enough, the birds will not get all of it, no matter how tremendous the flocks may seem. The bird problem will, however, be minimized by fall seeding. Though birds are always ready for a tasty snack of grass seed, they are not particularly hungry in the fall, when the hedges are full of seeds and berries. In the spring, however, birds are often ravenous, particularly if the winter has been hard. If you have not been able to get the lawn seeded in the fall, your only chance of success with spring grass is to get to work as early as you can tread on the ground without sinking in, and at that time the attack by birds may be quite serious. For spring seeding or patching, I usually spread vermiculite very thinly over the newly seeded area as a final gesture. Vermiculite is an expanded mica; from a distance it looks a little like seed. Spreading it over the newly sown area confuses the birds, and they don't dig in so hard for the seed. Their disgust at finding vermiculite sometimes discourages them from further efforts.

The aftercare of a new or existing lawn is fairly simple. In the spring, round about the time that the crocus are out in the North, fertilize heavily. I don't use chemical fertilizers on grass, particularly on new grass. Instead, I use organic fertilizers, and I prefer a product called milorganite or sludge. It does a wonderful, slow-release job of fertilizing lawns, and I name it specifically because the reuse of waste material may be the only way in which we can dispose of waste safely and effectively without further polluting the streams and the sea. There are other slow-release organic fertilizers, all of which should be our first choice in this day of urgent environmental crisis.

A second application of fertilizer should be put down around the end of August. At this time of year, if you insist upon using chemical fertilizers, turn on the sprinkler immediately after the compound is put down; this is the only way to avoid getting the grass burned. Because of this danger, most people avoid hot weather fertilizing, but it is extremely important for the sake of the grass. Up to this time, it has been growing very fast and has been mowed constantly, which reduces the amount of leaf surface available for photosynthesis. Regularly cut grass is therefore expending tremendous energy just to keep on growing with the ferocity that is such a nuisance to those who have to mow it! It is a bit of a vicious cycle. If we never cut the grass, it would not regenerate so fast, but in that case we should not have a lawn. And, when it was eventually cut, there would be nothing but brown stalks until new growth came in. But with all this strong growth, the roots have used up a great deal of the nourishment that went in with the spring fertilization. By

Concrete block mowing strip. The rampant background vine is bittersweet.

midsummer, when the heat is really on, grass goes dormant; sometimes it even browns off until the nights are cooler, and it stops that frantic growing. Fertilizer should be applied so that it is there for the roots to take up before growth starts again in the fall.

Organic fertilizers can even be put down during the heat of the summer without any fear that they will burn the grass or any need to water them in. All fertilizers are best laid with a spreader. But again, you should know the area of your grass so that the correct aperture rate can be set. Be very careful at the turn of the line when using chemical products. It is easy to give a double dose at this point, which will not only brown the grass but kill the roots as well. A wise precaution is to shut off the hopper just before you reach the end of the line and not reopen it until you have made the turn. I have seen appalling damage done to lawns through the careless use of spreaders.

Thankfully not everyone has to make a new lawn each year—I can think of nothing that might speed up the spread of Astroturf more. But most of us have to do some patching of bald spots year after year, and we should plan a regular annual rejuvenation of existing grass. Once again, the best time is fall, and it is a good idea to get to work some time after Labor Day. This is not only because the natural factors are good, with cool nights and heavy dew, but also because the job should be done before the grass has to be raked clear of leaves. If fresh seed is added to an existing lawn long before the leaves fall, the rains will carry the seed out of reach of the leaf rakers.

Even a perfect lawn should be reseeded each fall; grass, after all, is not immortal, and some invariably dies out each summer and should be replaced. Unfortunately, there is usually more to fall reseeding than just putting down an extra layer of fescue grass; there is usually clean-up work to be done where there are weak spots or bad invasions of crabgrass and other weeds. You cannot, however, just sow seed on top of crabgrass, hoping that new grass will replace the annual pest when it dies in the winter; things just don't work out that way. Dead crabgrass that shows up in the spring is thick and matted like compost, and, like compost, it heats up, so that fresh seed will not germinate in it.

If you have the time and energy, get to work to cut out the bad weed patches in the fall. Never mind the unhappy knowledge that there are hundreds of seeds lying in wait in the lawn, ready for action next year; concentrate on those you can see! Bad spots in a lawn are almost always irregular in shape, and I have found it simpler to square off the spoiled area with a line and four stakes. It is easier to repair a small rectangle than a wavy patch, and exact seeding is also simpler. Dig out the weeds, or the bare soil, and fill up the rectangle with compost. Tread this down firmly and make sure you tread the new soil in close against the edges; pile in more soil until it mounds up a little above the surface of the lawn. Water this heavily and leave it for at least a week. This will give the new material time to compact and sink; to bring it to surface level you may have to add a little extra compost. Seed the open area thickly, far thicker than when making a new lawn, for you need a thick stand of new grass in established lawns. Put on a thin layer of topsoil, tread that down lightly, and then sprinkle on vermiculite. This treatment usually takes care of the worst of the summer weed patches, and the rest of the lawn can be seeded in the usual fashion, only far less heavily than when making a brand-new one.

If for some reason you are not around to do this fall patching, it can be left until the spring, when even more winter damage will show up in the grass. For some years I never did any fall patching; it seemed to me that it was a waste of time when the grass inevitably looked even more tattered in the spring and had to have a lot done to it. But this was mistaken reasoning. Fall patching gets the grass off to a strong start, and though the lawn may still look poorly in the spring, the seed at least is already in the ground waiting to come up. You can reseed a lawn right into the depth of winter, even over the snow. I sometimes think this is a good time to do this annual chore. You can see where the seed lies very clearly, the birds cannot get at it, and the melting snow will carry it deep into the ground, ready for action in very early spring.

If you put off repatching until the spring, get to it as soon as you can walk on the ground. A spring lawn can be a most depressing sight. The dead crabgrass is an insult to the eye, and there may be many other spoiled areas. Some of the winter damage to lawns in this area comes from a fungous disease known as snow mold. This is a new pest to add to our troubles, and the only controls are a special fungicide or a regular spray schedule, which is better done professionally. Snow mold is made much worse when ice caps form on grass. These sheets of clear ice follow a fall of light snow, which then thaws but refreezes on the ground as sheet ice because the frozen land cannot absorb the water. Ice sheets or caps cut off all the oxygen from the area underneath them. This kills the grass and makes the nearby areas weak and vulnerable to fungous attacks. The result: when the grass greens up in the spring, it is deplorable. Nothing can be done about ice caps; they are natural phenomena, and do not happen every winter. But if you have hollows in your lawn in which ice always forms, you will never grow grass successfully in these depressions. If I see small sheets of ice forming in what were up to then unnoticed depressions in the grass, I make a sort of "pirate map" for myself—"five paces from the purple beech and three from the katsura," so that I will recognize the place in the spring if the grass survives. When the ground is workable, we raise the level of these vulnerable areas and reseed them.

Another problem for lawns is thatch, which does great winter damage. Thatch is a thick layer of matted grass that slowly accumulates on the surface of the lawn. It is the result of leaving the grass clippings lying around instead of catching them in a mowing bag or raking them up. You cannot reseed over thatch—again it heats up too much. Thatching machines can be rented that will loosen and tear it out, but to my mind this is work for a professional. If you do hire a thatcher, get one that is also equipped to get air into the lawn with spikes. Air around the roots of grass is just as important as air around the roots of any other growing thing, and lawns that are heavily used often get so compacted that aeration is needed. Our lawns are not used hard enough to need spiking, and I have not had it done. Nor have I had much trouble with thatch. We always get rid of all our grass clippings, for I do not think that the advice about leaving them lying on the grass to shade it makes any sense. All it does is spoil the look of the grass. If you are a demon about lawn care and you are going to the trouble of having the grass thatched and aerated, it might well be worth your while to have the weak places patched with sod instead of seed. Sod used this way is not too expensive and usually gives a better return than spring seeding.

Whenever weak places are patched in a lawn, weeds are the first growing things that appear. We leave these alone. If you rush to pull these first, rather minor weeds you will do a lot of damage to the underlying grass seed that is just getting started. The unimportant weeds usually do not survive the first few mowings; the more truculent offenders—dandelions, plantain, and docks—don't appear upon the scene until later. When these show up, if you are lawn-proud they should be dealt with, and there are various broad-leaf weed-killers, known as herbicides, available for the purpose. I have rather mixed feelings about these weed-killers. The first, rather simple form, known as 2-4-D, did an excellent job, though it is a bore to mix and carry around in a heavy sprayer, which must be done several times each season. The sprayer, incidentally, can never be used for any other purpose. But the product has now been reinforced and made more powerful by the addition of another element, and there are some questions about possible side effects, not only on the environment but also on those who are overexposed to it. This is the defoliant spray that has been used for wartime purposes, and I think we need some careful reconsideration of its qualities before it goes into regular use. The old broad-leaf herbicide was and is an effective product, and you should specify exactly what type you want when asking for sprays.

I do not happen to use herbicides; that is the kind of extra lawn care I have given up. We do cut out docks, plantains, and dandelions by hand in the suburban garden if they are too obtrusive, but that is as far as I will go. In the country garden with its big acreage of grass even that minimal care is impossible. As a result we have a great many very bad grass weeds; in some places the ground is a plantain rather than a grass lawn. Our one main concern is to prevent these pests from going to seed, and this is achieved by regular mowing. For the rest, they serve as my lawn in the places where they predominate. Also we do not do much liming; there is evidence that it is not necessary for established lawns. At most, we give a light top-dressing of lime about every three years.

Crabgrass worries gardeners terribly, more than I feel is

necessary. If it has made heavy inroads on your lawn, the chances are that it is there for your lifetime. If you can increase the thickness of the grass by regular seeding and feeding, the revitalized turf may crowd out the crabgrass. Crabgrass cannot grow in the shade that a thick lawn provides, and it will not germinate until the weather is really hot. One of the many reasons for fall seeding is to get a thick growth of grass well established before the crabgrass can get going. The preemergent crabgrass-killers sell so heavily in the spring that I presume they are effective or people would not buy them. However, I no longer use them. If crabgrass only revived as early in the year as the rest of the lawn we wouldn't worry so much about it. It's the bare patches where it grew last season that offend us in the spring. But if you are patient, these will soon fill in again, and one way to get over the worries of grass is to make the best of the crabgrass when it does appear and treat it as your lawn!

The question of watering a lawn is full of complications, and "if's" and "and's." In very hot, dry areas of the country, watering is essential to keep the grass alive as a lawn—a situation which leads me to wonder why one even tries to have a lawn under such circumstances. Whenever grass is watered it must always be done very thoroughly and regularly. Once watering is begun, the grass roots rise near the surface to take advantage of the extra supply, and if it is withdrawn, say, when you go on holiday, the roots are by then too shallow to search for the deep-lying moisture; as a result, the grass will die. Sprinkling the lawn for half an hour in the evening may make you feel cool, but it is an open invitation to crabgrass, which loves slightly damp soil but does not flourish so well or move so quickly into deeply watered grass. New or weak lawns that were reseeded in the spring need regular watering all summer, for the roots have not yet gone deep enough to survive the heat. New or weak lawns that are reseeded in the fall may get safely through the next hot summer in a New England-like climate, even if watering is never started, for roots established during the late fall weather will run deep enough to search out whatever ground water is available. It's the on-and-off, inadequate sprinkling that does the damage, and it is better never to start than to do a poor job of watering.

We have so much grass in the country garden that watering is impossible. We sit tight, and if the grass browns off with the heat we wait very calmly. Since the lawns are old, the roots are strong and deeply established, and we have no fear that they will die. And sure enough, as soon as the drought ends and the cooler weather returns, the grass comes in green again. I often look at those sprinklers waving to and fro on other lawns and wonder about the water bills, as well as the damage they are probably doing to the very grass they are supposed to save. With the ever-increasing problems of our population growth, I don't feel that it is right to use water in this way. Water is beginning to turn into a scarce commodity; within a short time we will have to use recycled water if there is to be enough to go around and preserve our streams, ponds, and lakes. To me, a brown lawn is no more of a disaster than a bed of petunias spoiled by the rain; both will come back when the weather improves, and I think we make unnecessary trouble for ourselves trying to beat nature.

However, I don't take quite such a casual attitude about the suburban grass just at present. The grass there has been so bad in recent years that we are making a long-term special effort at rejuvenation. We have taken a great deal of trouble with this grass in the last few years. Yet we now have more snow mold, worse lawn weeds, and poorer germination of seed each year, and I am at a loss to explain it. There must be some new factor at work discouraging the healthy growth of grass in our cities, and I am beginning to wonder whether this is but one more adverse side effect from the ever-increasing air pollution.

Apart from being seeded, fertilized, and watered, grass needs to be kept clear of leaves in the winter, and it must be kept mown all summer. By late spring when the grass is up and running hard, it needs regular, weekly mowing. While the weather is still cool, the blades can be set low. It is always a problem to know when to give a haircut to those hopeful spring-seeded patches, we only run the mower over them when we can no longer see soil underneath. In the summer the lawns are cut once a week and the blades are set high. All grass in America should be cut high; this still goes against my English grain, but I know it is necessary. The blade of the mower should be two to three inches off the ground; close cutting is an invitation to brown lawns when the weather is hot. But don't keep the grass so long that the weeds in it go to seed. This will only add to your problems, and the grass itself will show brown stalks when it is cut.

Where the actual cutting of the grass is concerned almost everyone today uses a rotary mower—usually a noisy, air-polluting self-propelled vehicle. This machine, which has come into general use since World War II, has almost entirely displaced the reel types of mower which are still in use abroad, though also mechanized. This I think is a pity, for by and large, a reel mower does a much more even job of cutting the lawn. A good reel mower usually comes accompanied by a small, built-in wooden roller, which trundles along behind the cutting blades as a safeguard for the operator. This roller is a great aid in compacting the newly mown grass and makes those lovely stripes. It is possible to get mechanical reel mowers in America if you search, but they are not as cheap or as easily serviced as the ubiquitous rotary. Also, American reel mowers throw the grass backward, over the feet and ankles of the operator, which may be one of the reasons for their lack of popularity, and a grass catcher for them has to be balanced rather precariously between the back of the cutting blades and the legs of the operator. It is a great mystery to me why this design is universal in this country. Foreign reel mowers throw the grass forward, and the grass catcher sticks out in front like the hood of a car. A good English lawn mower is a wonderful machine to operate—unfortunately the same cannot be said of its American equivalent. Most rotary mowers are sold without any attachment for catching the grass—these are an expensive (and rather inefficient) extra. I find this deplorable. If all rotary mowers were sold with a bag for grass clippings attached to the chute, not only would the hazard of flying debris be prevented, but there would be no need to go over the lawn afterward raking up the grass. True, the job is a little slower since the bag has to be emptied fairly regularly. But there is nothing to prevent you from having a wheelbarrow beside the lawn and tipping the clippings into that. Then everything can be wheeled away at once for mulch or to the compost pile.

The use of a bag would also prevent another all too common hazard with rotary mowers, damage to the fingers from sticking them in the grass chute. The rotary mower is one of the most dangerous pieces of household equipment around, and it horrifies me to see it as carelessly handled as it often is. When using them, always wear heavy shoes. Since the machine, when being used in hard-to-get-at places, is often pulled to and fro, the operator sometimes pulls a machine over his foot, and unless heavy shoes are worn, it is easy to lose a toe. All this may sound like rather heavy weather about a simple activity, but I don't think the dangers of rotary mowers are stressed enough. Not all of them run on gasoline; there are electric mowers which are just as dangerous though blessedly silent. Small mowing tractors are now in common use and are a great work-saver. Some come with an electric starter and are well worth the extra cost. Mowing tractors do, however, tip easily; they are not, after all, jeeps, and anyone using one to cut grass on a bank should be extremely careful, for they are very hazardous under such conditions. I wish in this age of technology something less lethal could be devised for grass cutting—or that some kind of grass catcher could be made mandatory. I worry whenever I see a small child running alongside his father while the grass is being cut. This I consider an unhappy state of affairs; the nostalgic smell of freshly cut grass is a delight and it should not have to be associated with so many warnings.

In spite of the appearance of power mowers and electric edgers, some of which are battery-operated nowadays, some hand-trimming usually has to be done where the grass lawns meet the drive or flowerbeds. But we do as little of this as possible in our gardens, for we have worked out a few small compromises that save us the burden of unnecessary hand-trimming. Where we have growing areas that run alongside grass, beside the edge of the flowerbeds, for example, we put down concrete blocks, butted together as closely as possible at surface level. The blocks are laid straight on the ground after the grass has been stripped off, and any weeds that work through the joints (and invariably some appear each summer) are cut out with a pocketknife in the course of our daily rounds. The line of blocks cuts down the need for sharp edging for the beds. The grass running up to the blocks also never grows high, for the wheel of the mower can run on the blocks and keep it cut. The blocks serve the additional function of being visually interesting.

We apply the same principle to feature and save work around extraneous objects that sometimes exist in lawns as, for example, the rocks that rise like humpbacked whales out of the grass in the country garden. Wherever there is an immovable object that needs grass hand-trimmed around it, we cut out the soil around it to a considerable depth and fill the cavity with sand and blocks. Sand offers an easier solution for irregularly shaped objects; like blocks, it will take the wheel of the mower, and it saves a certain amount of hand-trimming. But sand does support weeds, and it either has to be cleaned off several times each summer or a strong weed-

Decorative mowing strip of concrete block and sand defining a rock.

killer has to be poured over it. In irregular areas we often use smaller blocks that are triangular in shape—they are in actual fact the sections for circular cesspool bases. Laid down around rocks or trees, these make an extremely pleasant feature out of a possible problem. We have used the entire circular stone bases of cesspools for decorative stone circles and also as the mowing strip around young trees. They have been highly impressive in these positions, and no one ever guesses their true function! However, these blocks are much thicker and heavier than concrete paving blocks, and you will have to dig much more deeply to get them level with the surface of the grass so that the mower wheel can ride over them.

Often as a result of careless mowing or in an effort to cut down hand-trimming, trees get bumped from all sides, and eventually the bark is destroyed. Since the nourishment a tree takes in rises through the bark, the tree will die if all the bark is removed right around its base. For that reason alone, mowing strips around valuable trees are very important. They can range from elaborate brick circles to more casual arrange-

Base of cesspool used as decorative mowing strip.

Stones as a mowing strip.

Sand and cement block mowing strip.

ments. I have often seen stones suggested as a mowing ring, but of all the possibilities I am the least enthusiastic about stones and sand. No matter how good the mowing strip, if it is set into grass, the lawn will slowly creep over it, so once or twice a season it must be edged back. This is a boring job but not at all hard when it is done against concrete blocks or bricks. There is a half-moon edging tool that, kept properly sharpened, will trim back invading grass, and there are other tools, including a curious contraption like an enormous pastry roller, which we use. The electric clippers also do a good job. But none of these tools is effective against a mowing strip made of loose stones or sand. Then the job can only be done on your hands and knees very laboriously with hand trimmers. I recently tried using stones around a small dogwood tree that had an untidy tuft of grass growing at its base, but I am going to take them up next season and replace them with bricks; life is too short for trimming grass in this primitive way.

In another effort to make the upkeep of the grass simpler, we have reorganized the layout of the lawns so that most of the acreage can be cut by the riding tractor. The old-fashioned way of cutting a lawn was to walk to and fro, making a sharp turn at the end and returning with a slight overlap. Rotary mowers do not make this sharp turn so easily, and mowing tractors, not being built like English taxis, cannot do it at all. Today, therefore, grass is better handled, though not necessarily more attractively or even as efficiently, by allowing the mower to go round and round the area that is being cut, rather than to and fro. This circular method of cutting a lawn leaves unreachable corners if the grass is still laid out in a plain rectangle. Special efforts have to be made subsequently to get into the uncut square corners. It is better to redesign a grass area so that it too curves, and shape the flowerbeds and shrubs that run alongside it so that they dovetail with the curve of the grass.

In the suburban garden, all the grass that remains is kept cut as lawn. In the country there is too much grass for this, and we keep as lawn only the areas close to the house and guest house. The rest is cut much more roughly and less often, and we don't do any special recutting of unreachable corners. I let this grass grow high and tall and full of the wildflowers of the hedgerows, and it looks like a fine sweep of herbaceous wild plants from a distance. The seeded grasses and the tall ox-eye daisies nodding in the wind are restful and a pleasure to the eye. About twice a summer, I arm myself with a sickle and a hooked stick, and cut these wild patches by hand, for as the grass withers it turns brown and unpleasant. I still wield a rather neat sickle and I know the countryman's trick of pulling the swathes aside with the hook of the stick which I hold in my left hand as I work. This means I can advance steadily forward, seeing what I have cut down without having to stop and rake away the cut grass. There is a knack to handling this tool which is easily learned, but it does have to be learned —otherwise you'll find yourself heading off to the doctor for a tetanus shot. I should be very sorry to run a garden without a well-sharpened half-moon sickle, even though it involves a lot of stooping. It's an invaluable tool for reaching the tall grass that gets in around the base of shrubs or the walls. We also cut down the hostas, daylilies, and other deciduous material with it. We don't own a scythe, and I don't think there is much place for one in a modern garden. Instead we use a heavy, mechanized, shuddering monster called a sickle bar. This cuts high grass, and it will sweep through stands of poison ivy or young barberry. Sickle bars are dangerous objects, not to be used carelessly, for they can get out of hand rather easily. I took down half a valuable beach plum when we first got ours before I found out how to stop it.

The sickle bar was bought in the first place to cut the meadow—one of my labor-saving schemes about grass that was not a complete success. When we took on the third garden and pulled down the house, we were left with a huge open piece of land that had once been a well-kept lawn. It was much too much for us to keep as shorn lawn, so we let it turn into a hay field with a path mown through for us to reach the waterfront. It was a great pleasure going down to swim through a field of hawkweed, buttercups, tall

The rough-cut lawn of the third garden as a meadow.

grass, and innumerable daisies. Hay fields are rather rare today in small towns, and I often saw cars stop while the occupants watched the wind ripple across the meadow. The problem came with cutting the hay. We are in a zoned area where cows for grazing are not allowed, even if any are available, and the meadow is not sufficiently enclosed for horses. For some years we hired a man with a small reaper, and eventually we bought the sickle bar. This did the job, but it left us with long strands of unmanageable hay. This could not be used as mulch; it was too difficult to put down and too untidy after it was in place. It was also unpopular on the compost pile, for the long strands made turning difficult. So we gave up the lovely country feel of the meadow. Instead we now cut that grass about once every three weeks using the mowing tractor, with the blade set at the highest level. This makes for a rather rough surface, and as a compromise between a close lawn and a hay field it works fairly well and gives us excellent grass clippings for mulch. But I still regret that waving grass, and so, I am afraid, do all those families of field mice that used to weave their nests from the stalks.

Grass must be kept cut as long as it continues to grow. Don't put the mower away when the children go back to school or you will ruin the grass. A lawn that goes into the winter too long will suffer much more damage from lack of oxygen than will a close-cut winter lawn. Grass still has to be cut even after the first leaves fall, for this usually happens long before the grass slows down. There are huge garden vacuums now available that will suck up the leaves off a lawn so that it can be cut; most garden services use them, and I daresay they can be rented. But I find all this machinery just one thing more to look after, and we don't use them. In the country, the leaves are gathered in by a brush and bag contraption that is hooked up to the tractor. In the suburban garden we use an old-fashioned bamboo rake. Raking is good for the grass, it pulls out dead material and also serves the very useful function of working the fall seed yet deeper into the ground. Leaves should be swept onto a large square of plastic, which can then be gathered up by the four corners and carried to the compost pile. In corners where the plastic can't be used, the leaves are swept into mounds which are then gathered up between two old car license plates and dumped into a wheelbarrow. I use a small bamboo rake, which slows me up, but suits me better. Leaf raking is a tranquillizing occupation, requiring neither hard work nor mental effort. I regret the nostalgic autumn smell of burning leaves, but those were always someone else's leaves. From my early years, ours were always stockpiled for compost, which is how it should be.

During the winter there is not much that can be done about the grass except to try and prevent people from making a steady track across frozen ground. Regular tracking of this sort wears away the grass, which will be damaged whether there is snow on the ground or not. If the mailman persists in taking a shortcut across the lawn, it is worth roping the area off as a preventive measure. If you must cross frozen lawns regularly—we have to do so to get to the working areas—it is wise to put down an old-fashioned boardwalk. That rare and expensive bird, a handyman, can make one easily, otherwise you may have to hire a carpenter. Boardwalks are worth the money, though you need someplace to store them in. They can be shoveled clear of snow, they keep the feet dry in winter, and as long as they are taken up and stored before the grass starts growing, they do the lawn no harm. Without them, a winter track across a lawn degenerates into a mud track in the spring and a bare patch in the summer.

The other vital concern about winter lawns is the salt slush from the roads. The heavy increase in the use of salt in recent years may well be damaging many of the roadside trees, and it most certainly is ruining a lot of adjacent grass. If you are laying out a new lawn don't forget this danger. Either put a shrub barrier between the grass and the road, or an artificial floor, such as cement blocks, that can take the worst of the splash. Do not try and run the lawn right up to the sidewalk or you will be in trouble.

At this point, it may sound to the nongardener almost impossible to get anything green and smooth around a house. If I've given that impression, I've overdone it. Grass *is* a problem and its upkeep takes a lot of attention, but as long as you don't take it all too seriously you will be all right. In recent months I have been peering at all the neighborhood lawns to see if they are much better than mine. By and large ours came out of the comparison pretty favorably in spite of our relaxed attitude. Most of the neighboring lawns have all the same problems as ours—and some have difficulties that have not yet appeared in ours. But I only notice these defects when I look very closely at them; from the distance the grass everywhere around us looks green and pleasant. Far from bewailing our lawns, we would be wise to congratulate ourselves on doing as well as we do. Meticulous upkeep of lawns is a thing of the past for most people. I have had a far simpler gardening life since I ceased expecting that my houses would repose in the middle of something like the center court at Wimbledon. Why not profit from my experience and let your standards relax a little too?

VI | Weeds & Mulch

Weeds, which have been defined as any plant growing in the wrong place, are the reason why many people cease to be enthusiastic gardeners. Nothing looks worse than a so-called garden overrun with weeds, and nothing is more frustrating than trying to exterminate them. Furthermore, nothing in a garden regenerates as strongly and as enthusiastically as weeds. Weeds haven't the slightest interest in the concept of zero population growth. They multiply unendingly, not only during the summer months, when you are at work struggling to control them, but also insidiously at periods when you may think the garden is dormant. Weeds are hard at work establishing new colonies long before the gardener has got around to admiring the first snowdrop. Weeds are not really discouraged by the first fall frosts. Low ground-hugging weeds continue to thrive long after the more interesting spectacular flowers of the garden have been blackened by the cold.

Many weeds are attractive plants that can turn into a pernicious nuisance if they get established in a flower garden. Violets are an outstanding example. They have delighted poets through the ages, both for their scent and for what I consider a rather mythical attribute of a certain shy quality. I am prepared to be quite sentimental about clumps of sweet-scented white violets, a heritage from my gardening predecessor in the country garden, when I find them clustered together at the outer edges of the old boundary hedges. But when they come up in the heart of a valuable perennial plant, and then cannot be extracted without digging up their unwilling hosts, I cease to feel affectionate or to find them at all unobtrusive or shy.

Weed plants, whether they are misplaced pleasant things like violets, or strangling menaces like bindweed, are a fact of gardening life, and it is quite impossible to set up a quarantine station to keep them out. Their seed is in the loam you buy, in the compost you make, and in the root ball of the plant brought home from the local garden center. Weed seed is blown into a garden by wind, deposited there by birds, carried in on the shoes of visitors or on the coats of animals. Not all weeds are even intruders. Often they were in fact the original inhabitants of the site from which the gardener is now struggling to eradicate them, and they only came to be considered weeds when garden plants were introduced. The New England fall aster, for example, which can be found in corners of the most meticulously kept gardens in the Northeast, is the ancestor of the magnificent hybrid versions of this same plant that we grow today. Like the Indians, the native variety was here first, and it is not prepared to be completely shouldered out of its homeland. We pull it out by handfuls every year, and each year, equally tenaciously, it reappears somewhere else.

In these days of nonexistent labor, it is rare to see the kind of weed-free garden that our parents took for granted, and it is necessary to be much more tolerant and flexible about weeds if we're to enjoy our land. Nevertheless, there are still some areas that should be kept reasonably weed-free in any yard if it is to qualify as a pleasant place. But the effort will be more successful and far easier on the temper if you concentrate on keeping just a few specified areas clear of weeds and are casual about the rest of the yard. As long as the places that matter most to you are in order, weeds elsewhere will seem unimportant. Everyone obviously will have his own idea about which part of his particular ground is the most important to keep clear. I like driveways and paths as weed-free as possible, for I think these areas set the tone of a place. Weeds should be suppressed where flowers or vegetables are grown, otherwise they either overwhelm the better plants when they are small or later detract from the overall effect of the flowers themselves. I don't like weeds at the base of a clipped formal hedge or, for that matter, in any formal area. Nor do I like the verge between the edge of a lawn and the start of a boundary hedge to be full of weeds. Weeds in the lawn itself have already been discussed. And as a particularly personal reaction, I also resent seeing a luxurious crop of weeds stealing the goodness from my compost piles.

These are the places where I resent weeds, and where I am prepared to battle them. Further than this I am neither able nor willing to go. I cannot possibly attempt to keep weeds at bay in every part of the two large yards, and I have, in consequence, flourishing weed crops in the working areas, along the boundary walls, and among the boundary hedges. But to me these are not weeds; they are part of the natural landscape, and I should not feel at all at home in a manicured garden in which nothing was left of the wild out of which it was carved.

In the areas where I do fight weeds, I go about it in several ways. In growing areas I try to suppress them either by preventing the seeds from germinating or by smothering small seedlings. If and when some escape me, I hand-pull them. In man-made areas, such as paths and driveways, I try to exterminate weeds. Both our drives give us considerable weed problems. One is blacktopped, but weeds appear cheerfully and regularly in the inevitable cracks that occur in any blacktop over which huge snow plows must go in winter. The other drive has a heavy annual top-dressing of gravel through which the weeds positively love to grow. Along the gravel driveway I deal with weeds by the highly old-fashioned method of hoeing them out. That is, dragging them out with a long-handled sharp-bladed tool. This, I realize, is not a "now generation" solution, but in small driveways and gravel paths, a sharp-bladed hoe can cope faster and better with weeds than almost any other method. What's more, this action takes place standing up, which is a considerable advantage! To be effective, the hoe must do more than behead the offender; it must also tear out the roots. I should be very sorry to be ordered to hoe any large area regularly, but kept properly sharpened, this tool is very useful in small gardens.

Hoeing is not, of course, possible in solid areas such as a blacktop drive; here when weeds creep in, we have to try to exterminate them. One of the tools I use is a rather alarming little flame-gun that burns very savagely under pressure on a cup of kerosene. This is an imported tool and when it works, which in our case is not always a certainty, it's extraordinarily effective. The pressure generates an extremely hot flame so that the roots of even the most deep-seated weeds are killed. Old plants do not regenerate in any area properly burned-over by this method. New weed seed will eventually reappear, but the flame-gun is also extremely effective in destroying weed seed that has already floated in and is just getting ready to germinate. The flame-gun is also selective; the operator can choose exactly where to burn, and there is no danger of killing valuable plants nearby. The disadvantage is that mine, at least, gets too hot to hold if it is used over too long a period. Because it works under pressure, it also roars in a rather alarming fashion which gives me a slightly un-easy feeling, and I insist, no doubt foolishly, that grand-children stay indoors when we are using it. But if the design could be strengthened and the tool made easier to handle, this method of burning out weeds would be a strong first choice for solid driveways and paths. I am not particularly in favor of using it on terraces or patios, for it leaves a smoky residue that is unattractive and rubs off on the shoes.

Another method of weed destruction in man-made areas is the use of chemical weed- or brush-killers, brush-killer being the best for stubborn weeds in a driveway. Like all chemical gardening products, this needs to be handled with great care. The instructions suggest spraying it over the area to be treated, and they recommend a calm day for fear wind drift might injure good plants and trees in the neighborhood. Most of us have seen the devastation produced along the roadside by careless chemical brush-spraying, and I now never use it as a spray. Inevitably, whenever I started to spray with weed-killer, no matter how calm and bright the day when I began, a strong wind sprang up with disastrous side effects. I now use this material, mixed according to the directions, in a watering can, and that particular watering can is kept solely for that purpose and carefully labeled as poison. It is impossible to clean all the residue of these potent poisons from either a sprayer or a watering can, and, if either is used subsequently for watering, plants will be seriously damaged. Weed spray is a potent poison and should always be stored under lock and key. Just before we leave town each spring I use a very strong dilution of this killer between the cracks in the blacktop, around the paved concrete block terrace, and in the paving-stone walk to the front door. This application in early summer holds most of the obtrusive weeds in check until I return, when I go through the routine a second time before winter sets in. It is important not to allow the residue of this mixture to run into any planted areas alongside where you are working. If you do, it won't be only weeds you kill.

Chemical killing of well-established weeds takes a little time to work, and the killed material subsequently has to be pulled out. For that reason I prefer to use the chemicals early or late in the season as a preventive to sterilize the soil and keep seeds from germinating, rather than as a control when the enemy is established. I dislike the slow browning off of the dying material and the fact that eventually I shall have to root out their carcasses.

Weed-killers that can be used on growing areas are available. They attack only the foliage of the weeds, and the material becomes inert and harmless the moment it touches ground. By this means, weeds underneath roses can be controlled without damaging the rose bushes themselves. I have never experimented with this material, but I know many excellent horticulturists who use it regularly.

If you don't like using powerful poisons, and people with pets or very small children should be extremely cautious, rock salt and boiling water can do a reasonably effective job of killing weeds in a driveway or path. Spread the salt over the place you want to clear, and water it in with the hottest water available. This does mean a good many trips to and from the house, and the results are not as effective or as long-lasting as those with chemical weed-killers or a flame-gun. I used the salt method for years when our children were running around with bare feet. During a recent long visit of small grandchildren, I reverted to it. And I'm not sure my weeds were any more obnoxious during that particular year than at any other time.

If a garden has been laid out with brick walks, terraces, or flagstone patios, an attractive moss often forms in the crack between the bricks or what have you. If you use either salt or weed-killer on these areas the moss will vanish with the weeds. To keep the moss and still have no weeds you can buy a spot weed-killer, which is a little like a walking stick with a poison tip. These are sold at almost any garden store and are reasonably effective as long as there are not too many weeds and they have not got too much ahead of you. Otherwise, you have to return to the primitive method of digging out the intruders by hand. We have brick walks and a brick courtyard in the country garden, and the moss, which is now slowly intruding, is rather dear to me. So I carry an old knife whenever I'm walking around, and each time I notice weeds among the bricks I dig them out. In the spring I sometimes have to spend a couple of hours working over the courtyard, but after that one intensive effort, the handy pocketknife seems to keep me ahead of the weeds there and also in the cracks of the cement block patios.

For most people, incidentally, this is probably the best way to garden. I have always found two or three days of intensive work to get me ahead of the worst of my problems are far more relaxing in the long run than long drawn-out weeks of limited activity. But it is important to make sure that you are on top in the struggle to keep paved or brick areas clear of weeds. The speed at which wild growing things advance and obliterate artificial flooring is surprising. Any terrace or paved area should always be kept swept clean of leaves and debris at all times, otherwise weed seed will start growing in the rotting material. It is also important to prevent grass or ground covers, both of which will be discussed in later chapters, from encroaching over the boundaries of any artificial flooring. This again is a form of weed growth, and, even though the material itself may be handsome, it gives an untidy effect to what should be a sharply defined area. Exceptions are paths, steps, and mowing edges besides flower gardens. Here, as long as the artificial flooring is wide enough, the ebb and flow of low-growing plants along the margins can be a delightful feature and not just a readvance of the wilderness. The deliberate use of creeping plants, such as the various thymes, on paved or bricked areas will be discussed more fully in Chapter IX. But their mention is also appropriate here in this section on weeds. The delightful spreading mats that these plants form when well grown are the perfect hiding place for pernicious little weed violets and other horticultural inequities, and these, once established, will forever remain to plague you unless you pull out the thyme you have so laboriously established. If spreading, creeping plants are to be grown on paved or brick areas, do keep a very careful watch over and under the live mats to see that intruders are not using them as a form of Trojan horse.

In growing areas the main aim should be to prevent weeds from ever getting started. This can be done with very great success by the use of mulch—that is, a layer of sterile or near sterile material laid thickly over the bare soil and pulled up closely around the stems of plants that are already in the area or are expected to grow in this position. Weed seed cannot germinate under a smothering layer of inert material, though of course there are always a few intrepid spirits that somehow manage to find a chink to burst through. But with a heavy mulch on the ground, these successful adventurers are remarkably few, and better still are extremely obvious so they can be tweaked before they mature and send up a second generation of intruders. For flower- and vegetable-growing mulch has many more uses than just repelling weeds, but this will be discussed in a later chapter. Here I'm only concerned with the excellent results that can be had by using it as a weed-suppressor and work-saver, and I do not think this aspect of gardening has been stressed nearly enough to the new gardener. It is far the most labor-saving idea available in the whole new bag of gardening tricks, and it can be used with equal success on large and small areas by inexperienced horticulturists and cagey, knowledgeable growers.

The lack of knowledge about mulch comes, I think, from the fact that it is a relatively new idea for suppressing weeds, though it is a very old gardening practice for keeping strawberries clean and weed-free. In my youth, weed-suppressors were gardeners who worked carefully with a hoe among the rows of the vegetable garden or stooped, knife in hand, to deal with the intruders among the flowers and in the asparagus beds. But when these helpful hands vanished forever, the owner-gardeners themselves had to take over the chore of weeding, and I am sure that part of the present-day precipitous decline of interest in the growing of flowers and

Grass clippings as a mulch.

vegetables comes from a natural disinclination on the part of most people to spend hot summer days pulling weeds in their flowerbeds. I want to make the point extremely strongly that this is neither necessary nor even desirable. A good thick mulch can control weeds equally successfully and improve your garden in the bargain. Mulches can be organic or inorganic in origin and are available in neat, unobtrusive materials that will not spoil the look of a front yard. There are cheaper, coarser mulches that are equally effective for the less noticeable areas. All that is required for success is to clear the ground thoroughly of weeds in advance and apply mulch to a depth of four or five inches wherever you want to keep the weeds out. There can be very few gardeners who would not undertake that much effort for such a huge return if the process were only made sufficiently clear. Mulch also must be replenished or renewed faithfully at the end of each growing season. But given these guarantees, mulch can relieve everyone everywhere of most of the boring chore of weeding that has put so many people off gardening.

Oddly enough, the only mulching material for flowerbeds that has won any sort of general recognition is peat moss, and, unfortunately, this is one of the least effective of the available mulches. Peat moss is exceptionally hard to get wet if it is once thoroughly dried out. It also takes a great deal of peat moss to put a layer of four or five inches in depth over even a moderate-size flowerbed. And once it is laid, supposing the gardener has by hook or crook got it adequately wet, peat moss soon dries out under the influence of hot sunlight. When dried out, the peat moss will shrink again, and weeds will soon come through it. There is also another disadvantage. When peat moss is dry, it repels water, and rain cannot penetrate it and get to the ground underneath. A peat moss mulch can therefore be a serious contributing factor to overdry ground that will harm the plants growing there. Of all the possible ground mulches, peat moss is the one I would vote the least likely to succeed, and I wish garden centers would cease suggesting it for that purpose. Even its color is not good when dry, for it takes on a desiccated, light appearance. Peat moss has many very important functions in gardening, so perhaps I can be forgiven for being so emphatic that it is not good for mulching.

Buckwheat or cocoa hulls are also available for mulching, packaged in rather unwieldy bags. I have used them both and have found them excellent, and contrary to what I read, my buckwheat hulls have never blown away, even though we get plenty of wind in the garden by the sea. Buckwheat hulls have the mild disadvantage of being extremely slippery when they are first put down, and there is a slight danger that your feet may go out from under you during the process of mulching. But this is a temporary danger and passes as soon as the mulch is heavy with water. I like the dark gray color of the wet buckwheat hulls or the warm chocolate color of cocoa hulls, and I've found both of them excellent as weed-suppressors; they even hold down those pestilential violets! The main disadvantage of both these materials is the price. But then none of the most attractive mulching material is cheap. Another difficulty with these small loose hulls is that they run like water and make it hard to put in extra plants after the mulch blanket has been put on. I used both types for years in the front beds and I would still be using them if we had not abolished these particular flowerbeds. I now use a deep buckwheat layer as a mulch in big round containers in which I grow succulents in my courtyard, and I never see a weed come through. The color blends well with my formal areas; the hulls are clean to handle. They also do an excellent job of water retention when eventually they are incorporated with the earth. These hulls or husks do not add fertility to the soil, but they keep it cool and in excellent health. Unlike peat moss, they let moisture through, and plants growing with hull mulch will not be splashed and muddied by the rain.

Many of the same advantages hold for a mulch of fir bark, without the minor disadvantage of slipperiness that exists with the buckwheat hulls. However, fir bark is also expensive and much heavier to put down, for it is sold in large, unmanageable plastic cartons. Fir bark looks and

Firbark as a mulch.

smells delightful, but I don't think it does quite as good a job of suppressing weeds as do buckwheat or cocoa hulls. The material is much coarser and more likely to spread unevenly; it disintegrates faster than hulls, and for best results needs both a spring and fall application. We use it in the suburban garden to mulch the verge area between the lawn and the shrubbery in the front of the house; we also spread it between the stepping-stones that lead from the drive onto the front lawn. These are both very prominent positions that catch the attention of any visitor to the house, so we needed a particularly good-looking mulch. Since the whole front lawn slopes, buckwheat hulls would wash out, but the heavier bark stays in place. Fir bark is the professional manicurist's best friend; you can't live with your hands after working with it, and I now use gloves. Nevertheless, it is an excellent if rather expensive product, though I wish it were marketed in smaller and more manageable containers and in a less compressed form.

Various kinds of wood chips are also available as mulch. Occasionally wood chips can be had for nothing from tree-pruning men who have a shredding machine as part of their equipment. But these windfalls are becoming rather rare; tree companies are now selling some of their better wood chips to retailers. If you have a large naturalistic area where you want to lay a deep mulch, wood chips bought in bulk, which is possible from some retailers, save money. If you live near lumber yards, it is also possible to get chips in bulk at much lower prices. Their light color is an initial disadvantage, but like shingles on a house; the wood soon weathers. Sawdust can also be used for an unsightly but effective mulch, though I am not too enthusiastic about it. As sawdust decomposes it draws nitrogen out of the soil, and this mineral element must be replaced artificially or the neighboring plants will suffer. All wood mulches take some nitrogen out of the soil when they are first laid down, but the coarser the material the less is taken up. Finely ground sawdust is by far the worst offender. We can get occasional loads of free sawdust, and when these are offered, we use it to raise the ground level in swampy paths through the woods, where the color and the nitrogen-robbing aspect do not matter. Sawdust is soft to walk on, holds water extremely well, and smells very pleasant.

We make the most use of the green mulching material that is available to every gardener who has a compost pile and saves grass clippings. To suppress weeds in the flower- and vegetable-growing areas, we use half-decomposed compost that is already dark-colored but still in a very rough, unfinished state. This is piled on in a thick layer and covered with an inch of grass clippings—spread out this way, grass will not heat up and the color fades fast. A layer goes on in early summer after I have planted out the annuals and weeded the ground. By this date, which is usually mid-June, a considerable pile of grass clippings, stacked to one side, has already accumulated.

Around about August, weeds begin to show where plants that have finished flowering have been pulled out. These weedy places are then covered with additional spot mulching. After the garden has been cut down in the fall, we remulch it very thickly with the same combination of half-made compost with a topping of grass. All the books warn against putting on winter mulch before the ground has frozen; there is a danger that field mice may make winter nests in it. But we leave the country garden long before the ground freezes hard; mid-October is the latest we are free to put this mulch down. So far we have never had any difficulties with wildlife, nor have our plants been suffocated by the early application, though we avoid this peril by keeping the mulch away from the stems.

Putting mulch down is tiring work. The mulch has to be brought from quite a distance, which is done with a cart attached to the mowing tractor. If I had to barrow it all in by hand I am sure I would reduce the size of the area that needed it! There's also a great deal of stooping and bending. Putting down a successful layer of mulch cannot be managed standing up and heaving it onto the ground; you have to get right down and spread it around evenly by hand. I used to complain a great deal during this operation and wonder whether it really was worthwhile; surely the spring mulch was enough? But one year we went abroad before the end of the summer and left the flower garden to be cut down by our helper. He did it admirably, but he didn't entirely understand the principle of mulching, so he wasn't prepared to undertake that. The weeds the following spring could have provided cover for a baby elephant. Since then, though I have complained just as much, I have had no doubt about the efficiency of fall mulch!

We would not be able to mulch nearly as freely or as heavily if we had to depend on buying it; the cost would be too much and also we would not have space to store so many

Winter mulch on cut-down growing area. The path and small block of evergreens provide winter interest.

Grass and leaf winter mulch in vegetable plot. The privet hedge still carries leaves in midwinter.

bags. Free mulch material is yet another side benefit of making compost and one that is not mentioned enough.

We also use seaweed as a mulch as it comes off the beaches; the salt benefits the ground rather than harms it. Seaweed breaks down, that is, decomposes extremely slowly, and when we used it in the flower garden I found it made a springy layer on top of the soil that was hard to pull aside and impossible to set plants out in. Now we use it to keep the ground weed-free below the clipped hedges, where it slowly adds fertility to the land. Seaweed is an excellent mulch to put down on land that is going to be rototilled, if and when you can induce the man with the rototiller to put in an appearance! When it is spread very thickly and left in place over a hot summer, with just an occasional watering, seaweed cleans the ground beneath it of weeds. Incorporated into the soil mechanically, it makes good humus, but don't try and dig it in yourself. It will tangle around the shovel, cling to your legs, get into your shoes, and generally prove impossible to incorporate into the soil. After you have labored for hours, strands of seaweed will still be sticking out all over the recently dug area, like hairs on a monstrous half-shaven chin.

If you are lucky enough to have access to large supplies of pine needles these make an excellent acid mulch for naturalistic areas or for shrubberies containing azaleas and rhododendrons, which love acid soil. Pine needles on a path in the woods have a soft, secret feel; I envy my neighbors who can use them this way.

I am slightly less enthusiastic about either salt hay or sugarcane residue for mulch. Both these materials have their patrons who swear by them, but salt hay is now expensive and rather rare, and sugarcane is costly in the North. Furthermore, the color always remains light and unattractive, and since the material has to be put down extremely thickly to be effective, it stands out too much for my liking in the garden. It is also harder to spot the inevitable adventurous weed on a light surface.

In recent years, black plastic has been heavily advertised

as the perfect mulching material. In the proper spirit of inquiry I invested in a roll and tried my luck. The first problem was getting the material down and taut. As soon as one side was pegged, the other flapped up. It was a three-man job before we were done. Stones alone would not hold it down, and to keep it in place earth had to be thrown over the outer edges. The weeds that subsequently grew on these earthern dikes were quite spectacular—the reflected heat from the black plastic was an elixir to them! Following the instructions, I cut slits in the material and set annuals into the ground below. The plastic did a very good job of suppressing weeds, for they could not grow through it; the plants also grew well in their slits. But the overall effect was curiously unpleasant; flowering plants floating above that black space looked artificial and wrong. Also, when the season was over and I rolled the material up, the ground underneath was dry, powdery, and in poor condition; no moisture had reached it for several months, and this had done it harm. One experiment was enough—I have no burning desire to try it again. But I do have a horticultural neighbor who swears by black plastic for growing melons and squash. In his experience the fruit ripens faster and with fewer blemishes when the vines sprawl over the plastic and take advantage of the reflected heat that enchanted the verge weeds so much. I read that aluminum foil or newspaper can also be used for mulch, but I have had no experience with either.

A stone mulch is sometimes used by specialist horticulturists for growing delicate alpine plants that loathe wet ground beneath their leaves. A pad of small pebbles keeps away leaf rot while still helping the ground remain moist and cool, but a heavy layer of stones is not a good all-over mulch no matter how much you may admire gardens in the Japanese style! To keep an all-over stone mulch weed-free, a considerable depth of soil must be removed, the area lined with a very heavy plastic, and a fill of sand added. The stones are then piled on top of the sand. But even with these precautions, dust and windblown debris lodge among the stones and provide a toehold for weeds. A loose stone mulch is also uncomfortable to walk on, and no kind of cart can be taken across it without a great deal of effort. If you are determined to use stones (and I do in fact have a small stone-mulched area in my courtyard), use a strong chemical weed-killer regularly on it, spring and fall, to prevent weeds from ever getting established.

There is, as you can see, an enormous diversity in the number of materials that can be used for mulching. Whatever is employed will be successful if it is applied thickly enough and if the layer of mulching material is regularly replenished. Mulch is a lifesaver for the harried gardener, even though the actual process of putting it down can be tedious and hard work. It keeps a garden looking neat in winter and free of summer weeds; mulched ground also does not need watering in the hot summer months. And, as I shall explain in a later chapter, in some instances it serves as a perpetual source of fertility for the ground.

The one weakness for early-bird gardeners is the fact that ground covered with mulch does not warm up as fast in the spring as open ground, thus delaying early planting. The easy solution is to pull aside the mulch along the rows where peas and so forth are to go in, a few weeks ahead of planting. This will warm the ground. And when you pull aside the winter mulch you will be in for a delightful surprise. Ground that has been covered by it does not need any digging; it will be in perfect condition. Since we have used mulch covers in the winter, we have never had to dig the ground. Once used, mulch becomes as essential to the owner-gardener as a shovel. I only wish I had understood its effectiveness years ago, for I have come relatively late to an appreciation of its use. If this account serves no other purpose than to introduce novice gardeners to the blessings of its use I shall be entirely content.

Boundary Hedges | VII

For many years one of the most unusual aspects of small American gardens was their openness—the neighborly concept which considered any form of enclosure to be a sign of unfriendliness. The unfenced, unhedged front yards of suburban communities never failed to surprise visitors from abroad, who admired the goodwill this suggested, while occasionally deploring the sameness and conformity this attitude imposed upon a community. In some places these open yards were an unwritten law; in others they were enforced by local ordinances, but, in either case, the thinking behind this style of almost communal front yards was a deeply ingrained, traditional habit. Today, however, a trend seems to be developing against the idea of a yard open to everyone who cares to look in. The reasons are many; some are sociological and do not concern us here, but others are practical and stem from ever-increasing traffic on the roads, private swimming pools, new dog-leash laws, etc. But whatever the reason, there certainly exists a new feeling for enclosure and privacy in the home lot, and this in turn has brought about a great interest in fences.

I have always considered a garden a private domain and not community property and, therefore, have the greatest sympathy with those who feel the same way. Everyone should have the right to be as secluded as they want in their own yard, but I am not too happy about seeing it accomplished by tall fences. This should not be taken as a condemnation of fences in general, for there are very handsome ones available, though these usually have to be custom-made. But no matter how elegant a fence may be, it is rather intimidating to those on the outside. There are conditions, of course, in which a solid barrier is the only answer: a place with small children that fronts a busy highway, for example. But in such a case, try and keep the actual fence rather low and get privacy by planting tall shrubs behind it. A tall fence says "Keep out" in an abrupt manner, no matter how well designed, and the more common utilitarian types manage to combine this vaguely unfriendly attitude with considerable unsightliness! In time, all fences can be softened on the inner side by the use of shrubs growing against them, or vines, or espaliered plants. All these solutions help the visual impact of a high fence upon a small lot from the garden side, but they still do nothing about its appearance to passersby, and in this respect I think they have not improved the American landscape.

If the only function of the fence is to provide privacy, then the boundary of the yard can be equally well defined by fast-growing shrubs. These can shield a garden effectively—and with a little horticultural ingenuity almost as fast. Shrubs used for boundary hedges give a sense of definition no matter how small the grounds. They provide privacy, absorb sound, and give shelter from the wind. Shrub borders also serve as a natural barrier against drifting snow—and generally speaking, they perform all these functions far more attractively than the kind of fence the average homeowner can afford to put up.

We use fences combined with shrubs in our gardens. In the suburban garden we are protected from the road by a thick shrub border which provides the necessary privacy and is set behind a low stone wall. Fairly recently, however, we added about four feet of rustic fencing to rise above the level of the wall. This was not put up for privacy's sake, or to absorb the noise; the shrubs took much better care of both those functions. The extra piece of fencing went up to act as a deflector against the ever-increasing menace of the salty slush thrown up by passing cars in the winter, which was rapidly ruining valuable bushes. In the country, where this particular problem has not yet arisen, we have magnificent shrub boundaries that protect us completely from the road without any artificial additions. Since they are freestanding and get the light from both sides, they grow better than the suburban planting, which has had light blocked off by the fence. This is a matter of some importance when considering the overall density of a planting: bushes that are set against a fence will not be as well shaped or grow as thickly as those that stand free. In the country we also have a shrub boundary planting that was originally set out to shield us from a rather raw stretch of rustic fence put up by a neighbor. The fence is long since gone—it was eventually replaced by a stone wall—but the bushes we used to soften its impact on our eyes are now a great feature of the place.

Whether you are planning to soften a new fence or laying out a boundary line of shrubs, most of the same ground rules hold. For maximum privacy the most suitable plant material is evergreens which grow upward in a dense thick form rather than spreading outward—and these will be the most expensive of your purchases. To avoid an unnatural, stilted look, a row of evergreen shrubs should not be planted side by side in a straight line, but zigzagged with an irregular profile. If possible, a second irregular row of deciduous shrubs that spread, rather than grow upward, should be set out in front of the evergreens—also planted irregularly and not in

Surburban garden. Boundary hedge in winter, and with far greater privacy when leafed out.

a formal row. A very simple combination in the North could be arborvitae at the back, with forsythia, althaeas, and peewee hydrangeas in front of them: the latter all capable of being kept under fairly strict control by pruning. Similar inexpensive combinations can be produced in any area of the country. The jagged outline relieves the possible monotony, while the deciduous prunable shrubs can be trimmed to varying heights to form a more interesting effect. A planting of this sort will cost far less than a fence, even if you buy quite large evergreens, and, properly planted (see pages 151–7), will grow extremely fast and make an excellent visual barrier far sooner than people expect. But don't try to speed up the effect by buying extremely tall evergreens; these cost a disproportionate amount and are not necessarily worth the extra price.

Today many plants are container-grown and therefore can be moved at any season with a reasonable certainty of success, and the science of digging big bushes and trees has been highly developed. But young plants move better and recover faster and often in a short time outgrow bigger, older shrubs and trees that have been lifted and moved. Present-

day landscaping tends to be instant—I am just as guilty of this as anyone else—but if new gardeners can just wait a little, the results from using young plants often outstrip the temporary advantages gained from using larger specimens, and the cost will be astronomically lower. Putting in huge trees and shrubs is fine if you can afford it or if you are no longer young and want desperately to have a mature garden while you are still around to enjoy it. But, in point of fact, old large stock, no matter how carefully it is lifted and later replanted, suffers such a shock in the process that it may regress, that is, die back, for several years afterward unless it is enormously reduced at planting time by pruning—in which case it seems a little foolish to spend so much on a large bush in the first place! Big bushes also need far more careful aftercare, and it may be several years before heavy new growth regenerates. In contrast, healthy young plants moved into planting holes full of rich soil grow on without a pause. They don't die back or stand still but rush ahead with enthusiasm. So don't think of small shrubs as growth stock, only to be enjoyed by your grandchildren; you will get dividends in far less time than it takes a child to go through high school.

A few years ago a devastating series of wet, heavy snowstorms did tremendous damage to many valuable shrubs in the suburban garden. Specimen trees and evergreens that had been in position from the time we first owned the place were smashed beyond repair. After we had cut out the broken material we found that there were two very serious gaps in the planting that protected us from the road. To fill in the worse hole, a large yew was bought at huge cost and professionally planted. Some distance away from it a seedling yew about three feet high was set out. This had originated in the suburban garden under one of the mammoth English yews which remained from the original ground plan, and had been grown on for many years in the nursery area. English yews are slow starters and do not grow at the speed of the modern Japanese hybrids. However, during the four years that both trees have been in place, the big one has stood

The rampant leaf-less vines of the big hedge in the country garden still providing privacy in winter.

A grown-on, self-seeded English yew in the suburban garden.

Katsura planted in 1956 as a four-year-old cutting.

still; there has been a heavy needle drop each fall, and the new growth is still a poor color. But the homegrown yew has developed enormously. Clearly it had passed the standstill stage and was just getting ready for a spurt of growth. The move did not bother it at all, and it is now over five feet tall, with a wide pyramidal growth, and is covered with red berries; in a very short time I shall have to start pruning it!

For better immediate effects, it is also important not to plant small stock closely together. The more air and light a bush or tree can have, the faster it will grow. Grit your teeth and let people laugh at your idea of a thick hedge; you'll have the last laugh far sooner than you expected! Knowledge of the distance plants should be set comes through understanding their growing habits. But for a rough guess, take a look around the immediate neighborhood to see how close together the well-grown plants of the same kind you are contemplating have been set out. This can serve as a very useful clue to what otherwise can be a complete mystery. Do this before you go to get the plants; it is a mistake to buy anything with the idea that it will be a long-term asset to the yard without having a good idea of how it looks fully grown. This may seem obvious and preposterous advice, but most of us have made grievous mistakes along these lines in our time. In fact, I have committed this particular horticultural sin twice, planting small trees far too close together without taking sufficiently into account their eventual potential. In one instance, where I set out two small crab apples in an area that now can hardly accommodate one, the extra tree had to be cut down. In the country I decided to have the extra tree moved, for it was an unusually beautiful katsura. It took the tree six years to recover from the move, and it took my purse even longer to recover from the cost of such an undertaking!

If you do decide to buy big expensive evergreens or other plants, it is worth the extra cost to get them professionally planted by the nursery that sold them. The amateur gardener often does not have machinery capable of lifting really big bushes into position. Furthermore, when you have bought material from a good garden center, it is usually possible to get a written guarantee that they will replace the material if it dies—as long as they planted it. This guarantee usually does not cover a very long period, for bad cultural aftercare can kill even the best-planted bush within a few years. But any large and expensive shrub that dies immediately after being planted professionally—immediately being within a year of purchase—ought to be replaced by those who sold it to you. If they won't give you any such guarantee, go elsewhere for the material.

Big plants need large planting holes, and to grow well they also need good soil at the bottom of the hole and thrown in alongside the root ball. If you don't possess a spare supply of good, rich compost that can be used for the purpose, order some loam from the same place where you buy the plants. This is a protection against any suggestion that if the plant dies it was because nothing could be expected to live in your poor, starved soil! Also be sure to be around when the material is planted. You can learn a lot by watching trained men at work, and you should also be there to see that the job is done properly, that it is put in the exact place you want, and faced correctly. This is just another job to the men, but your presence can turn it into an exact operation. And it does not matter how inexperienced you may be, the owner's eye at planting time has a salutary effect on how the work gets done! The only exception to this rule is if you have handed the supervision of the entire work to a landscape architect. In that case, suggest that he be there when the plants go in, so that the work is not carried out by a foreman.

Evergreen shrubs that have been carefully dug and had the root ball wrapped in burlap can be safely moved at almost any season when the ground is open, as long as the owner is around to care for them during the first critical months after they are planted. Deciduous shrubs are most successfully moved when they have no leaves. In most areas, the best time to move either type is the early fall; evergreens are semidormant after August, and deciduous shrubs will lose their leaves and drop into dormancy if lifted soon after Labor Day. Fall is particularly suitable because the ground remains warm and mellow for several months after the move, which gives the roots a good chance to establish themselves. The ground is cold and wet in early spring and therefore less acceptable to the injured root systems of the lifted plants. Fall-planted shrubs also have at least two months of moderate temperatures. In the spring, newly planted stock is in constant danger from sudden fierce heat and drying winds.

Unfortunately, most garden centers do not have nearly so much stock dug in the fall as they have available in the spring, or in nearly such variety. But there is a way out of this difficulty. If you do not want to buy bushes in the spring, go to your local garden center to check the sizes and colors you want and then ask to see the same material growing in the fields. Choose and tag the bush you want dug specially for you in the fall. There are several advantages to this practice. In the spring, garden centers are terribly rushed and are inclined to expect the customers to take what is offered. But by tagging material while it is still in the ground you can be sure that the plant chosen has been locally grown and is therefore used to your particular climate. Arborvitae, for example, grows well in the North and also as far south as Virginia, but southern-raised stock would not survive a New England winter, even though these are the same species. Plants are sometimes offered for sale that have been shipped a considerable distance, and there is always a chance that they may not be able to survive your local growing conditions. Imported material also often gets badly dried out during the long journey and has been out of the ground too long to make a proper recovery. To make sure that any pre-dug plant you buy is local stock, it is best to deal only with garden centers that grow their own—not with distributors of plant material. Before paying for any pre-dug plant, take a careful look inside the burlap bag underneath the knot. If the earth is pale in color, with a powdery texture, the root ball has become dried out and the feeding roots may have been incurably damaged. Even local stock that has been standing around a long time may have suffered too much drying out to make it a good buy. Don't be taken in by a skim of damp earth on the top of the root mass; squat down and poke a finger deeply inside the soil. There's no other way to tell.

Whether the stock is specially dug for you, or whether you buy it as is, always put the plants into a shady place when you get them home—don't stand them around in the sunny position where you hope eventually to plant them without a little preliminary conditioning. Line them up in the shade and spray the foliage; then let the hose trickle very slowly into the heart of the tied-up root ball until water seeps out of the entire base of the burlap. Treated this way, and kept in the shade, the stock can wait several days in safety while the planting holes are readied. Ideally the holes should have been dug before you got the plants, but this is not so simple. For good growth, the holes must be about twice the diameter of the root ball and half again as deep, and it is a little hard to judge this unless you have the plant on hand. Once you actually have the wrapped roots you can make rough measurements with a stick which can be marked or notched. Never plant anything in a hole that only just accommodates the root ball. To thrive, the shrub must have plenty of fresh soil all around the root ball, and the only way to provide this is by digging a large hole. Put a thick pad of compost mixed with damp peat moss at the bottom of the hole: peat moss encourages the growth of feeding roots, though how and why is not entirely understood. But remember, the peat moss must be wet; dry peat moss incorporated into a planting hole never takes up moisture and can harm the new hair roots as they thread into it.

It is important to make sure that there is enough fresh soil at the bottom of the hole to bring the root ball up to the exact level at which the plant grew previously. Usually it is easy to see on the stems or the trunk of a small tree where the old surface of the soil rested against them, for the bark is a slightly different color. If there is no indication, a very rough rule of thumb is to set the plant so that the knot in the burlap is about an inch below the new soil surface. Try to make sure the bush faces the same way it did before. Most plant material has a front and a back, the front being where the strongest light fell upon it. Evergreens show which way the light fell by the way the leaves face; conifers are harder to judge, but the side that faced bright light is usually denser. With deciduous shrubs the tip ends point toward the stronger light. Apart from the fact that most shrubs look better if they are faced the same way they grew previously, there is a horticultural reason for making sure which side is which. The bark of a tree or shrub that is suddenly exposed to full sunlight, where once it faced the other way, is liable to sunscald in the summer or to crack in the winter sun. Some growers shield newly planted trees against this danger by wrapping the trunks spirally in special paper which can be bought at good garden supply houses. But since a many-stemmed bush cannot be wrapped, it is better to try and deal with the problem by the more practical method of resetting it to much the same exposure that it grew in originally. Any bush that has firmly oriented itself in one direction and then

*Newly planted
shrubs with earth
dikes.*

is turned around when it is replanted recovers much more slowly, even if there is no danger to the bark. Often it never looks as well as it might, because the original pattern of growth was too fixed. This is something to watch even when the bushes are being professionally planted. In the suburban garden there was an enormous Royal azalea that outgrew its position and had to be lifted. It was reset in my absence the wrong way around, with the buds facing toward the shady side of the new position; it has never flowered well since, though previously it was a mass of bloom. It now presents an odd appearance as the new growth tries to twist around to the light.

Once the bush is properly positioned and at the right depth, add rich compost halfway up the root ball all the way around until the shrub stands upright alone. This often calls for getting down on your knees and pushing new earth underneath the root ball by hand. The soil must be firmly pressed against the burlap at the lower levels so that the bush will not settle later. Once the new soil has been thoroughly pushed in around the lower portion of the root ball, tread it down. New soil sinks unless it is compacted, and it is important to prevent this or the shrub will sink with it and change the proper ground level at which it has to grow. This treading down is the equivalent of those thumps that are given a newly potted plant. It settles the soil, eliminates air pockets, and firms the new material against the root ball. Roots need this sense of pressure against them to stir into action; if the backfill of the planting hole is loose, this advantage is lost. When everything is firm, cut the cords that hold the burlap, untie the knot, and roll the sacking back so that the top of the root ball is exposed. Don't try to pull the sacking away. It will soon rot, and left alone at this early stage it serves a very useful purpose by swaddling the original soil mass in which the plant grew tightly against the injured roots. Any big shrub that is not moved with a dense mass of original soil is far more likely to die. Only very young trees and shrubs can be transplanted bare-rooted, and the new gardener had better not try to do this, for it is a skilled process that has to be done at fixed seasons of the year.

After the sacking is rolled back, fill up the hole with water and let that seep slowly away; this carries the new soil into any small crevices you may have missed. When the water has gone, fill up the remainder of the hole with new soil and cover the entire root ball. This soil can also be tramped down, but only lightly. Don't put much weight on it, for the water will have made the lower level very squishy and heavy; compacting of wet earth damages the soil structure. Finally, make an earthen dike about four to six inches high and equally thick in a ring around the outer edge of the planting hole. This creates a saucerlike depression immediately under the bush which can be filled from the hose, and it also serves to catch the rain. If the appearance of the dike bothers you, it can be raked away after a year.

Once the bush is safely settled in, spread a heavy mulch in the saucer. This can be anything you want to use—we happen to use grass clippings because they can be added whenever the grass is mown, without bringing special material from a distance. The mulch serves the double purpose of keeping the ground underneath the bush weed-free and moist in the summer, and protecting it against the first light frosts. All this is a benefit to the new root system. Roots get going faster in cool, moist ground during hot weather, and the longer the roots can stay at work in the fall, the better the plant will establish itself. To avoid any danger of stem suffocation from the deep mulch, do not allow it to touch the trunk or lower branches.

Otherwise, the immediate aftercare of a new shrub is simple. In hot weather, spray the foliage. This is better done in the morning to get the plant through a very hot day. While the roots are struggling to reestablish themselves, the bush will take in some needed moisture through the leaves as long as they are misted in hot weather. But don't do this every day. Plant leaves, like roots, need to dry out a little; they can't survive if they are constantly drenched. Go easy on ground watering. If there was moist peat moss in the earth fill that went around the root ball, there is good water retention below ground, and the mulch will keep the surface soil from drying out. Roots are extremely sensitive to rot after the traumatic experience they have gone through. No matter how careful everyone was at every stage, the roots are in shock. In this condition, sodden earth around them is the last straw. To recover quickly, roots need plenty of oxygen for healing, which they will find in the soil if overwatering does not drive the oxygen out. I know this has been said before, but it cannot be too strongly stressed. With any planting, old or new, don't be overenthusiastic with the hose; water only when the surface soil looks dry and is either powdery or hard to the touch. In the fall, not too long before the first frost, give the shrubs a very thorough ground watering. This is extremely important whether the planting is new or old and well established. Some activity takes place in all growing things even in the depth of winter; evergreens, for example, continue to evaporate moisture at a slow but quite steady rate. It is important, therefore, to make sure that the plant tissue is well supplied with reserve moisture before the ground freezes so hard that the roots cannot extract any from it. If frost is delayed, and there has not been much rain, re-water newly planted shrubs late in November.

Pruning at planting time should be kept to a minimum. With deciduous shrubs, cut off any broken branches or anything that is growing at an odd angle—but don't do any enormous cutting back, particularly with spring planting. The plant needs the leaves that will break along the existing branches to carry out the process of photosynthesis, and it also needs leaves to take in airborne moisture to assist the injured roots. With evergreens, shear them lightly to keep the growth compact if it looks loose and weak, though it would be more sensible not to buy a straggly evergreen in the first place. Any regular pruning program should be put off until the plants have begun to send out heavy new growth.

My experience has led me to be against using arborvitae for tall evergreen protection where there is regular heavy snow; these bushes often get bowed down and, if they should break, this shrub does not regenerate well. Arborvitae is, however, the plant that is the most often offered for sale for screening purposes, and it does have some assets. In temperate zones, arborvitae grows to an enormous size and keeps green growth right down to the ground. It also transplants successfully even when large. Don't, by the way, be alarmed when arborvitae turns brown in the fall. As long as this is not tip end material dying off, the browning is the natural leaf drop and is not abnormal. Shake the bush vigorously to get off the dead fronds and use the debris as mulch or put it on the compost pile. In places where arborvitae does get bent down by snow, the bushes sometimes do not break, even though they lie almost flat on the ground. The main stems of arborvitae are very supple, and unless it is an extremely old specimen the bush usually pulls up of its own accord after the worst weight of the snow is off. But anything tall very rarely gets entirely upright again, and once it has been bowled over in this manner, arborvitae remains vulnerable to future storms. It should, therefore, be cabled in some way to prevent a repetition of the disaster. Our big arborvitae hedge was constantly knocked flat by heavy storms, and I got into the habit of assuming that it would always pull up, for each spring the trees rose very nearly to their old height. But luck eventually ran out—a few seasons back five or six mammoth arborvitae snapped off halfway down their main trunk, leaving jagged stumps like broken teeth. Cabling back tall shrubs is a professional job; done inexpertly, the next storm may break the branch where the cable has been attached. It is also an expensive job, and the wires that have to remain sunk into the grass or attached to other trees are unattractive. What's left of our arborvitae hedge looks miserable tied up to a heavy framework, which has had to be the final solution. This is why I am not overenthusiastic about using this particular shrub in areas where there is strong wind or a great deal of snow. So in spite of its other advantages, it would be nice if garden centers would not offer this particular bush with quite such enthusiasm to the uninformed novice.

Having learned a lesson with arborvitae, we steered clear of it when suddenly confronted with the need to hide that raw new fence in the country garden. This time we decided to forgo instant results; we would make haste much more slowly by using native junipers. These grow fast and thickly into a pyramidal form like arborvitae if they are planted in a sunny place, although as they age they lose their lower branches. We used junipers partly because they are more resistant to wind and snow than tall arborvitae and are far less inclined to break since the branches grow more densely together. They are also more exciting, for their colors vary through dark green to a pale blue-gray. Moreover, they carry blue and gray berries which the birds love. We were fortunate in having access to as many as we cared to dig from an open meadow belonging to a friend. But the job was not all that simple. The area was filled with numerous elegant four- to five-foot specimens, and in my innocence I decided that this size would be the best compromise between the rather bigger bushes which were also to be had for the taking, but which we might not have the capacity to move, and tiny little bushes that seemed hardly worth the bother. It didn't take us long to discover that the basic problem in digging junipers in the wild is that they throw an almost unextractable tap root to China. What's more, if the tap root is broken, the plant dies within the year. This became clear after we moved a few experimental bushes the first season, planted them out with exquisite care against the fence—and found them all dead the following spring! The next time we were more careful. We took trees about eighteen inches and we planted these out in a staggered row against the fence. To be on the safe side, we dug a good many more little bushes than we needed, and these were set out in a special growing-on area. Junipers, once moved, never throw that pestilential tap root again; instead they develop a thick, fibrous root mass, and then can be safely moved as far larger plants. We were fortunate in having a very sunny place to set the small bushes, for under those conditions they grow very fast and need almost no care. In time, junipers lose their lower branches and turn into small, dignified trees, but time with junipers is a slow process, for they are extremely long-lived plants. The second lot of bushes was planted farther back from the fence to give them the best possible circulation of air and light. This is a precaution that should always be taken whenever shrubs are used as the boundary line be-

The juniper hedge twenty-five years after planting.

tween two properties, and not only for the sake of having the plants do better. Even the friendliest neighbors do not always want your bushes growing over their property line, and you should allow a considerable leeway for the spread of even tall, upright material.

To give us privacy and to screen out that slightly undesirable fence until the junipers increased in size, we set in a few perennial sunflowers alongside the fence itself. These are coarse, very fast-growing, tall plants which need to have the growing tip cut off when they are about four feet high, in early summer. This treatment makes them bush and throw out a great many extra branches instead of confining their growth to one monstrous ten-foot stalk. The flowers are profuse, last well in water, and the seeds attract birds, particularly flocks of goldfinches. The plants took over the temporary job of enclosing our side of the yard with enthusiasm, though with great perversity almost all the flowers faced away from us, for they turned toward the western sun! The sunflower is a plant that can run you out of house and home if you are not strong-minded. The root mass can be pulled apart by hand in the spring and separated into individual plants, each with a single stalk attached. The new

Sunflowers as a screen.

sections turn into multiple-stemmed plants in a single summer, and the following spring you dig them up and redivide again. If you can't get the perennial, try annual sunflowers, which can be sown where they are to grow as soon as the weather warms up. Don't get the immense Russian variety; buy some of the new hybrids that have much smaller but far more interestingly rayed flowers. Nip out the growing point of these in just the same way you do the perennial variety, and you will again get far bushier plants. Sunflowers make excellent temporary screens in sunny places and should be used more for the purpose.

Most of the junipers planted beside the fence survived, but inevitably there were a few casualties, so those extra bushes set aside in the growing-on area were very useful. Long-term planning has a rather depressing sound when it is applied to gardening in a small yard, but it pays to set aside a small strip of land (somewhere sheltered and sunny) where small plants can be allowed to mature. Every outdoor gardener should make the construction of a little nursery area for young plants a very high priority on his list of what must be done at once. Following in the family footsteps, I had always had an experimental plot wherever I gardened. When the suburban garden was in year-round use, the place was the old dug-up laundry yard. When we moved to the country house for the summer months, this was grassed-over and the material in it, which by then was mostly specimen shrubs, set out in a far larger experimental lot. The soil in the country garden was in shocking condition, and though there was plenty of space for the plot, the lack of nourishment in the ground was a problem.

If your land is poor and weak, the method we used might also come in handy. In a sheltered place—wind is a great danger to young stock—we enclosed an area with lengths of railway ties. During the first summer in the country almost all the time was spent cutting down and pulling out rampant trash vines and weeds. At that very early date a compost pile had not been started, so all the green material from these rescue operations and all the grass clippings were tipped into

Growing-on area with buckwheat hull mulch. The small yews to left are some of those now surrounding the entrance court.

the long narrow bins formed by the railway ties. It is never wise to make any growing area so wide that you have to step on it to get at the plants at the back; ours, therefore, were about five feet across, half the width of a railway tie, which was sawed up to make cross beams. Railway ties are now hard to find; they are much in demand for their durability. I can vouch a good deal of first-hand information about this famous durability, for they are exceptionally hard to saw! In the fall, we filled the bins right to the top with seaweed from the beaches and instructed the man who was to keep an eye on the place to pile in all the leaves as these were swept up. By the following spring the piled-in trash had sunk very considerably, and purchased loam was brought in to top up the beds. Being local loam, it was very sandy, and after it had been watered heavily and we had trodden the beds down, like vintners in the vat, sackloads of our own compost from the suburban garden were added as the final fill. Such heroic measures may not be necessary in a lot with good soil; just set aside a special area, and go to work.

The enclosed bed was necessary to increase the fertility

Self-seeded English yew ready for moving to growing-on area.

of the ground and also because of the dreadful weeds that were rampant in the summer garden. Only by smothering them with a huge depth of soil could they be eradicated— and there was far too much else to do in that garden for the growing-on area to have any special attention after it was made. We did reap a most unexpected dividend for having used raised beds. When the 1954 hurricane swept the sea across the yard, the little bushes in these beds were above the level of the salt water and were among the few new plantings that survived.

Once made, this new area was far larger than the one we had had in the suburban garden, and there was plenty of space for extra stock. A great many tiny evergreens, conifers, deciduous shrubs, and infant-size flowering trees were therefore ordered from one of the many excellent mail-order nurseries that sell immature material inexpensively if it is bought in quantity. Some of those baby plants were less than six inches high when they first arrived, but everything was lined up in the sunny planting area and left to its own devices—

except for occasional watering. After the country compost piles were well established, a top dressing of this was added each fall, and the ground kept constantly covered with a thick mulch, at first buckwheat hulls and later a mixture of grass and leaf clippings. The mass-purchased seedling shrubs took hold well and fast, but they were not the only plants lined out in those nursery rows. There were also cuttings of shrubs grown from stock kind friends had let me clip in their yards—a method that will be described in Chapter XII. There were also numerous small seedling bushes which had been found struggling to survive in both gardens where they had been deposited by the birds. This home nursery has paid off unendingly. It is kept updated with new material, and it still serves its original purpose of providing a reserve stock of well-rooted and properly acclimatized plants. I cannot stress strongly enough that without it our three gardens could never have been restocked and replanted. It is never too late to start such a place in the home yard and, once made, it will never outgrow its usefulness.

For anyone looking for a quick answer to a screening problem the rather despised privet should not be overlooked. Privet has been much overplanted and has got itself rather a bad name as a rapacious, greedy grower that does not offer much in return except to require constant clipping. But in the newfound desire for privacy, privet is due for a comeback, for it is a most accommodating plant. Varieties exist for every climate, and in the North some hold their leaves so long as to be almost evergreen. Privet can be allowed to develop naturally, in which case it will soon turn into a very tall bush, or it can be kept trimmed to any shape that suits the gardener's particular need. Privet is used a great deal to form a dense, low hedge, and since it is a very sturdy grower, there is a tendency for it to spread out at the top while the lower part becomes open and bare. To prevent this, always prune so that the top is narrower than the bottom and so that the hedge slopes inward, like a triangle. In this way, the topheavy look of the average privet hedge can be avoided. The other method is selective pruning, like layering a haircut, so that there will be new growth at the foot of the hedge as well as at the top.

Privet hedges became unpopular because they were over-used and badly handled in the past. They do need a considerable amount of attention if they are to be grown clipped; you must expect to have to shear them back three or four times a season. Privet also has a tendency to two rather tiresome though not fatal pests. Red spider attacks the underside of the leaves, giving them a grayish tinge, and white fly can rise in clouds from it. Both these minor irritations are far less likely to occur when privet is planted in rich soil. The fact that privet is so accommodating has led to its being used in very poor soil. Under these growing conditions it is far more vulnerable to attack. If either pest hits, spray the bushes very hard, right into the center and under the leaves, with the strongest possible water pressure from the hose. And keep the process up until the problem diminishes. Privet is a greedy feeder and if you are planting a hedge around or near a flowerbed, sink a six-inch strip of metal down the side of the planting trench on the garden side. This should always be done when hedges are planted beside flowerbeds. The metal strip will block the feeding roots of the bushes from growing into the flowerbed and making a nuisance of themselves.

Planting a hedge is very similar to planting an individual shrub. The area where the hedge is to run should be laid out with a cord and stakes and stripped of turf or topsoil while the cord is down. This makes it possible to get a really straight line for the planting. If the hedge is to be planted beside grass, put sacks or even thick sections of newspaper on the grass alongside the trench, and pile the earth you take out onto that. Soil thrown onto grass makes a dreadful mess and is far less easy to handle. Privet is usually sold bare-rooted in bundles, in which case the trench need not be more than eighteen inches wide; this is the minimum width for easy digging. Go down at least two spits' depth. If the place where you are planting has fairly good soil, throw some damp peat moss at the bottom of the trench, as much as two inches if you can manage it, and then put back a great deal of the earth you have taken out and mix it and the peat moss together. This is far easier than trying to mix huge quantities of soil and peat moss in a wheelbarrow beside the trench. Fill the trench three quarters of the way up, and untie the bundle of privet. To measure the depth the soil will have to rise inside the trench to bring the bushes up to their old growing level, take one of the little bare-rooted plants, measure, and then poke a small stick into the wall of the trench. Once you have undone the bundle of privet, which ought to be bought with all the little roots bundled together in burlap, always keep the bare roots covered with damp burlap as you work. Don't take out some and leave the remaining plants lying around with their roots exposed. Drying out can be fatal even to tough privet at this stage. For that reason it is better to try to get the planting job done all at one time and the trench entirely prepared before unwrapping the bundle. When the fill is the right height for the new bushes, tread it down very hard, and then add more earth to bring it up to the proper level once more. Planting bare-rooted shrubs takes a little more finesse than just bundling a burlapped root ball into a hole. The bare roots should be spread open like fingers

Metal strip to block roots of privet hedge from entering vegetable plot.

and soil trickled in among them and firmed until the bush stands steady. If there is spare compost available, use this around the bare roots themselves. Privet should be planted about two feet apart, with the same rather finicky care given each bush. After they are firmed-in, fill the trench with water and let that seep away. Then fill up the remaining space, but let the new surface be an inch below the ground level. This will provide a natural saucer to catch the rain, and, like other shrub planting, this depression should be filled with mulch.

The extra trouble is well repaid by the speed with which the bushes will take off. We drive tall, heavy stakes into the ends of the trenches and form an enclosure with heavy green twine. This serves to control the first of the new growth and keep it compact; it also acts as a guide for the mechanical shearers—so long as you don't cut the twine! A new privet hedge should not be allowed to grow too fast the first season—growth should be trimmed back evenly—and not more than four inches of fresh stems and leaves allowed to accumulate by the end of the growing year. This rather harsh treatment leads to a stronger root system.

Venerable privet hedge that once enclosed rose garden.

We found a very old privet hedge still in reasonably good condition in the country garden, where it had been originally planted to provide shelter and a sense of enclosure for a rose garden. It had been kept roughly clipped where everything else had been allowed to run wild, and it stood tough and unamused at the desolation around it. The little garden room formed by this old hedge was the first place where I felt able to make some real progress in getting the garden back into shape, for the hedge provided me with a limited and defined area that was possible to tackle and produce immediate results.

When we decided to take over the country house, a list of garden priorities had to be drawn up, and since the privet hedge was one of the few areas still presentable, helping it to survive the dreadful condition of the ground in which it grew was important. At that time there was no compost available and the hedge was too large to resuscitate with loam. Instead, seaweed from the beaches was trucked in and spread in huge piles underneath the clipped bushes. Over this we put a thick layer of cranberry vines. These are difficult to handle as mulching material in a growing area; the vines are wiry and resilient and usually more trouble than they are worth. But under the hedge, on top of the seaweed, they served the admirable purpose of keeping in the moisture, looking neat, and giving no toehold to weeds. This did the trick; the hedge, which had been a poor color, darkened up the subsequent spring and has never given us any worries since. We still use seaweed as a mulch, but this now is put on top of a heavy layer of compost—a job which is done about every third year.

The capacity of the old hedge to withstand the famine condition of the land in which it grew impressed me very much, and, since I knew it had withstood seawater around the base, I planted quick-growing privet elsewhere in that garden wherever I wanted fast growth, a neatly defined area, and protection from the wind. It is still a great bore to trim, it would be absurd to pretend otherwise, but I never allow it to get ahead of us. We use the mechanical shearers on it almost every month, and this constant regular trimming is reinforced by one heavy, hand cutting-back in the fall. Used this way, privet can be invaluable. For example, a tall, narrow hedge of privet could easily be grown between a front yard and a busy street within three or four years. Privet can also be planted effectively beside a chain-link fence and allowed to grow through it to soften the outline. Allowed to grow unclipped, privet has white flowers with a distinctive scent that not everyone likes, but the hard black berries make excellent winter feed for birds. Privet grows in sun or light shade, and it does not seem to be particularly susceptible to air pollution. All these advantages outweigh, in my estimation, its rather dull appearance—for a fast, trouble-free return for money invested, "plant privet for privacy" might be a good slogan!

The summer garden had originally been enclosed by a boundary planting of blossoming shrubs and small trees. Some time, possibly after the 1938 hurricane, the pruning of the boundary hedges must have been given up. When this happened, trash vines got into the hedges and largely took over. By the time we appeared, the original bushes and even the trees were entirely covered with a choking growth of wild roses and bittersweet. Fighting equally savagely for supremacy in the tangle were wild grape, Virginia creeper, and Japanese honeysuckle. When fall came, and the colors gleamed, that hedge was undeniably picturesque, but the rest of the year, though it was in excellent health, it not only looked extremely untidy but also was rather menacing as it advanced steadily across the lawns. It was also very full of gaps: the vines fought their way upward to the light, forming a high jungle canopy that inhibited growth in the lower levels by shutting out the light. Our first intention was to get the vines out and restore the hedge to some semblance of its original form, and to that end we pulled, tore, cut, and dragged at the vines for several years. But it all was just so much wasted effort. While we cleared one stretch, the growth got worse in another. When we turned our backs and returned to town, the vines reappeared in the part we had so painfully cleared. One summer my husband spent weeks freeing a huge tree of bittersweet. It was a rather fine specimen of fringetree and it was no longer possible even to see the flowers. With immense effort, he cut out the invader—and the next season the tree was worse off than before; the bittersweet had been rejuvenated by the hard pruning!

Eventually we reversed ourselves and decided to live with the vines, but to prevent them from growing so tall that they made that dark canopy. To do this, we took to trimming and shearing both sides of the hedge and cutting the climbing vines off at about shoulder level. This decision was one of the more sensible labor-saving actions we have taken. The immense boundary hedge still takes a lot of controlling, though here again the regular use of electric shears makes a great difference. The pruning forces the vines to thicken out instead of just scrambling upward, there are no longer any gaps in the hedge, and it is green right down to the ground. I would never have chosen deliberately to live with a horticultural mishmash of this sort, but the close trimming has given it unity and density which it did not have before and has turned it into a feature of the yard. It protects us from the violent northeast wind, provides magnificent shelter for birds, and still looks dramatic and technicolored in the fall. I do regret the bulbs, which I can still sometimes spot in the spring struggling for light, deep in the tangled growth, but life has been a lot simpler horticulturally since we have joined this hedge, rather than fighting it.

The success that followed cutting back the big hedge and my newfound interest in privet in turn led me at long last to use sheared material in the suburban garden. In the following chapter the making of the flowering shrub border will be discussed, but here perhaps is the place to say that during this process, which at first was intended to be all laid out naturalistically, I suddenly realized that a sheared hedge was needed to run alongside the drive and cut the grass off from a new ground-cover bed. Privet was no good, because evergreen material that had strong winter interest was needed, so some of the innumerable little Japanese upright yews were moved to town from the growing-on area to see if they were the answer. They did exceptionally well in the suburban garden; it was impressive to see the speed at which they blended into a fine hedge. At first they needed training, for they had been left to their own devices in the country. Once this was accomplished, which was only a matter of some stern hand-clipping, this hedge has needed nothing other than regular clipping in the spring and again in the fall.

With the great success of the yews before my eyes, a much more ambitious project was undertaken. In a later section I shall discuss the huge old flowerbeds that existed in the front of the country house and the struggle it took to redeem them. Part of the problem was the wind which lashed across that area, requiring tiresome, unattractive staking. Also the flowers, which took a great deal of work, did not show off as well as they should just standing in the open; they needed a background. It was decided to enclose the outer perimeter of the area with our own small yews. The planting procedure was exactly the same as the one outlined for making a privet hedge, and here the intervening strip of metal was also set in on the flowerbed side of the planting trench. I had taken the largest of the yews for the suburban garden, so the average height of the bushes was about eighteen inches. But even so,

Entrance through clipped yew hedge in suburban garden.

they were a great success; they outlined the borders and gave them definition even while they were still so small that there had to be a new family rule that no one could walk over the hedge! Then disaster struck. Two years after they went in, the 1954 hurricane covered them with a tidal wave and all the young shrubs in the garden that were not deeply rooted died, including all those little yews. It took two years for the salinity to drain out of the land, for this part of the garden is at the lowest point. In 1957 we replanted the enclosure exactly as before, using what remained of our own stock and some extremely expensive purchased material. It is still quite obvious where I decided I had spent enough and called the project off! Fifteen years later, there having mercifully to date been no more tidal waves, that particular hedge is over seven feet high and rising; we now have to use a stepladder to cut it. It looks venerable enough to be in an English churchyard and I am extremely proud of it. Keeping it in order is complicated by thin, wiry strands of bittersweet that insinuate themselves unnoticed in the lower levels and suddenly break through the clipped top like an exultant, and insulting, green finger. Getting these out involves searching around under the bushes and trying to find the ground source of the flaunting banner.

Clipped yew hedge around old flowerbeds in country garden.

Unless the bittersweet is pulled out, orange root and all, it would soon ruin the hedge.

Not everyone wants a huge hedge surrounding flowerbeds, but any clipped material, whether it is deciduous or evergreen, makes an accent in the winter landscape. Pines and big spreading evergreens, for example, make excellent individual accents. Flowerbeds often present rather a dreary appearance cut down in the winter; this effect can be greatly improved if one end of the bed is finished off with a half-circle of clipped bushes. Clipped hedges are also excellent to form the walls of courtyards or as windbreaks for patios and cookout areas.

I stayed away from sheared materials too long. My gardens would have been more effective if I had not been so set against them. Trimmed hedges are a nuisance, they must be cut to look their best. But then so must the grass, which we somehow get done without all that fuss. It is important to understand that constant clipping, just like regular lawn mowing, puts a considerable strain on the plants, for they have constantly to expend a great deal of energy putting out new growth. This in turn calls for plenty of rich food in the planting trench and continued top-dressing to keep the fertility of the land up. For greater ease of upkeep, a mulch under them seems a sensible idea.

Clipped hedges are excellent as visual barriers to give a small yard privacy; they absorb sound and heat and filter the wind. Kept dense through pruning, they are not too vulnerable to snow damage. Used as accents in a yard, they add distinction. I am not too keen on seeing flowering bushes treated this way, but forsythia, sasanqua camellias, pittosporum, and althaeas, to name only a few among many, can all be used successfully as clipped material. There is only one warning —don't take on clipped hedges without electric shears. Battery-operated shears are now available if you don't have an electrical outlet available. This I consider the one absolute necessity for successful clipped hedges—beyond that, their use is up to you.

VIII | Flowering Shrub Borders

Almost everyone who owns a yard would like, at least in theory, to have some color in it, and the most obvious way of getting this is to use flowers. Flowers and flower borders can be a delight, but they are a nuisance to plant and demanding about their care. If you go away, they look bedraggled on your return; to do their best, flowers need almost daily inspection. Many homeowners do not want to be tied down this way by any one aspect of the yard; and some do not have the knowledge, even if they had the time, to serve as nursery maid to outdoor plants.

Fortunately there's a way out of this dilemma. Instead of the yearly struggle with annual or perennial plants, it is possible to get a very long-lasting display of flowers from blossoming shrubs and trees. Many of these also have good fall foliage and, if they are combined with evergreens and bushes that carry bright berries into the winter, an attractive shrub border can be produced that will be an addition to the yard all year long—and still not demand too much work. I got into the act rather late, but the fact that our shrub borders have already given us enormous pleasure, in spite of being relatively new, is proof that it is never too late to start.

Timid gardeners should realize that making a shrub border is not difficult, for the term sounds intimidating and might well put a novice off. Experienced horticulturists should use them more so as to give themselves time to concentrate on the other bothersome matters that crop up in running any garden. Shrub borders do take a little planning, but any good garden center can help you with this as long as you buy the stock from them. There is some financial outlay involved; shrubs and trees are not inexpensive, though there are ways of getting around this a little, which I have discussed earlier. But once the job is done, all the gardener has to do is sit back and enjoy the results. The initial cost is a once and only item, not to be compared with the regular expenditure of time, energy, and money that goes into planting seasonal flats of annuals and perennials year after year.

Our first shrub border was in the suburban garden and making it was slightly forced upon us. For some years after we had acquired the country house, the suburban yard remained much as it had always been except that there were no longer flowers in the flowerbeds. For spring color we depended on bulbs and the blossoms of the apple trees, which had been reinforced by the purchase of other small flowering trees that had been set out behind the house. Winter interest, however, was not particularly good. What did exist was provided by the bare silhouette of the big trees and the deep colors of the huge old evergreens we had retained near the house. Then within the space of two years we lost several of the venerable apple trees from old age. It was sad to see them go, but they had had a long and honorable career. In fact, all the propping up and cabling that had been necessary to keep them going had begun to ruin their appearance. But the death of the huge elm along the road boundary, which happened at the same time, was another matter. The tree succumbed to Dutch elm disease after a prolonged and very costly effort to save it. Having to take it down was a great blow, for it was at its magnificent prime and one of the outstanding features of the yard. And it wasn't just the visual appearance of the garden that suffered, there was another problem. When the big trees sheltered us, the front yard was exceptionally private and very quiet. With them gone, we were suddenly open to every passerby and far more conscious of the noise and fumes from passing cars.

Clearly something had to be done quickly to shield us again from the road, and, since some of the old boundary

Flowering shrub border in the suburban garden in early spring.

shrubs still remained, I was not inclined to force a fence in among them.

We decided to replant the newly opened-up areas where the trees had grown with thick, fast-growing shrub material. To solve the other problem, the uninteresting unfocused appearance of the yard, we hit upon the idea of greatly increasing the density of the existing boundary planting, and laying it out in a more interesting shape than just a straight line marching along the wall. And by doing this, we could provide ourselves with additional space into which we could incorporate a great many new flowering shrubs to give us spring bloom and fall foliage colors. In this way we would make a feature out of a necessity and bring accent and style back into the yard. But spring-flowering shrubs and fall foliage, though delightful in themselves, are not enough to make an impressive shrub border. To achieve that, evergreen material must also be incorporated, because this gives a sense of stability and depth which would otherwise be lacking during the leafless winter months. In the suburban garden, this particular shrub border had to be one-sided, so we worked the tallest evergreens in the back of the planting. In the third garden, where we later made another such border, the design is freestanding, so the tallest evergreens were set down the central spine.

All the shrub borders are in sunny areas, so much of the tall evergreen material has been native junipers and arborvitae. But the principle holds good for shady positions where Canadian hemlocks or yew could be used. But no matter what is chosen, these plants should never be set out like guardsmen on parade. In a shrub border, more even than in a boundary hedge, tall evergreens should always be spaced informally, sometimes two or even three to a group and sometimes as a single accent. For these positions, material with dense foliage that grows upward like a pointing finger was the first choice rather than trees like the pines, which spread outward. Steeple points are attractive in any type of planting, and these were intended to catch the eye at every season. Spreading evergreens with a more bushlike form were incorporated into the middle layers of the borders, for, to deserve the term "shrub border," the material must be at least four tiers thick. Needle evergreens like spreading yews and shrubs with shiny leaves such as the various ilex make exciting contrasts of texture when seen in conjunction with leafless branches. They also are a cohesive force to any planting. Spaced at irregular intervals along the middle of the border, evergreens tie otherwise diverse material together into a single feature. Without them, there is far less sense of deliberate unity of design.

During the winter months, evergreens also come into their own as a delight to the eye. The great variation of color that exists among them, ranging from the bluish green of the Pfitzer juniper to the cold black of the yews in winter weather, is usually not appreciated until they are set out in quantity. This subtle shading of color adds a winter dimension to every garden, particularly where winters are snowy.

Any shrub border that is to look and last well must have careful advance thought. It should always be planned to improve with age and not just become a crowded muddle. If you put yourself in the hands of a good garden center, they will choose the appropriate material for you. However, most of us prefer to do our own choosing, or at least be able to have a say. For that reason, it is important to know how tall and how wide any shrubs or trees you may be contemplating will grow if everything is to their liking. Most plants exist in a great variety, with a range that varies from huge and fast-growing to small with an almost imperceptible growth pattern. Potentially big shrubs grow much faster than anything small and spreading. This kind of knowledge makes a great difference as to what you should choose and how you plan to use it, and is the reason why the work of trained landscape architects often looks so much better than equally careful work done by amateurs. The professionals know the plant material and how it reacts in an average garden, and this can make all the difference in as short a time as two or three years.

But there is no need for even the newest gardener to lose out in this respect. There are numerous shrub catalogues available which list all the information, let alone horticultural societies with excellent libraries, and local field stations. If the thought of that sort of research puts you off, there's still a way out. To discover what to expect from the material on sale locally, ask the man who sells it. Don't be put off by vague generalities. This is a long-term expensive project and you have the right to get specific information before you buy. Write your questions down. No matter what the plant, you need to know whether it likes sun or shade, how fast it grows, and if it has special requirements, such as quick drainage or moist soil. Success or failure with your planting depends on your knowledge of those matters, and you should get straight answers to direct questions. It is also a good idea to find out whether bigger or smaller versions of the same plant exist. There are, for example, huge

Country garden shrub border in the spring.

rhododendrons and small, slow-growing varieties, also big, coarse philadelphus and new, smaller, more sweetly scented varieties and double forms. I don't think it wise to go out with the intention of bringing plants straight home. It is much better to shop around a little and see what is available and how much you can find out about the possibilities before you spend money. If you can't track this information down at the gardening center (and in all fairness it must be pointed out that the help situation being what it is, a great many of the salesmen simply don't know the answers), then leave the list of what you hope to buy and the questions you need answered with someone responsible and say you will come back later. If, when you return, the information is still not available, go elsewhere. Impulse buying or settling for so-called excellent substitutes is always a mistake—and never more so than when buying plants. We have all seen disastrous examples of forest trees mistakenly planted underneath a house window or by a front door. The same mistake can be equally unfortunate in a shrub border, and with so much more information available for the asking there is no excuse for it.

Planning and planting a shrub border is not in the least beyond the capacity of a novice gardener, but for most people it is more sensible to spread the work out and take your time. The suburban border took several years to complete and the country equivalent even longer, but the slow progress is not frustrating because the first bushes to be set out give a good return before the last go in, and this produces a sense of reward and achievement from the very start.

The first stage is to lay out the shape of the border and decide just how thick and large it is to be. To look important and add style to a yard, the front of a new shrub border is more successful curved in ripples and bays—a magnified version of ebbing waves lapping a beach. This effect is equally important for shrub borders that are enlargements of old boundary plantings, as was the case in the suburban garden, for this is the only way to eliminate the dreariness of original straight lines.

The problem with curves and bays, or indeed with any horticultural sweeps, is to make them bold enough and yet stay in proportion to the rest of the yard. Small curves look mean and ineffectual while a dramatic sweep that is too large to allow for an equally big reverse curve loses its point. The trick is to find the happy medium, and the way to do this is to lay the curves out along the ground with lengths of hose. This sounds rather simpler than it will turn out to be. Hose can be extremely intractable and about as cooperative as a snake; laying out well-proportioned curves with stiff plastic hose is not an occupation for the short-tempered or a job to be undertaken in cold weather when hose can be almost unmanageable. At the same time you must be careful if you are working on grass in hot weather not to leave your potential line down for several days or you will ruin the grass underneath it. But with all these disadvantages, hose is by far the best thing to use. Heavy cord does not show up so well when you come to survey the job, and a row of small stakes stuck in the ground cannot be adjusted nearly so successfully. Hose shows very plainly if the curves are too small or disproportionately large, and in spite of all the irritations, the effort is worth the trouble, for nothing else shows up the contemplated outline as effectively.

Putting the line down must be done rather slowly. The hose itself will probably ensure that but, in the unlikely event that everything goes like a dream, still take your time. Leave it and come back again to look at it many times from every angle. You need to be absolutely sure that you like it, that you have left yourself enough room for your plants to expand, and that the space the outline encloses really serves your purpose, whether it is for privacy or just as a decorative feature. If it is possible, look at the outline from an upstairs window; this is the best way to see if the curves are in proportion to the length of the lot. A bird's eye view is also excellent for discovering how well you have meshed the new design with the rest of the yard. Once you think the curves are correct, peg the hose down with lengths of wire cut from coat hangers and bent into large-size hairpins. Getting the hose in place is such a tiresome job you don't want the outline spoiled. If you don't peg the hose down before you set to work, either children will kick it out of position or dogs romping across the lawn will rearrange it for you! In my case, after days of struggling with the problem I went away for the weekend, leaving the hose down in its final shape. The weather was rather hot, and when I came back, I found our choreman had rolled it up. He was afraid for the grass underneath and thought I had just carelessly left it down. But even without these hazards the hose line should be held in place, for you will have to cut along it to open up the planting area, and unless it is pegged down, your work will be much harder.

Getting the curves the right size and at the right angle is only part of the laying-out job; the other is integrating the new design successfully into the rest of the garden and other established features of the yard. Shrub borders do not look

Suburban garden flowering shrub border with its curved outline and newly opened edge.

The old curve is marked by the leaf mulch.

their best floating aimlessly; they need to be anchored to existing structural or even horticultural features. In the suburban garden the shrub border begins immediately beside the gate, curves along the property line beside the front and side boundary of the lawn, and finally connects up with one of the huge old evergreens left over from the original planting plan. In the country, the shrub borders serve a different purpose. Here they are not intended to shield us directly from the street but to break up a large expanse of open ground and carry the eye toward the waterfront, which is off to one side of the rest of the property. The first border we made in the country was tied in to a group of enormous arborvitae that had been part of the foundation planting of the torn-down house. But this was too abrupt a start. The border never looked right until we prolonged it so that it snaked back toward the small guest house. The moment it ceased to be free-standing and was visually linked to a structure, it was more satisfying, for you could see its purpose. This projected tie-in should always be established from the very start while you are battling with the hose.

Once the curve and size of the border are satisfactory, strip off the grass or clean up by weeding the open area where the bushes eventually will be planted. I do not think it is necessary to rototill, particularly if you are going to take your time over the actual planting. The land can be prepared and kept in excellent condition by spreading a very thick layer of half-made compost on the surface of the soil and covering that with a thick mulch. In the suburbs we used fir bark as the mulch until everything was planted, for the open area was immediately under everyone's eye. In the country, where the borders were to be in a much less obvious place, we kept the cleared ground weed-free and fed with a constantly renewed layer of thick seaweed. If you do decide to have the whole area rototilled, it is still important to cover the open ground with a mulch. This will make a pleasant feature of it before the shrubs go in, and the change of surface material will also give you a chance finally to make up your mind whether you like the shape.

The next step is to experiment about where you are going to set the plants, so that they will look the most effective. I did this by hammering stakes in the ground and constantly shifting them until the groups looked right. So that I knew exactly what each stake stood for, I bought small cans of enamel. A dab of blue meant a tall evergreen, pink a medium-size flowering bush, yellow a spreading evergreen, and so on. This is why that preliminary knowledge of the ultimate size of the plants you want to grow is so important. The position of the stakes was changed dozens of times, which is how it should be—but we always knew how much space should be allowed between the various dabs of enamel. The ultimate success or failure of a shrub border depends on how the material is arranged; to get that right takes time.

In the suburban garden the final position of the hose outline was fixed in September and the ground was stripped and mulched immediately afterward. The experimental staking went on most of the winter whenever we could get outdoors. In the spring we set out the first of the tall evergreens, which led to some final alterations in the position of the remaining stakes. After that I drew a very rough plan, for I am no artist, and outlined on it the positions we had decided upon for the later material. When that was done the stakes were pulled up. You don't want them staring you in the face over a long period of time; what's more they may fool you by being changed. Children knock them over, they get pulled out or rot off, and then they are often put back in a different place. It is far better to have the final decision down on paper. But it is important to stake out the entire potential shrubbery at least once, for this gives you an idea of how many plants you will need. Don't, by the way, lose the plan; it is a clue to your intentions, which can very easily be forgotten as you slowly fill in the border. On the other hand, there is no need to treat it as gospel. After all, it was tentative and just an outline! What's more, as the shrubs go in you may find you have to make modifications; once in the ground, plants give a very different impression from stakes—always be ready to adjust your scheme ac-

Newly planted shrub border and vegetable plot in country garden and after eight years' growth.

cordingly. If you skip the stake stage and try and arrange the plant material after it has been delivered, you will find it much harder to make a calm assessment of where the plants will look best. Big bushes with their roots wrapped in burlap weigh a lot and are hard to move around. Incidentally the usual practice of dragging them about by the neck does them no good. After a little of this, most people give up and say "That will do," and that's not the way to make the best use of expensive plant material.

A new shrub border should always start off looking slightly ridiculous, with the bushes far apart. With proper planting, and if plants are allowed to grow at will, a border develops extremely fast. Shrubs fill open spaces far sooner than even experienced gardeners sometimes realize. Crowded plantings soon degenerate; the material loses its natural form when it is jostled by nearby bushes and has to fight for light and air. If you try for a thick shrub border from the start, you will soon find yourself faced with the necessity of digging out the very plants you labored over. This happened in the suburban yard. The need to muffle the noise from the road and regain privacy led us to plant too closely, and a lot of expensive material has since had to come out. And having once been crowded this way, the dug-out bushes are no longer well shaped and are therefore hard to fit attractively into another position. Were I to do the job again, I would still plant thickly, for we need the protection. But if I did, I would use slower-growing material. This is why it is so important to discover whether there are varying types of the plants you want to use. Unfortunately, slow-growing shrubs often cost more, for it has taken the garden center much longer to bring them to a salable size. Only the owner of the land can judge this situation. If you can afford to wait until the border fills in naturally, it is far better to plant the material far apart. If you must have instant density, choose narrow bushes that will not spread outward, and dwarf varieties for the front of the border, and set them closely together—but be prepared to pay more. Whether you are starting from scratch or redesigning an existing line of bushes, always begin with the tall evergreens; they are to be the backbone of the planting. In a brand-new border these can be fairly small, but the biggest specimens you can afford make the best impression.

Small flowering trees such as dogwood, laburnum, and the many varieties of flowering cherry and crab apple make excellent accents if they are included in a flowering shrub border. They look most effective brought forward into one of the outer curves of the bays and allowed to dominate the space immediately around them. The planting treatment for trees is identical to that given shrubs, except that a strong stake should be driven deep into the ground beside the tree trunk when everything else is finished. Don't just push a stake in the ground, this will not be nearly strong enough. Get a hammer and drive it in hard. The little tree trunk should then be fastened to the stake at several places. Not so tightly that it presses up against the wood, but close enough to keep it closely attached. To prevent injury to tender bark, we use rags for these ties, and to prevent them slipping, I draw on my ancient training as a Girl Guide and tie them in a clove hitch. Staking a tree prevents the wind from rocking the root ball; small trees are particularly vulnerable to this danger because they carry a mass of foliage on a slender stem. Rocking can do more damage to newly set-out trees than anything else, for it dislodges the feeding roots just as they are trying to reestablish themselves. If a newly set tree, which was well handled in every way, wilts after it is planted, in spite of proper misting and watering, always consider the possibility that it is suffering double jeopardy from wind, which dries out the foliage as well as shakes up the roots. The strong stake will take care of the wind rock as long as the truck is tied to it in at least three places. To protect new shrub or tree plantings against the hot, drying winds of summer, a temporary summer windbreak can be a help—and a windbreak should always be put up to protect valuable new shrubs over the winter if they are in very exposed positions. Rather dreadful-looking windbreaks can be made by stretching lengths of burlap between stakes. I find that burlap usually tears, particularly in the winter, and not only ceases to function but also flaps around horribly. It is simpler and neater to buy lengths of snow fencing.

Wind is less damaging if it is filtered rather than if a solid obstacle is put in the way. Confronted with anything solid, wind roars over the top and crashes down hard some feet beyond the windbreak. This can do the bush more damage than no shelter at all. Some time when a hard wind is blowing, go and stand by a fence. Immediately alongside it the air is calm; a considerable distance from the fence, you will feel the normal force of the wind; in between the normal force and the calm provided by the solid barrier, you will feel tremendous turbulence where the air that climbed up and over the obstacle in its path is tumbling down. If you are planting behind a fence, bushes should be set right up against it or a considerable distance away; in between, which is where most of us set shrubs so as to give them space to develop, is the worst possible place, because of wind damage. This problem does not arise when wind is filtered. If the onrushing air can work its way through the barrier, it will

Dogwood in bloom in suburban garden.

do so, rather than pouring over the top. The filtering of wind absorbs a great deal of its force.

Wherever there is deep winter snow, it is important to try and prevent shrub branches from getting so bent down under the weight of a heavy fall that they are broken or permanently distorted. While everything is still very small, snow often covers the entire shrub. This is all to the good; snow serves as a protection and your bush will emerge unscathed. The danger comes when the shrubs rise above the snow cover and huge drifts settle deep in the heart, spreading the bushes open and bowing down the branches. If you can shake off some of the weight while the snow is still light and fluffy, well and good. But don't try and knock hard-frozen snow off anything. Cold makes the stems and barks of trees and bushes extremely brittle, and misguided efforts to free the plant of the frozen snow often do far more harm than good. Bright days follow even the worst storms and then usually some of the weight will slide off of its own accord and the branches regain resiliency. Even if they remain bowed over, all is not lost. The tip ends of the branches frequently get frozen down when the plant is pressed against the ground. You should wait until the thaw comes and they are freed naturally. Don't try to pull free any branches that are frozen to the ground. You will only break off the tips if you do. Unless they have been cracked or broken, healthy shrubs usually pull up on their own accord when the sap rises in the spring. Don't work among shrubs when the snow is deep unless there is some very obvious disaster you must cut out because it is injuring other plants. You may trample on an uninjured branch that is entirely covered with snow. If there is no sign of recovery by the time the deciduous shrubs are leafing out, the bent-over branches should be cut back to a point where they are still upright. If not, a dreadful tangle of deadwood will eventually build up under them. Even if the upper surface of bent-over branches is leafing out, cut them back; your shrubbery will be ruined otherwise. Evergreens that were spread apart by the snow and have not recovered shape can be tied together. I prefer this to staking, which spoils the natural look. Use insulated electric wire for this job, it hardly shows and will not cut into the bark as you pull the stems close together.

One of the troubles with our flowering shrub borders has been their spectacular success. The careful planting paid a huge dividend with very fast growth, and every bush was soon a mass of long stems. Since we live where there is regular heavy snow, our shrubs rapidly became extremely vulnerable to serious damage, and, as we cannot control the weather, the only solution was to try and institute some kind of control over the bushes. This we did by keeping them sufficiently trimmed back so that the new growth was thick and sturdy rather than long and whippy.

Shrub pruning is one of the most misunderstood processes in all of home horticulture; done badly it can ruin the shape and character of a bush forever, and done at the wrong season you can deprive yourself entirely of flowers. Both these sins unfortunately are regularly committed by far too many gardeners. Before even contemplating pruning a flowering bush decide how you are going to allow it to develop. This applies equally to those that are freestanding as well as shrubs planted in a border. If you are going to keep them heavily cut back—almost sheared—do so from the start. Once a bush has been allowed to develop along naturalistic lines, it is a form of mutilation to shear it back. I am not very fond of flowering bushes trimmed hard back each year, but there are circumstances when this is better than having no shrubs at all. Bushes that are regularly trimmed back develop a thick, dense outline and a rather unnatural shape, but they are the least liable to snow damage. Our shrub borders were deliberately designed to be informal, but they still had to be controlled. This was and is done selectively; overlong branches are trimmed back with hand clippers to keep the characteristic outline of the bush, and each year some of the oldest growth is cut out with heavy hand-pruners right at ground level to keep the overall spread under control and to encourage the bush to send up new growth from the ground rather than spreading by constant extensions of the existing branches. This treatment tightens up the pattern of growth and prevents the loosely growing shrubs from getting out of hand.

You can prevent yourself from cutting off the potential flowers by understanding their habit of growth. Every shrub that blossoms falls into one of two categories. If it flowers in the spring, the flower buds are formed during the previous summer, and winter over as small knobs on the branches, ready to burst into bloom when the weather warms up. That is why in mild fall weather flowers occasionally appear on shrubs like forsythia and even some of the flowering cherries. The buds are already set, merely waiting to go, and the late appearance of cold weather tricks them into abnormal bloom. In this category—which technically is described as material that flowers on old wood—come all the shrubs that bloom up to the middle of June. Summer- and fall-blossoming shrubs, those that bloom after August, do not make their buds ahead of time and carry them through the winter; they have been too busy flowering late in the season to set buds. These shrubs are described as flowering on new wood, for the buds appear in the spring on brand-

Flowering plum in suburban hedge.

new branches. If you can remember this fact of horticultural life you are safe, and you will know better than to cut back a spring-flowering plant just before the buds swell.

Rather mysteriously, there exists in almost every household members of the family who will always go out and prune in the early spring even though they never do anything else in the garden. To avoid this annual disaster, and for the sake of greater domestic serenity, try posting a few guidelines near the gardening tools. Shrubs that flower in the spring should be pruned immediately after they have finished blossoming, never before. There is a huge spurt of growth after the flowers fade, and unless the bushes are taken in hand at that time they will sprawl about and look extremely sloppy. If you can hold off your overeager helper until after the flowers are gone, no lasting damage will be done. But don't let this pruning be put off too long. If the cutting back is postponed until midsummer, the subsequent new growth will not be sufficiently mature to make flower buds, and there will be far less bloom the subsequent spring. The alternative is to set your eager helper to work on the bushes that won't bloom until late in the summer. These actually need to be cut back hard in early spring. If this isn't done, they will bloom only at the top of the bush. With plants like althaeas, the flowers sometimes are so high up as to be almost invisible. When the urge to trim comes over the nonhorticulturalist in the family, and the moment usually coincides with the appearance of the first crocus, take the time to tie red wool onto the bushes you want pruned. It really does not matter how fiercely these are attacked, new growth will burst out when the days lengthen, and a summer-flowering shrub can hardly ever be prevented from growing back into a naturalistic shape. All the winter frustrations can safely be taken out on these plants without lasting damage! But do make crystal clear that the unmarked bushes are not to be touched at that time; then you will get your bloom.

One of the few (but inevitable) exceptions to this rule is the rhododendron. It needs time to regenerate after being cut back; new growth does not come very quickly. If a bush has got too big and must be pruned, it is better to do so in early spring, even though it means sacrificing the fat green flower buds on the tip ends. If you wait to cut back until after the bush has flowered, the new growth may not be sufficiently hardened to get through the next winter safely. Rhododendrons that need cutting back should be done bit by bit; they will recover in time even when cut to the ground, but there is no need for such drastic measures. Take out or cut back a few overgrown branches each spring for several years until you have brought the bush down to a manageable size. In very cold areas, new wood on rhododendrons winter-kills quite badly, and this serves as a natural control. Where the bushes do not die back, don't be afraid to prune. Too many people treat rhododendrons rather gingerly and let them get out of hand. A well-proportioned bush with the flowers where they can be seen is infinitely preferable to a monster with enormous outstretched arms.

Lovely as many of the hybrid rhododendrons are when in bloom, I am not too enthusiastic about setting them out in any blossoming shrubbery where they are very obvious from the windows of the house—particularly if the garden is in a cold area. Instead, use them where the border turns away from the house. In bitter weather, the leaves of rhododendrons roll into thin black cigars of misery and present a singularly depressing appearance. There is no need for a thermometer to judge the temperature if these particular plants are within sight.

If you let evergreens of any sort grow naturalistically you should be sure not to allow this liberty to degenerate into license. Long, loose branches should always be hand-clipped back. Most of the needle evergreens such as yews and arborvitae need occasional hand-clipping, but they should always be left with a naturalistic irregular outline. To keep the pines under control I halve the candle-like new growth each spring as long as I can reach them on a stepladder. This again is a tree that improves greatly in appearance with control; it can be prevented from growing wildly out of bounds for many years by this simple, if sticky, process. If the growing tip of a pine wilts, a fearful pest called tip borer has invaded the tree and, without control, will eventually kill it. This calls for professional spraying on an exact timetable, so as to catch the borer during the very short period it is vulnerable.

Generally speaking, I am anti-spray, for it is impossible to overlook the damage done by indiscriminate use. But selective spraying for a specific pest such as the pine borer is rather a different matter. The spray is not broadcast, as it is, for example, when used for roadside weed control, or against mosquitoes; properly applied, it is an exact, successful operation. What is important is that you and your tree man understand each other before he goes to work. If, as I hope all gardeners do, you have strong feelings about casual or incompetent spraying, you should make this very clear so that he is careful. It is also as well to be around while the job is done so that you can see exactly what goes on. Conscientious professional firms are as much aware of the problem as the rest of us; it is, after all, their livelihood. What is our business is to make sure we are dealing with responsible firms.

In general, don't prune in bitterly cold weather; frost can crack the bark at the open cut. The only time I break this rule is when I cut the winter greens for the house at Christmas. I usually put off trimming the yews, chamaecyparis, and other decorative evergreens until late in December so that the clippings can be used indoors. So far, this has never damaged any of the bushes, and I enjoy using my own greens for this purpose because it is part of a family tradition.

Any informal shrub border inevitably slowly encroaches on the areas alongside it no matter how much you may attempt to control the spread. This is bound to happen unless the front of the border is regularly sheared back, which produces a completely different style of hedge. But if a naturalistic appearance is required, or preferred, you must expect this creeping forward and bend with it. In the suburban garden I have recut the grass verges a great many times since they were first laid out, to accommodate the expanding lines of the shrub border. The curves have always been kept in the same proportions, but if there was a mistake in the original outline, the time to set it right is when you have to redo the grass edging. Our once large front lawn has diminished steadily under this annual encroachment, and in a later section I shall discuss how to handle the grassless areas which appear under the outermost spread of the branches. I don't particularly mind seeing the grass eaten up, I prefer the sinuous curves of the shrubs. But I had not realized quite how far the process had gone until a visiting daughter remarked a little sternly that no one today would ever guess that that particular lawn once had been large enough for baseball. If you treasure large expanses of grass, you should perhaps bear this in mind before you plant an informal shrub border.

Flowering trees, or indeed almost any trees planted on a small lot, are less of a problem if they are high-pruned. This process involved cutting off all the lower branches to a height of about five to six feet, depending on the age of the tree, and allowing no lateral leaf-bearing branches to grow below that level. High pruning has several practical advantages. Trees with low sweeping branches kill the grass underneath; the ground usually is too dark and dry for anything to survive. Sweeping branches also make mowing a menace. Nothing is more aggravating than twigs poking at your eyes every time the mower passes by. High-pruned trees also open up the look of a lawn. You can see past the bare trunks and cleaned-off branches to the grounds beyond. I like to see the skeletal underpinnings of a tree. The contrast of bare lower trunk branches with the leafy upper stories is always interesting and often structurally exciting.

I was forced into high pruning in the suburban garden. The remaining crab apple on the lower lawn flourished mightily and drove everyone mad whenever the grass had to be cut. One day I could take it no longer; every branch that hit my head when I walked underneath the tree was sawed

High-pruned crab apple with an unwanted lateral bud breaking.

off. Acting out my hostilities, as the situation would now be described, did my disposition an immense amount of good, but I need not have bothered with the job. The following winter there was one of those terrific ice storms that do trees so much harm, and major damage was done to almost all the remaining branches of the crab apple as well as a dogwood that grew nearby. In consequence, both trees had to have a great many smashed branches taken out—a process known as "opening up," when it is done deliberately. Again, I was amazed at the distinction the trees gained from drastic surgery. They took on a controlled dignity that they had lacked before.

When we outlined the plans for the construction of an entrance court in the country garden, described in Chapter II, the design turned in part around an existing pair of matched kousa dogwoods. These had grown fast and well; I had planted them as very small trees, and the branches had spread widely almost from ground level upward. The spreading branches did not fit into my ideas about the courtyard; they were going to spoil the vista, and the informal style of growth also was not in tune with the projected formality of the area. But the trees were so symmetrical and lovely that I could not bring myself to cut them out—pruning of any sort would have seemed like mutilation.

The problem was solved most unexpectedly. The area had to be dug out by hand to save not only the roots of those trees but also the yew hedge that surrounded it. The contractor whose men were to do this job spoke fairly good English; his workmen spoke none. The landscape architect in charge of the proceedings, egged on by me, made a very strong point of the necessity of saving every possible tree root. Dogwood bleeds easily if injured; bleeding, incidentally, means an unchecked flow of sap from injured roots or bark. We therefore had good reason to be nervous about those trees and to make our wishes very clear. The contractor was warned several times of the care that must be taken, and I stood there while he translated our admonitions to his workmen.

Digging out took place the week our local baseball team was in the playoff for the World Series. In consequence I was not outdoors as much as usual; moreover, I had turned the responsibility over to someone else and I did not want to seem to interfere. One afternoon, the very moment, in fact, in which the home team clinched the pennant, there was a knock on the door. It was the contractor. He wanted to explain that his men had misunderstood his instructions, or rather had reversed them (maybe his command of his mother tongue was not as good as he thought). Instead of saving the roots, they had understood that I wished them pruned, and he held up a large bundle of sad, white lengths as ghastly evidence. Sap was already pouring from the severed roots when I reached the spot. Both trees had been strongly root-pruned in a wide half-circle to within six feet of their trunks on the courtyard side. As a holding measure we packed clean, wet sand as tightly as possible against them to try and staunch the flow. To compensate the trees for the bleeding, we immediately pruned them severely, cutting off all the lower branches and opening them up by taking out a great deal of the high growth.

It was not the proper season for pruning dogwoods, they prefer the work done in late February before the sap starts to run, and I was not optimistic. But even in the middle of my worries, it was impossible not to notice how much the appearance of the trees had been improved by our emergency work. Cleaned off, they looked far more striking. I also took in for the first time the attractive manner in which the bark peels from the trunk of this particular species in the fall. We saved the trees, in fact I believe that savage root-pruning did them good, though I would never advocate it. Not only have they fruited and flowered even more profusely ever since, but they have also gained in distinction.

The experience led me to high-prune a great many more trees in recent years. By cutting out lower branches it is often possible to grow bulbs and ground covers in what hitherto had been bald patches. In mixed shrubbery, high pruning makes it possible to underplant a flowering tree with dwarf shrubs and still have them get enough light. High pruning, or any cutting out of branches, should be done with a sharp saw and the cut made flush to the trunk. Amputated stubs should never be left; they are an invitation to invasions of pests and disease. Large wounds should be covered with special tree-wound dressing. This can be bought at hardware stores and at garden centers. In a pinch, cover the wound with paint. Any tree that has been high-pruned or opened up will always try and make up for the injury it feels it has sustained by throwing out new branches. The new growth forces its way through the bark of the denuded branches. It is part of the backup system of all trees, shrubs, and plants to have dormant buds hidden under the bark that will only grow after an emergency. To these lateral dormant buds, high pruning constitutes an emergency! The new growth is thin and whippy; it appears at the base of the tree and along all the branches. For good appearance it should be cut out. I prefer to rub them out while they are still soft green promises, rather than waiting until I have to cut them out. But they will need watching out for. I have two golden-rain-trees in the country garden that I recently put in as a feature. I want them to grow into single-trunked matched trees. About every third week all summer long I rub off the soft pink growth that is breaking out along the trunks. If I go away for a summer, there will be a thicket on those trunks when I return.

The only trees that do not look well high-pruned are those that weep. The branches of weeping trees are supposed to sweep the ground, which is fine for those who like them. I am not enthusiastic about them. Weeping trees look well at a distance by a stream, but I find them inappropriate in a small yard. This is purely a matter of personal taste and has nothing to do with their usefulness. If you plant a weeping tree, let it be. That is the way it must grow to look its best.

Main sweep of freestanding shrub border in 1963, 1965, and 1969.

In spite of a few minor problems, the border in the suburban garden has been a success from the day it was begun. It cost more than I liked, because it was necessary to buy large shrubs for immediate privacy, but under the circumstances we did not begrudge the expense.

But when eventually we were able to set about redesigning parts of the country garden, we used very little large stock. The freestanding shrub border that was constructed in the third garden called for a great deal of plant material, and an almost equal amount was needed for a second curve that was laid out several years later to make some sense out of a group of old swamp maples that were standing forlornly at the far end of the grounds, not connected or aligned to anything else. We did buy some Japanese black pines, for these are impervious to salt spray, and that end of the yard is susceptible to salt damage from gale winds off the sea; otherwise at first we used our own material entirely. Most of it came from the growing area, but some was moved in from other places in the yard where it had become crowded or inappropriate. Only when everything was finished, several years after the two projects had been begun, did we go to the extravagance of getting some late-flowering calendula azaleas and a few specimen Japanese red pine to add character to the design.

The first curve looked pretty pathetic when we got it in, and I was not at all optimistic about the speed at which it would grow—or indeed if it would grow at all. That first shrub border was set out over the foundation of the pulled-down house. In many places over the filled-in cellar, the planting holes had to be pickaxed out of a mass of brick rubble. On this occasion the bushes did not go into exactly the place I intended; they went in wherever we could make the nearest hole in the ground! To brighten up the appearance of that planting while it was still so small and new, tall perennial asters and sunflowers were set out in the bays together with clumps of daylilies. Ten years later there are hardly any survivors of these plantings, for the shrubs have taken over entirely.

Since this was to be a winter sheltering area for birds as well as a summer border, there is not much emphasis on spring bloom. Instead, for midsummer flowers there are bushes of clethra, althaeas, buddleias, shrub roses, vitex, and caryopteris. Whatever spring-flowering bushes are there, we included less for their bloom than for their fall berries. Unless you are going to spray everything in sight indiscriminately—in which case this book is not for you—a large bird population in great variety is an extremely helpful way of controlling insects—and for best results you want birds to be around not only in summer, but in winter too, when there is less natural food and they are forced to hunt down every available insect. But a large bird population cannot be maintained in a long cold winter by the insects available; some extra food has to be provided to keep them around. One way to do this is to put out food and water all winter long and also to grow a great many fruiting shrubs and plants with hard, long-lasting berries that will sustain them. And there is also another factor in keeping birds happy. There must be thick cover to provide shelter against predators, bitter cold, and heavy snow. This is where careful planning can make a difference, and this is what we had in mind when we laid out the country borders. We wanted them to look decorative—and in this we succeeded—but above all we wanted them to be a winter-long attraction to birds, since we would not be around to set out food.

Long before the suburban shrub border was finished there was a great improvement in the general appearance of the garden. The sense of design was better, particularly in the winter, and the flowers were more abundant and far more satisfying than any I had been able to produce so early in the year in the old flowerbeds. And there were other benefits. The thick, dense planting absorbed the noise from the road and gave us the same privacy we had enjoyed while the old trees lived, and they have continued to serve as an excellent sound barrier, even though the traffic outside has quadrupled. This is particularly true when the deciduous shrubs are leafed out, but the planting still traps a great deal of noise even when the branches are bare. I don't think this factor is stressed enough to new homeowners. Many houses today face on streets that are increasingly heavily traveled by cars, and the volume of noise rises steadily. A thick shrub hedge can be a great help in shutting out the swish of passing cars, as well as preventing you from seeing them. A fence is not such a successful barrier to sound and is far less pleasant to look at than evergreens and flowering bushes.

A shrub planting can serve as well as a fence as a fixed limit for all but the smallest children. When a garden opens right onto a street, the forbidden areas are hard to set, and there's always the danger that someone will chase a ball into the road. A thick hedge is an easily defined limit: children can be forbidden to go past it, and it will also stop a ball or tricycle just as effectively as a fence. I am still not done with the advantages. A thick shrub planting reduces the temperature in its immediate vicinity because in the process of its life cycle it constantly exudes moisture. It also helps in the battle against air pollution, for plants give off oxygen as a spare product during the daylight hours and absorb carbon dioxide.

Every time a tree is cut down or open land paved over for parking, the supply of oxygen available to us is diminished. The only way we can remedy this is to plant living material in our grounds which can counteract in a small way the general damage that is being done not only to the environment but also to our very lives. This is rather heavy talk, rather big guns to bring to bear on planting a few flowering bushes and some evergreens. But hasn't the moment come to leave generalities aside and get right down to the specifics as to what we can do in the present environmental crisis? A very small solution does lie near at hand for all gardeners if they will but take advantage of it by planting trees, shrubs, and evergreens.

IX | Ground Covers

Fashions come and go with plants just as they do with everything else, and at present ground covers, which are low-growing perennial plants used in masses, are very much in. Ground covers can be dull and uninteresting, a gardener's cop-out from taking trouble. At the other end of the spectrum they can serve as a highly important element in garden design. Generally they fall between the two extremes and are used to save the gardener work while also giving pleasure to the eye. This is the way I try to use them, and I find them invaluable. In fact, I am not sure that I could run two gardens with so much absentee ownership without making extensive use of ground covers.

Evergreen plants that carry dense foliage are popular for ground covers though there are conditions in which deciduous plants can be used equally effectively. Some plants used as ground covers carry flowers and berries, but, generally speaking, this is an additional bonus and not the primary reason for using those particular plants. To qualify for ground-cover use, a plant must not get much taller than about two feet at maturity—though the outward spread can be any width. Dwarf and low-growing shrubs are the most elaborate ground-cover plants and also the most expensive. More frequently the phrase "ground cover" means the use of plants that spread along the surface of the ground and increase in number.

The present popularity of ground covers comes partly from the modern interest in design and partly from the fact that it is possible to use dense blocks of growing plants to provide texture and very subtle color values with a good deal less work than would be involved in getting the same effect with flowers. The fact that ground-cover plants are available for every kind of climate and every type of soil has added to their tremendous popularity. Since ground covers can be used for ornament and at the same time work for us by smothering weeds, there are very few gardeners who would not be wise to make use of these plants. There is more information available today about how they should be handled than in the past. But a few warnings are still in order, for in spite of all their many excellent points, there are misconceptions about the use of ground covers, as well as problems in handling them.

Ground covers cannot be considered as a substitute for grass if you think of your lawn as a place in which to walk, sit, or play. With one exception, which I shall mention a little further on, the most useful ground-cover plants in the Northeast cannot take this sort of treatment; the stems and leaves get broken, or at the very least badly bruised, and the planting cannot survive heavy traffic across it. No matter how terrible your grass, you cannot replace it with a ground cover unless you are going to admire the planting from afar and never step on it. A stretch of ground cover must be thought of in terms of a flowerbed rather than a lawn substitute. If you are not interested in using the place where normally there would be grass and you plan to put it down to a decorative ground cover, it is important to realize that any large expanse of land covered with a single type of plant invariably looks uninteresting. Massed dwarf spreading junipers are a favorite modern ground cover in front of public buildings. Beds of junipers fulfill the standard requirements: they are evergreen, grow quickly and very thickly, and soon produce a rolling, irregular outline that is harmonious but heavy enough to smother weeds. But the overall effect often is monotonous and dull; the eye longs for a contrast of color and a change in texture.

In California and other mild climates where ivy flourishes without winter die-back, the plant is used extensively as a ground cover. When ivy is massed in small blocks and care is taken to include varieties with slightly different shapes to the leaves and variations of color, it can be a delight. But huge stretches of plain ivy in front of a house is monotony personified, and this unfortunately is the way it is often planted. Anyone who wants to use nothing but ground-cover material, where normally there would be lawn and shrubs, must be skillful enough to use them in variety, choosing plants that are compatible—that is, enjoy the same growing conditions and develop at much the same speed—and this takes considerable horticultural know-how. Furthermore, to look really well, blocks of ground-cover plants should also be set out in an interesting design and to an exact pattern so that the various plants blend and give a lively but not spotty effect by changes in color and in the shapes of leaves. To lay out a large area of ground cover, you have, therefore, to be an experienced gardener with a very sophisticated sense of design, and the average homeowner usually does not have both qualifications—if indeed he has either! Ground-cover gardens are not an easy way out for nongardening gardeners; on the contrary, a successful planting of this sort is exceptionally hard to bring off unless you are prepared to call in professional assistance from a landscape architect. Once down, it can be relatively easy to maintain, but first you have to be able to afford to get it properly laid out.

I have seen many delightful front yards given over entirely to ground covers, but I do not know of any that were done by untrained amateur horticulturists with no outside advice. The best I have seen used a variety of plant material, and the danger of monotony, which lurks near any ground-cover garden, was avoided by changes of level produced by steps and paved or mulched paths. These gardens were almost all small, for this type of ground plan is extremely expensive to plant, and they were all in shady positions. A ground-cover garden with a variety of plants in a sunny position, with the exception of heathers and heaths, would be even harder to achieve. Those I know use a great deal of masonry and brickwork to minimize the use of plants.

All this calls for money as well as expertise. If it lies within your reach, beautiful places can be achieved with ground covers, but you must always remember that any such garden has no place where children can play and has to be kept immaculate to look its best. For this reason I would be inclined to suggest that young or novice gardeners steer clear of putting their lot down exclusively to ground-cover plants.

I started using ground covers without really understanding enough about the need for careful design. When we ceased to use the suburban garden in the summer, many of the flowerbeds were abolished but not all. To have nothing but grass and tall shrub borders was going to produce a very dull effect even though we redesigned the boundary plantings to try and improve the overall design. Something more was needed that looked well in itself and produced a good effect in the winter to bridge the gap between the flat green grass and the big shrubs. I had been very much taken with some ground-cover borders I had seen in the neighborhood, so it was decided to construct the same kind of trouble-free planting in some of the old flowerbeds as a sort of permanent halfway house between flowers in flowerbeds and nothing at all. The first attempt was alongside the terrace that runs up from the drive to the front door of the suburban house. This area is three steps above the level of the lawn beside it, and when we first owned the place the path was a flagstone walk along a narrow grass terrace. The change of level between it and the lawn was filled with a large shabby flowerbed. Keeping the grass in condition on that terrace proved impossible after we were no longer around to do it ourselves—hired grass-cutters invariably "forgot" it. In despair, a helper and I dug up all the sod and replaced it with flagstones, a piece of herculean activity I now look back on with amazement. And as we were never around when the plants in the bed flowered, it was decided to clear them out during this reorganization and replace them with a ground-cover planting of dwarf shrubs. These included miniature spreading yews, dwarf rhododendrons, variegated euonymus, azaleas, cotoneasters, leucothoe, and some extremely slow-growing dwarf pyramidal pines for accent. I went to an enormous amount of trouble chasing down plants that would not grow too fast or too large, and they were put very carefully into deep planting holes full of rich soil. The method has been described in Chapter VII, and we followed it exactly.

The long-term result has been only moderately successful. I was correct in trying to avoid monotony by getting different types of plants, but it was a mistake to mix deciduous and evergreen material. The leafless azaleas add nothing in winter, in fact, in this context they give the impression of being dead. Also instead of concentrating the varying plants in solid masses, I dotted them in and out and around about. This weakened the very effect I was after, the change in leaf texture. To get that contrast, similar plants must be massed together for a strong visual impact. The change of level was easy to handle, for the bed was, in fact, a sloping bank. But even here I did not make the most of a natural advantage. Though I understood the plant material, I did not always choose the right variety; I substituted when I couldn't get exactly what I wanted. This was a great mistake. Some of the substitutes turned out to be much larger and to grow faster than my original choices and in consequence have masked the sloping ground and reduced the entire planting to a flat plane. The plants that grew too fast have also had to have regular hard pruning to prevent them from smothering slower-growing, better specimens. This has ruined the interlocking natural effect I wanted in the foliage. To cover the bare ground after the shrubs went in, I planted pachysandra, which I shall discuss in detail later on. This is now overexuberant and ruins such design as remains by creeping over the terrace.

The planting is not a complete failure in spite of my grim description. It gives us good winter color and is far more interesting than the worn-out daylilies. But the overall effect does not show the amount of thought that went into it. Above all, it is not restful. The mistaken choice of some of the plant material and the thrusting pachysandra give much more the effect of a battleground in which I must serve as umpire. Perpetual vigilance was not at all what I had in mind when I laid out that bed, and I was an experienced horti-culturist when I undertook the job!

Unluckily for my self-esteem, but fortunately for my gardening education, I soon had firsthand knowledge of how much better the job could have been done. The salt thrown on the grass by the snow plow had made it impos-sible to continue to try and have a lawn alongside the drive. Again, a planting of sturdy ground-cover shrubs seemed the best solution. But here material had to be chosen that could stand the tremendous weight of the snow as well as the run-off of salt, and I had no idea what to use. This, combined with the fact that I was going to be away at the proper planting time, made it seem better to turn the whole project over to a landscape architect. It was a small job that did not tax his skill, but the difference between his work

Ground-cover bed beside the suburban drive. The raised berm diverts salted snow water from the road.

and mine was revealing. He used plants with different leaf forms for contrast and emphasis, but he confined them to three different types, dwarf mugho pines, dwarf junipers, and heather, while I, in an area much the same size, had used an infinitely larger number. He massed each variety but fingered a few into the next block of plants. The little plants were set much farther apart than mine with a thick bark mulch between them. To lighten the effect and fill in the gaps, creeping plants like thyme and bearberry were used; these spread into thick surface mats which can easily be controlled. As it matures, the professional planting looks better and better, while mine is deteriorating with age and may have to be pulled out. Both beds have served their purpose, but both were expensive to stock, and in the second case the professional fee was an additional charge. I don't for one moment regret the extra price, the job was so much better done. Furthermore, from it I learned how to

Ground-cover bed years later.

handle work of this sort and I have since put the knowledge to better use elsewhere. But this cautionary tale does, I hope, explain why I do not consider ground-cover gardening practical for do-it-your-selfers when they first start working a garden. With this sort of job it is all too possible to repeat the same type of mistake we see everywhere in so-called foundation plantings—using the wrong material the wrong way in the wrong place.

Ground-cover plants that can be used for covering open areas and suppressing weeds vary considerably in the way they go about the job. These basic differences exist in all ground-cover plants no matter what climate they grow in, and it is important to understand the ways they develop in order to choose the right type for the place you have in mind. Limited space, or any area adjacent to a lawn, should always be planted to ground covers that are easily controlled; otherwise you can create more problems for yourself than you solve. Rough ground in unobtrusive places or big areas with no sharply defined boundaries can take far more exuberant spreaders. This may sound obvious, but far too many gardeners blithely set out ground-cover plants without a notion of how they spread or how fast, and horticulturally speaking, this is the road to disaster. I learned the hard way, and some of the mistakes I made will remain with me as long as I work in our gardens. So before buying (or even more important, accepting from a friend) any ground-cover plants, make sure you understand their growth pattern. This is essential background knowledge and the only way to be sure of not getting overwhelmed. Ground covers are chosen to spread. If they spread wildly where you don't want them, you may well let loose a monster in your yard, for it is one of the characteristics of almost all ground covers that they are very hard to eliminate once they have taken hold. When this piece of horticultural information is clear in your mind, then and only then is it safe to take your pick among the innumerable plants offered for sale for this purpose. This point is not emphasized enough in the present-day rapture over ground covers, and that is why I am belaboring it.

Generally speaking, ground covers spread in four ways. The simplest to control are known as mat plants. These grow into wide, ground-hugging mats of foliage that are unobtrusive except when they are in bloom. Usually they are slow growers and need to be planted in combination with a thick mulch. We use perennial candytuft this way, and when the foliage gets thin we shear it back. Mat plants are the most effective when they are used in a strictly confined area.

Dwarf plants and shrubs with dense foliage, those junipers for example, are popular as ground covers because weeds cannot get established underneath them. This type of plant spreads slowly by growing wider and wider. Part of their charm is the interesting shape and color of the leaves or foliage. But anyone using this style of ground cover must expect to set out a considerable number of plants if they want to control weeds over a large area, and this is where the danger of monotony comes in. Spreading plants are heavier feeders than most of the other candidates for use as ground covers. They need to be started off in very rich soil in large planting holes, and they also require supplementary feeding as they increase in size. All this can make them more trouble, as well as initially much more expensive than some of the alternatives.

Creeping plants that spread by forming new colonies are the best known and most popular ground covers; they also give the fastest return for the least cost. But it is essential to understand that creeping plants spread by two very different methods and that there is a world of difference in their suitability for various positions in a garden. Some, like ivy, spread along the surface of the ground, forming new plants by rooting sections of their long stems into the top layer of the soil. With this type the spread can be watched and directed, and when the new growth reaches the outer limits of the allotted area, pruning can keep it under control. The other much more dangerous type of creeping plant increases by underground runners called "stolons." Stolons, which cannot be watched, pop up through the ground, often at quite a distance from the mother plant, and start in turn to colonize the area around them. Plants that spread underground, pachysandra is an example, cover any given area extremely fast, but since it is impossible to know where they are going to show up next, the spread is impossible to control. They also have the additional disadvantage that even the smallest scrap of underground runner broken off and left in the ground usually lives and sends up a fresh tuft of leaves—just after you think you have rooted the entire pestilence out! Plants that creep underground form magnificent ground covers in large areas, but they should be used with caution beside a lawn or in any place that needs strictly defined limits for good effect.

Perennial low-growing plants with thick foliage that seed freely can also be used as ground covers. The dog violet, which spreads like wildfire in open ground, can, for instance, be used deliberately to form a pleasant ground cover. But any plant that throws out hundreds of seeds, all of which germinate with enthusiasm, should never be used near other growing areas or in the vicinity of bricks, paved walks, or gravel driveways. The seed will not remain within the designated area, and little plants soon become a nuisance, establishing themselves all over the place. We used all these varying kinds of ground covers in both gardens, and by trial and error, with a few dreadful exceptions which will be described in the appropriate place, the right ones now are in the proper places.

Many gardeners often find that in spite of careful planning they have somehow acquired narrow stretches of open ground where it is impossible to plant in a conventional way. These areas can be between a path and a house wall under a window or beside a sliding door, and they present a considerable problem. The suburban garden has several such spots. One exists between the edge of the asphalt path that runs behind the house and the back porch—the contractors could not bring the hot asphalt right against the wooden beam that supports the porch so they left a narrow gap the whole length. A little farther on along the same path there is a slightly wider area between the asphalt and the greenhouse wall. This route is in constant use, and it is not a place for thick shrubs even if we could get the roots into the narrow space, for they would brush against us as we walked by. At first we tried to control the weeds that filled those open spaces with a bark mulch, particularly after we had planted miniature bulbs in the narrow strips. But there was not enough space to hold the deep mulch in position and it regularly washed over the path with every heavy rain. In desperation we tried mat plants, using perennial iberis, thyme, and aubrieta in the sunny area and creeping sedum and sempervivums in the shade. This worked well. The mats held down the weeds and, being low-growing plants, they don't deluge our ankles when we walk by them in the rain. Too much adventuring on their part is prevented by the fact that we walk over the thrusting shoot ends. They need no care except a haircut after they have flowered and another in the fall if they seem to be getting out of bounds. They have softened the harsh junction between the house and path unobtrusively and successfully. The fact that the soil is very poor does not worry them, for most mat plants are not heavy feeders; their main concern is for good drainage. Given that, they can stand almost any growing conditions, though the best of them need full sun. I do not happen to like the colors of creeping phlox, but it would also succeed in a position of this sort. The secret with mat plants is not to put them in large areas; they look better rather strictly confined. Nor should they ever be combined with other ground-cover plants; the attraction is their low profile, and this is soon lost if they are in competition with more aggressive plants.

Other difficult places in the suburban garden are the open strips of land where the lawns lap up to the shrub borders. The grass grows quite close to the hedges, but under the outermost spread of the branches it is too shady for it to thrive. And even if we were to cut back branches to let in more light, we don't really want grass in these strips, for they are full of flowering bulbs and therefore cannot be mowed. For some years we used mulch to keep down the weeds after the bulbs were through flowering. This worked, but it was not very interesting in such a prominent position; also once the bulb foliage was up, it was extremely difficult to lay a thick enough layer to hold down weeds over the summer. Another increasing annoyance was the appearance of the grass verge alongside this mulch. I do not share my father's passion for immaculate grass edges, but the untrimmed fringe of grass that slowly encroached over the mulch irritated me. Since we do not have the gardening help for this sort of meticulous work, let alone the time or inclination to do it ourselves, another solution had to be devised. The problem was solved by putting down controllable creeping ground covers, mainly myrtle and ivy, both of which spread by rooting in the surface of the ground. These are still in the process of being established, for there is a lot of land to be covered, but where they have thickened they are very successful. The open ground looks neat all summer long, and the leaves of the ground covers hide the encroaching grass. In fact, in places they have turned

Vinca or periwinkle ground cover with small bulbs spreading into the lawn.

the tables by growing over the grass, but this is easily handled by just cutting the stems back. We now only edge the lawn twice a year, once in the fall when fresh bulbs go in and again in the late spring before we leave town. The grass still gets an untidy fringe, but it is far less noticeable and no longer annoys me. Being evergreen, these ground covers have also added winter distinction to the area. Their leaves show color and texture even during bitter weather, and they strike a rather elegant note under the leafless flowering shrubs. They also are a pleasant relief and contrast to the seemingly brown, dead grass of a winter lawn.

Myrtle—or periwinkle or vinca as it is sometimes called—is particularly useful in our cold climate for this rather prominent position. The leaves stay glossy and in good condition in the depth of winter, and there is no winterkill to be worried about. Myrtle is not a very fast starter, though once established it can surprise you with the speed at which it romps over open ground. A new planting has to have a lot of little plants to be effective. We use rich compost in the planting holes to speed the growth, and the ground under the runners is spread with a thick pad of the same compost. To get the plant to cover the ground where we want it to grow, the runners are pinned down into the moist compost; hairpins do the trick. Forcing the stems into this close contact with the soil speeds up the rooting process, which in turn helps the formation of new colonies. But it is important to remember that this same mulch is also a delightful haven for innumerable weeds that can easily smother tiny myrtle plants. Any new planting must be kept carefully weeded until it is thick enough to deal with intruders without help. Myrtle does best in light shade or with morning sun.. It does not like full sunlight nor will it grow in the deep shade. New and better varieties have appeared on the market with bigger leaves and better, long-lasting flowers, and there is also a double-flowered variety. But this is basically a foliage, not a flowering plant, and we don't take very much interest in the bloom, though it is attractive while it lasts.

Ivy, which we also use in this area, though not combined with the periwinkle since I have come to dislike mixed ground covers, is rather more of a problem. In mild climates ivy can easily get out of hand, and in the North its leaves often die from winterkill. This usually does no harm to the plant. In time fresh leaves appear, but the dead foliage, which clings to the stems just when everything else is bursting out all over, is not only unattractive but holds on for a very long time; fresh growth is always slow to appear. People who live in mild climates will not have this problem, but they should be even more careful where they use ivy. Given a chance this is a takeover plant, and to control it successfully requires heavy regular pruning. Ground covers are supposed to save work, not make it, and for that reason ivy should always be regarded with caution in climates where the winters are not severe. We had a lot of trouble with ivy in my youth, for in England there is not enough really cold weather to keep it in check. My father spent a lot of time and energy pulling it up; he considered it a nuisance and a sign of poor husbandry to have it in the garden. I had, in fact, never seen it used as a ground cover or treated as anything except a pest and a bit of a gardening disgrace until I came to this country. My father had never heard of ground covers; this type of horticultural shortcut was unknown, for with plentiful labor weeds were kept down by hand. But were he alive today I am sure ivy still would not be in use in any garden where he had a say; he would have considered the idea repulsive and ludicrous.

It wasn't only on the ground that my father objected to ivy; he disliked it even more passionately when it climbed up trees. In those days it was supposed to kill them—an idea which is now discredited—and every so often he would take a large saw and stalk off into the woods to cut out tree-growing ivy. No one was very enthusiastic about this expedition; for months the dying ivy looked dreadful in the trees, and the whole operation was utterly useless, for the original sinner at the base remained as vigorous as ever. Within a couple of years the plant was usually back

Mixed ground cover of ivy and pachysandra with old tulips.

up where it had been earlier, and my father, undeterred, had to repeat the whole process. I would never willingly encourage ivy to grow up trees; I think it makes them look whiskery and untidy. Furthermore, though it doesn't ruin them, it can mask dangerous conditions. This was recently brought home to us when a huge bough of an ivy-covered elm in the country garden was blown down in a very moderate wind. The tree men had just finished cabling and treating that particular tree so we were all much annoyed, particularly since elms today are a diminishing species. When we investigated, we found that there had been very bad decay at the junction of the branch with the main trunk, which had gone unnoticed and unrepaired for years because it was entirely hidden under a thick growth of ivy.

But, in spite of my vague dislike of ivy, we use it a lot. We mix several varieties together so that the slightly differing leaf shapes prevent monotony. There is nothing to be done about winterkill except try and find hardy types. These exist—Baltic ivy, for example—and when you see ivy that has come through a cold winter with its leaves intact, it is a good idea to increase your stock by taking cuttings from that particular plant. To do this, cut shoots about five or six inches in length in the spring. Trim the cut stems with a sharp knife or razor blade back to the first node—the place where the low leaf grows—and strip off the next two leaves. Put the prepared shoots into glass jars—baby-food jars are excellent—add aquarium charcoal, and keep the jars topped up with water, which should be changed whenever it begins to smell or look cloudy. The jars should be kept in a light, bright place—a sunny window indoors will do—and small roots will soon form along the stem. When these are about an inch long, shift the rooted cuttings, three or four in a group, into a wide-mouthed glass jar. Then slowly displace the water with fine earth over a period of about a week until the new roots are embedded in soil. Rooted cuttings should never be left too long in water or they will adapt to taking all their nourishment that way and will then be unable to stand the transfer to soil. The cuttings should be left in the damp earth until it begins to dry out; by then the roots will probably have taken hold. At this stage the root ball can be turned out intact and the cluster of cuttings planted outdoors without disturbing the earth around the roots. Once outside, cut back the stems an inch. This will make the plants bush out and will also help the new cuttings survive by shortening the amount of stem the roots have to sustain.

Ivy settled into the ground this way should be in good light but not full sun. The planting hole should be full of compost and the whole area must be kept moist and well weeded for the first summer. By fall the new ground cover will be well established and able to get safely through the winter. Next spring it will send out new growth which can be pinned down onto a compost pad just like the periwinkle. This may seem like a lot of trouble for a plant that I keep warning you about, but ivy is a slow starter and won't look like much for several years unless you use big plants in the first place or take trouble with rooted cuttings. Here in the North ivy rarely flowers; the leaves we see are immature. The plant carries flowers and berries only when it has climbed to the top of its support or when it has reached a certain stage of maturity. It never will flower, no matter how old it may be, as long as it remains on the ground. Flowering ivy attracts flies and bluebottles which serve as pollinating agents. Since the smell is distinctive and to many people slightly unpleasant, it is not necessarily a drawback if your plants never flower!

Pachysandra ground cover.

For ground covers in deep shade, pachysandra is in heavy use in our gardens. This is one of the plants that spreads by underground runners, and it can become a nuisance in very rich soil. Pachysandra should not be planted in a mixed collection of ground-cover plants, for it will overwhelm the others. It was already well established in the suburban garden when we bought the house, and the plantings, with sturdy green stems and a tuft of leaves at the top, are still a delight, filling impossible places under the big old conifers beside the house where nothing else survived. Huge stretches of pachysandra are uninteresting, but they

Pachysandra sprig rooted by knotting.

can be lightened by using some of the new variegated variety that has a silver edge to the leaves; this set out along the outer limits of a big patch of ordinary pachysandra makes an immense difference. The leaves never winter-kill, and they are reasonably tolerant of that modern menace, salt splash from the winter roads. As long as it is not overused, pachysandra has a great deal going for it. It prefers light shade and a moist position, but it is exceptionally accommodating and will make the best of almost any place it is planted except full sun, which it cannot take—the leaves will turn a dingy yellow.

For all its fast growth, this is quite an expensive plant to buy, and the variegated variety is extremely costly. This is all the more surprising, for pachysandra is an exceptionally simple plant to root. If you pull handfuls out of an established clump, the original patch will fill in so quickly that you can easily get a neighbor to allow you to ravage hers. Keep a basin of water beside you and put all the gleanings in it. The plants break off with long skinny stalks, sometimes with small-rooted stolons attached. Take a single stem and tie a knot in it: if there is a stolon, work this carefully through the loop. Ideally the knot should be six inches or so from the tuft of leaves, but I work with any length of stem that I can knot. Carefully tighten the knotted loop; you'll break a few, but gently does it. The pliable stems are inclined to try to work loose, so you must pull the loop tightly enough to hold it in position. Set the knotted stem into prepared ground which should have been dug over and had wet peat moss incorporated into it. The knot should be buried at least two inches below the surface of the soil, and the ground should be firmed around the stem so that the tuft of leaves stands upright unsupported. If there was a runner, this should be spread along the ground about an inch below the surface. Space the knotted material about five inches apart, and when every scrap is in, spray the leaves with water. If the planting area is kept moist, roots will form where the stem tissue was bruised by the knotting. What makes the process successful is the fact that the stem and leaves remain alive and healthy for an extraordinarily long time without roots; the plant is partly succulent and has a considerable supply of reserve moisture in the tissue.

I have found this method far simpler and much faster than the conventional advice about taking cuttings from this plant. Also it is half the work, for the new shoots are established from the first, in the place where they are to grow. The second planting-out process that has to follow the conventional method of taking cuttings is therefore eliminated. Spring is probably the easiest time for new plants to get established, but I have used this method in the heat of summer and just before the snow flies with almost a hundred percent success. Do try it; it's the understatement of the age to point out how much cheaper it is, and since it is so simple and so successful, this method will give a new gardener a great deal of self-confidence. Nothing impresses others more than being shown a large patch of ground cover and casually told that those are all your own cuttings. Success of this kind may be all that is needed to lead you on to try other horticultural adventures.

Pachysandra is so sturdy and so little trouble that it is sometimes abused by being used as a substitute for grass. This it cannot take. Walking over it leaves a trail of bruised plants, and if people track steadily across pachysandra it will die out under their feet. When happy, the plant has a white flower, but this is not particularly important. Slightly unexpectedly, pachysandra makes quite a good house plant. You can first try the knotting trick with a potful and use it for indoor greenery in a bright, warm window. Pachysandra has proved extremely useful as a ground cover under lawn trees that have very dense shade in which grass cannot grow. Specimen trees on a lawn almost always ruin grass, and the answer is to plant a ground cover and allow it to spread out to the limits where the grass can again take over. But it is important to use plants that are controlled by mowing in such a place. Ivy can do the job, but the problem is the slowness with

Ajuga—the
purple lawn.

which it gets going and its need for light. Pachysandra or even lily-of-the-valley will move into an area far faster and, though both will spread out of their allotted space, mowing will keep them under control. The soil under old, well-established trees is usually poor and very hard-packed, and it is a job to get even good-natured pachysandra successfully rooted. The trick is to get hold of an old, low-sided wooden box, knock out the bottom, and, if you are garden-proud, paint the sides green. Set this on the ground underneath the tree near the trunk and fill it up with rich compost. Then plant the ground cover in that. By the time the wooden sides have rotted and been removed, the plants will be thoroughly established. You can then train them to spread outwards by putting down the usual thick layer of compost on top of the soil. This is far the simplest way to get small ground-cover plants established in impossible positions.

Purple ajuga is another evergreen ground cover that will grow in impossible places and spread thickly. It too will take deep shade, and unlike pachysandra it can also be grown in full sun. In many ways it is almost an ideal ground-cover plant, for it is indestructible, fills in fast, and keeps a good color in its leaves winter and summer alike. Ajuga, however, has one appalling drawback; it is almost uncontrollable and, though we use it in the country, I have been extremely careful that none has ever found its way into the much smaller suburban garden. Ajuga should never be planted in small areas unless it can be strictly confined; planter boxes, for example, would be excellent near a front entrance, whereas putting it straight into the ground near your front door might be disastrous. I found all this out the hard way and I am still paying the price.

In the third garden the guest house is lent to our friends and our children in the summer, and we use it for fall, winter, and spring weekends. Guests in a guest house do not come there to garden, they want to laze around. Nor do they want to be made to feel guilty by the sight of untidy flowerbeds or their hosts weeding around their temporary domain. I was well aware of this and have kept the planting around the guest house plain almost to the point of austerity. But since we were there so much ourselves it seemed absurd to have no flowers that we could enjoy, so I compromised by planting beds of flowering and berried shrubs nearby. In order to keep these areas weed-free during the summer, a thick ground cover was needed, and, just because I had a lot running freely in our woods, I decided to use purple ajuga for this purpose. Ajuga in a naturalistic situation where it is on its own and ajuga in a restricted flowerbed proved two very different plants. It did the job required of it very fast, for it filled in under the azaleas and other shrubs so thickly that no weed ever shows its head. But then it looked for new worlds to conquer, and purple tufts began to appear in the grass that ran beside the guest house. At first we tried to salvage the situation by digging these trespassers out of the lawn and sinking a metal strip six inches deep between the shrub border where I had set the ajuga and the grass. But this was locking the stable door after the horse had gone, for, once free, the ajuga was determined not to be reconfined. In spite of continuous efforts we have never completely eradicated it from the grass. In fact, I keep finding new colonies in unexpected places, for it seems to travel enormous distances underground before coming up for air. It is cut whenever the grass is mowed, but that doesn't appear to bother it at all, and I am now rapidly acquiring lawn areas that are not green but purple! It does not suffer in any way from steady traffic across it, as long as the leaves are kept clipped. The place where the garden chairs are set out has now been invaded, and it seems to thrive under that hard treatment. It also remains impervious to damage from children playing on it. If you cannot stand your grass, ajuga might be the answer, but for those who are not anxious for yet one more intractable weed problem in their lawn, never allow ajuga to be planted where it could spread into it.

So far I have only mentioned the ground covers that hold their leaves all year. I have also deliberately excluded one, euonymus, which is often highly recommended, for I don't think it does a good job. Euonymus spreads extremely slowly, and the ground below it is not really shaded by the foliage, so weeds become a menace in it. It needs heavy pruning each spring or it becomes scraggly; it is also extremely prone to scale, and to control this several regular sprays are needed. I feel quite strongly that new gardeners should not be encouraged to plant anything that calls for a regular spray program. We inherited a certain amount of euonymous in the suburban garden and I have not had the strength of mind to get rid of it, but I would never deliberately plant it. The same holds true for pachistima. I have had it in the same place for years without getting anything out of it, and I cannot understand why it is on everybody's list as a good ground-cover plant. The rate of growth is slower than cold molasses, and though it has a pleasant form and nice leaves, the time it takes to develop puts it right off my list of useful plants. Gardening is an individualistic matter—we all have likes and dislikes, but to fill a specific purpose, the plant must at least have the capacity to function. Neither euonymous nor pachistima seems to me to fulfill the requirements of a good ground cover.

There are many excellent deciduous plants that have the necessary growing habits that produce good ground covers. They fill open areas with pleasant foliage, grow fast and thickly enough to suppress weeds, and can be cut down when frost comes and not given another thought until spring. In some ways deciduous ground covers are easier to manage than the evergreen varieties, though obviously they lack the useful function of providing winter interest. With a deciduous ground cover you don't have to worry about falling leaves smothering the foliage. This is a danger with new evergreen ground covers; this is one place where the leaves cannot be left to form a natural mulch. Young evergreen plants will die if dead leaves lie too thickly on them. Deciduous ground covers can also be given a top-dressing of compost when the foliage is cut down. Plants that grow thickly and in close association with each other take a lot of nourishment out of the ground, and it is far more trouble to top-dress evergreen ground covers than the deciduous types. There are quite a lot of these plants that can be used to form pleasant green blankets during the growing season. Violets have already been mentioned, bishop's-weed or goutweed—the name is curiously interchangeable—is another.

This plant, which is also known as ground elder, has a terrible reputation as a garden menace, and in mild climates it should be kept out of any cultivated area. Here in the North, the cold keeps it under a certain amount of control. Though I hardly dare admit it in print, we have found the pestilential green variety very useful as a ground cover in the rough land beside the waterfront. There is also a variegated variety that is far less intrusive and vigorous, and we use this in our brick entrance court where the green and white three-lobed leaves are pleasant and restful. Goutweed is a plant for light shade; the leaves turn brown in the sun, and it cannot survive in very poor light. The variegated variety was new to me; we found it growing half-wild in a completely neglected flowerbed in the third garden. I had been so burned by my experience with ajuga that I took my time before doing anything about the goutweed. It grew beside the grass and clearly had not been able to spread successfully into it, even though, like the ajuga, it increases through underground runners. Obviously this was a plant that could not stand regular mowing, so that danger was eliminated. But before allowing it into the new entrance court, I grew some plants in boxes to check on all its habits, and only when I was sure that I could control it sufficiently was it moved into its present prominent position. This is the route every gardener should take when confronted by an unknown plant.

It may sound ungrateful, but this is particularly important if someone gives you a plant. There is a cynical horticultural saying, founded alas on solid truth, which says in effect that if you get given it, it spreads! A deep wooden box set in the ground with a few holes bored in the base for drainage is an excellent proving ground for any unknown plant. Fill it with rich soil, put in the plant, and watch it for a couple of years before risking introducing it into your garden. The box, being portable, can be moved from sun to shade until you find the position in which the contents thrive the best. This means you will have a chance to observe dangerous tendencies before it is too late, and if the

Hostas as weed suppressors.

gift is a valuable one, the temporary home in a box will not hurt the plant so long as it is kept watered in hot weather.

There are many other deciduous plants that can be combined in a mass planting to make excellent ground covers—hostas or plantain-lilies being a prime example. These are exceptionally sturdy growers that are often used for accent in a garden or in a border along a difficult shady area, but they are not very often used alone as ground-cover plants, though they are impressive and excellent for that purpose. Hostas increase slowly but majestically in size; they do not make new plants. They have thick, dense foliage which arches right down to the surface of the soil and shades out even the toughest weeds. They will thrive anywhere, except in full sun, and have almost no enemies except slugs. They come in a large variety of sizes and leaf shapes, and the color range of the leaves varies from plain dark green to a shade that is almost lettuce color. There are varieties with variegated leaves and those that have a silver edging. Some of the larger species have leaves with a blue tinge. We use them everywhere in our gardens, but they have been the most effective and looked their best when planted very close together to serve as a ground cover. They do this job in the suburban garden in open spaces along the drive and beside the garage, where we never were able to get rid of a particularly virulent weed grass until we planted hostas. They also form the backbone of the ground-cover planting on the very shady side of the brick entrance court in the country. Hostas, particularly the numerous new varieties, are not cheap, but, as shall be described a little further on, they are easy to divide, and the initial outlay is soon absorbed by the number of new plants that come from one large specimen. For ground-cover purposes they should be planted in rich soil so as to get the maximum foliage spread, though individually used, hostas grow reasonably well, even in poor soil. It is important when buying them to discover how wide any particular variety is expected to reach at maturity, otherwise you will not be able to lay them out to get the effect you want. Hostas carry blue and white flowers which are pleasant though not overwhelming. I don't allow them to bloom, for I prefer the rounded billowing effect of the leaves unspoiled by spikes of flowers. If I have been lukewarm about other ground covers, perhaps I can make amends by my unqualified admiration of hostas.

The use of ground covers for filling in places where grass is weak under trees has already been mentioned, but it is also possible to use large deciduous plants for the same purpose. Oddly enough, big trees look best with low, creeping ground covers circling them, while small trees with less dense foliage are set off extremely well with big plants. In either case the all-around effect will be better if the lower branches are pruned off the trees so that the ground covers are seen against bare trunks. Hostas and daylilies are both very attractive in such a position, and, though daylilies are not ground covers in the usual sense, they do suppress weeds when massed together in light shade under a tree. Both plants have large root systems, so they are not amenable to planting above ground in a box; no matter how hard the ground or how full of roots, a planting hole has to be dug. As these plants have a wide foliage spread they can be set into the ground some distance away from the base of the trunk, but it still can often be extremely hard to dig a big enough hole. And if this kind of planting is to be done well, the hole must be big and loaded with compost, for there is tremendous competition for food underneath a tree.

One way out of the difficulty is to get a crowbar, hammer it in fairly deeply, and then bang it from side to side until it is sufficiently loose to come out. Repeat the process a number of times around the edge of your planting hole and eventually enough hard-packed soil will have been worked loose so that you can get a shovel in. Once you have reached that stage, you are on your way. But don't try and establish huge old plants in these planting holes; a strong, young division will settle in faster and do better. If you are going to use division from a plant you already own, do the work in early spring as soon as new growth shows above ground. To get the plant out of the ground with as little root damage as possible, take a spade or shovel (I prefer a long-handled shovel), and dig a circle around the root ball. Drive the shovel straight down, don't slant it inward. Once the circle is completed, reinsert the shovel and push it in under the plant, heave, and the entire root mass should come out like a plug. Shake off the soil—this, by the way, is a fearfully messy job, so don't do it on the grass. Lay the plant down on its side on a hard surface, usually in the path, and take a spade which has a flat, straight edge, not the pointed end of a shovel, rest it lengthwise across the center of the root mass, put your foot on the shoulder of the spade, and bear down with your full weight. This will cut the plant in half, which will probably be enough, though in some enormous old hostas and daylilies you can redivide the halves. But don't make the divisions too small; it's harder for them to recover. Always try and keep a fair balance between the amount of root and the foliage it carries; a plant will not survive if there is a lot of top-growth and very little root to sustain it. If you have waited to do the job until the foliage is already strongly up, you would be wise to cut most of it off after you have reset the division. As long as the new plant is kept watered, fresh leaves will come very quickly in the spring. If you divide in the fall, which is not advisable in cold climates, always cut the foliage back. We have used hostas and daylilies under lawn trees for many years. Hostas are probably the more satisfactory because the foliage stays neat right up to frost. Daylilies get a little ratty toward the end of the growing season. But the flowers on the daylilies are much more interesting, and if you want them, do not give in to the very natural inclination to cut off the daylily foliage early for neatness sake. For good flowers the leaves

Flowering heath.

must go full term; cutting them down prematurely will weaken the plant and reduce the amount of bloom considerably. The number of flowers on both plants will also depend on how much light is available. In general, tough older varieties of both these plants are the most successful under trees; almost all the newer hybrids need easier living and stronger light.

Sloping areas are a problem in most gardens because they are hard to mow. Here again ground covers are a solution. In the suburban garden we have a sloping rise between the lower and upper lawns in the back garden which for years was a problem. Nothing grew well until we set out some ferns. These proved a great success; they serve as an excellent ground cover, filling in the area so thickly that nothing else can grow. They look neat and tidy without any attention, and, when they do get blown over, we only have to cut off the broken fronds for dozens of new ones to reappear. But ferns are also plants with takeover tendencies. I don't think they combine well with other plants—they are too overwhelming. Used alone, and there are varieties for sun or shade and for every type of climate, they are excellent for banks. For a more formal ground cover on a sunny sloping area there are many varieties of spreading junipers, and some of the newer types creep along the ground rather than billow above it. These make good ground and bank covers, but the plants are not cheap. Make sure that the area into which they are to go is properly prepared with rich soil, for it is hard to add nourishment later. Junipers also need a mulch to keep down the weeds until they are strongly established.

If you live where the soil is slightly acid, heathers and heaths make delightful ground covers in a sunny place. They are also particularly successful on slopes because they enjoy good drainage. The only disadvantage is the cost—again these are not cheap plants. They come easily from cuttings, but they start off very slowly. When they are established you will love them, for there are varieties that can be had in flower almost every month of the year; but until they get going they will bore you by looking very uninteresting. Although minute plants that cost a lot of money and seem to be standing still can be a great irritation, don't pull them out in despair. That is the way all the heather family behaves. Sit tight, and one day you will notice with amazement that your heather bank is a thick delight. There is no upkeep with heather except trimming off the dead flowers after they have finished blossoming. I would like to see them much more freely used. Crown vetch, a member of the pea family, is now tremendously advertised for its capacity to cover banks. I have neither used it nor seen it in use, but it seems to have a great many advocates—apart from the people who want to sell it to us! You can also cover a bank in time with creeping forsythia.

In this section, I have only touched the outer fringe of the possibilities offered by ground covers. It is an enormous subject with an equally enormous amount of available plant material. The use of ground-cover plants is limited only by the gardener's imagination, and they can be the solution to gardening problems in every climate. Writing from experience, which is after all the basis of this book, necessarily limits the amount of information I can give about using them. But wherever you garden, and whenever you decide to take on ground covers, remember the importance of discovering the methods by which they spread before you put them in the ground. This is the key to using them effectively. Ground covers are not going to be a success, no matter how well they keep down weeds, if they are constantly adventuring into other parts of the yard. The use of them calls for more sophisticated horticultural knowledge than almost any other phase of outdoor gardening. I realize this sounds a little severe, but there is too much modern emphasis on ground covers as a cure-all, which they are not. Good ground covers, properly chosen, can be a delight; intrusive ground covers can be an incurable gardening disaster. As long as you bear this in mind you will be all right, for you will think before you plant—and that is the real secret of success with ground covers.

Bulbs | X

Color in a garden is produced in all sorts of ways. It can
come from trees and shrubs, from blossoming vines, from
roses in all their variety, and from cultivated plants. Any
such display is a great source of pride to the gardener, for
success depends largely on the skill with which these orna-
mentals have been grown. Fortunately, however, for the
new, the busy, or less dedicated gardener there is another
surefire way of getting color through flowers without having
to take too much trouble, or know too much horticulture.
Everyone everywhere can have flowers by putting bulbs in
the ground, and there are types that suit every climate and
a sufficient variety to give months of successive bloom.

The term "bulbs," or "bulbous plants," as I shall use it in
this section, will include not only the true bulbs but also
rhizomes, corms, and tubers—everything, in fact, that can
be bought with the embryonic flower already formed, and
surrounded with a reserve store of food so that a flower will
appear the first year after planting even under less than perfect growing conditions. Getting bloom in subsequent years
is something else again and will also be discussed. I am perfectly well aware that lumping together all these various
types under the single term "bulb" is a gross horticultural
inaccuracy. Plants with prepacked underground storage, are
not technically at all the same thing. A daffodil bulb is a modified shoot; crocus and gladiolus corms are modified stems;
the rhizome of an anemone or lily-of-the-valley is a modified
root; while the caladium is a modified branch. This information is highly important to the specialist—and possibly it
is important for those who write books to show that they are

aware of the differences—it is not, however, vital knowledge for home gardeners. All they need to know is when, where, and how to plant these different horticultural lifestyles, and, since the planting treatment is much the same for all plants with an underground storage system, it is far simpler in this rather general account to describe them all under one single term, no matter how much the purist may shudder.

Bulbs of every kind should be the beginning gardener's best friend as well as a standby for sophisticated horticulturists. They should be used freely and with complete assurance, for most bulbs are extremely undemanding. All they need to make at least one dramatic show is to be planted at the proper season and at approximately the right depth; after that, there's nothing more to do except sit back and enjoy the results. The rub, of course, for insecure gardeners comes with those vague terms "proper planting time" and "correct depth." But of all the many horticultural problems that can turn up to baffle or alarm gardeners, the right time to plant bulbs is not one to worry about; the matter is solved for you.

It is, in fact, impossible to plant bulbs at the wrong time of year, even though the variety of bulbs makes the planting seasons very different. This is because bulbs of all kinds are available from retailers or are sent by catalogue dealers only at the time when these particular species should go into the ground. Outdoor bulbs are simply not around to be planted at the wrong season. A rather useful slogan for the novice gardener would be "if you can buy bulbs, you can plant them." For the forgetful gardener, the sort who bitterly regrets not having planted any bulbs when he sees them in bloom in a neighbor's garden, the slogan might be changed to an imperative "when you see bulbs, buy them, and plant them." Unlike many other garden products, such as seeds or container plants, bulbs are highly perishable, and they cannot be carried over for another season unless the retailer possesses extremely costly cold storage designed especially for bulbs. Without this specialized equipment, bulbs shrivel and go to waste if they are out of the ground too long.

If you can't plant the bulbs as soon as you buy them, store them in the coolest place you possess, in open paper bags or in mesh bags, the kind used for onions. Bulbs must have free circulation of air around them while they are out of the ground and should never be kept in a tightly closed container.

In addition to ensuring you the first pick of the bulbs, early planting gives bulbs a chance to establish a strong root system before flowering. This applies equally to spring bulbs, which must be planted in the fall in order to make roots before the ground freezes, and to the summer bulbs, which need time to throw strong roots in before the ground is baked hard. New bulbs will flower even with a poorly developed root system—that is why they are the novice gardener's helpmate—but the flowers will last longer with good roots, and the plant itself be better supported against wind. And if you want your bulbs to put on a repeat performance in subsequent years, plenty of strong roots over a long growing season are essential, either to plump up the bulb so that it can build a new embryonic bud, or in the case of corms, which are annuals, to form an entirely new storage supply.

The exception to the early planting rule is the tulip. This, like all the other bulbs, is best bought as soon as it appears on the market so as to get the best. But tulips should not go into the ground before late October or even early November. While tulip bulbs wait, store them in a cool place. Newly planted tulip bulbs rush into top-growth the instant they feel moist earth around them; they would rather sprout than root. This premature top-growth, if it gets above ground too early, is vulnerable to cold weather, and the flowerbud can be blasted.

Though tulips are the most seriously affected if top-growth shows above ground in the fall, other bulbs occasionally do the same. Snowdrops, for example, often show a flash of white in very early spring. But as long as the shoots are still small and tightly closed, cold usually does not hurt other spring bulbs. Fall top-growth in bulbs can come

The suburban terrace in spring.

from a number of things, too shallow planting being one. The most usual cause is the weather. If the fall is wet and hard frost late in coming, bulbs become confused about the season and start into growth. If you spot a clump of bulbs that has got ahead of itself and it bothers you, throw a few spadefuls of compost around and over the shoots. If you don't notice them until everything is frozen hard, boughs off the Christmas tree make an excellent emergency cover for overenthusiastic bulbs. The exception to this first aid is the snowdrop. This bulb expects to be up and at work by the end of the year. If you cover up those little shoots you may kill them. Once snow has fallen you can relax. Snow is excellent insulation; under it, adventurous bulb shoots are entirely safe.

Planting the bulbs too shallowly has other disadvantages. If the bulbs themselves are exposed, they suffer debilitating dehydration from heat in the summer. Exposed bulbs are also extremely vulnerable to fatal damage from heavy feet! So what about "planting depth"; what is too shallow or too deep? Stores that sell bulbs usually pin up a chart showing the exact depth at which each type should be planted. This is fine, if you have a photographic memory, total recall, or can take the chart home—or even if you have a pencil and paper in your hand. Most of us don't have any of these things, and when we get the bulbs home, we feel confused, unable to remember whether to bury our purchases in a deep or shallow grave. If you are chartless and new to bulbs, there is a rough rule of thumb that can be used: plant the bulbs about twice the depth of their overall size. The inevitable exceptions are two: first, the tulip, which for reasons I will deal with later, needs to be planted six to eight inches below ground level; the other standout is the lovely Madonna lily. This is a plant that gives skilled growers tremendous trouble and often flourishes for the casual gardener. If you are one of the fortunates for whom this plant thrives, it may be because (and possibly by chance rather than through knowledge) you planted it just below the surface of the soil, which is the treatment it needs.

If you are prepared to put in new bulbs each season and treat them as annuals, it is possible to have them bloom for

Reused tulips with muscari and tritelia.

you in almost any place in the yard except swampy ground. The bulbs we buy come to us in superb condition, force-fed like a Strasbourg goose, with the embryonic bud bursting to go. This conditioning by the growers is the reason why we can be so sure of flowers. Some people find it simpler always to use fresh bulbs each season, digging them up when the flowers are over and throwing them away. There is nothing wrong with this, though it is a rather expensive way of gardening, but it does mean a fresh planting effort each year. But since most of us dig and replant summer bulbs, this is not an insurmountable objection. I don't happen to like spring bulbs used this way. New bulbs always look new; they grow unnaturally tall and in a stiff fashion. I enjoy most spring bulbs grown in an informal style, and I prefer established clumps rather than groups. Treated as perennials, and as a permanent feature of the yard, the spring bulbs spread into pools of color that bear no resemblance to the stiff solitary bulbs set out each fall. Temperamentally I am also always in favor of growing plants in a manner that does not call for any annual effort on my part!

But to use spring bulbs as a regular source of flowers, they have to be planted with a great deal more care than just figuring out the correct depth. For certain long-term enjoyment, they need to be set out in a position that suits their rather picky requirements for long-term health. Ideally, the spring bulbs, with which the autumn crocus and colchicum must also be included, need rich, light soil: that is, either sandy soil with compost added or a rich soil that also has extremely good drainage. But in spite of the need for fast drainage, bulbs will not flourish in a very dry place. They need plenty of moisture during their growing period in the spring and also in the fall when they are making their early roots.

This fall rooting begins far sooner than most of us realize —unless we have dug up a bulb by mistake in late summer. Bulbs are not available commercially here in the Northeast until after Labor Day, but those already in the ground do, in fact, start to root in early August. During this stage, moisture is extremely important. If your bulbs are planted in a dry place, you will get a far better spring show if you water the ground regularly from late August until the fall rains take over. Some of the bulbs in the suburban garden have been successfully carried over year after year in what technically is absolutely the wrong place—a very hot, dry little flowerbed in front of the greenhouse, which gets the full sun all day long. The reason for their continued good health is probably the fact that this bed has a long, slow watering every second week all fall.

For regular bloom, spring bulbs also need good light, preferably some sunlight, until the rather untidy foliage withers away. This does not mean full sunlight beating down on the bulbs all day long, for this dries out the leaves prematurely. They prefer light, dappled sunlight, or morning sun, and once their foliage has withered away, it doesn't matter how shady the area becomes.

Translated into growing terms, this means that spring bulbs, with the exception once again of tulips, flower and increase most successfully in a hay field or orchard where the grass remains uncut until June, thus shading the leaves slightly. Meadow grass also provides some protection from the summer sun baking the ground. But since meadows and orchards are not common in suburbia, light high shade under deciduous trees makes an acceptable alternative. In such a place, enough sun falls on the leaves during the ripening stage, and the bulbs rest in cool, shaded ground once the trees are fully leafed out. If you have no such place in your yard and the only possibility for bulbs is either full sun or deep shade, choose the sunny spot. Sun cannot easily be introduced into a shaded area, but dormant bulbs can be sheltered from baking heat either with a low ground cover or a very thick mulch. If you want long-term pleasure from them, too much sun is better for bulbs than too little.

But why this emphasis on allowing the foliage to ripen and why is this process so vital? Flowering literally takes a great deal out of a bulb and uses up the stored material so that it shrinks. In order to survive, let alone flower again,

Naturalized daffodils in "the glade."

this storage material has to be replaced. This replenishment comes from two sources, the roots and the leaves. The root system keeps the bulb full of stored moisture in the fall. In the spring it also sends moisture to the leaves. As long as the leaves are functioning and exposed to the sun, the process of photosynthesis can be continued, and this in turn sends proteins, sugars, and starches, the building blocks of all plant life, back to the bulb. If bulbs are expected to continue to produce flowers and spread in increasing numbers, it is absolutely essential that their leaves are allowed to grow undisturbed until they wither of their own accord or are cut down by frost. Any premature removal of bulb foliage is disastrous for the very survival of the bulb—let alone the expectation of future flowers.

I sometimes read the suggestion that bulbs cease flowering because they get too crowded, and that if a strong clump has no flowers it should be dug and separated in the fall. If you intend to try this, remember to stake the bulbs while you can still see them. I am not sure that crowding, which is the natural increase of a clump of bulbs by the formation of new offsets alongside, results in a lack of flowers. Bulbs growing in open meadows spread into tremendous thick clumps and still remain full of bloom. Whenever bulbs cease to flower, I am inclined to suspect other problems. They may not have enough moisture during the crucial fall rooting time, something that can easily be remedied by watering and which should be tried for at least the season before digging up the bulbs. Another problem could be lack of nourishment in the soil. Bulbs need fertilizing as much as any other long-established plant. If your bulbs are growing in woodland, or at the edge of a shrub border, spread a rich top-dressing of compost over them in the fall and fertilize them again in the spring. This may bring about a great improvement. Lack of sufficient light on the ripening leaves is, however, the most likely culprit. Nothing stands still in a garden; an area that once gave enough light for bulbs can imperceptibly over the years get too thick and overgrown for them. Often the flowering problem can be solved by having the trees overhead thinned.

To keep up the fertility of an established planting, where a regular top-dressing of compost is not possible, spread fertilizer over the ground in the fall and again on the ground around the bulb foliage after the flowers are done. A mixture of bone meal and dried cow manure has worked well with us. And, whatever you use, water the area thoroughly afterward so that the fertilizer sinks rapidly into the ground where the roots can make use of it.

The simplest, almost the most rewarding, of the spring

bulbs are the small bulbs that flower early. These do not produce nearly such a problem with withering foliage, for it dies away fast without giving offense. In the suburban garden, in light shade under the drip line of the shrub borders, there are snowdrops, chionodoxa, scillas, the yellow winter aconite—which comes with an Elizabethan ruff of green around the flower, grape-hyacinths, and triteleias. None of them gives us any trouble; in fact they deny everything I have written by spreading unconcernedly into the nearby lawns and continuing to set bloom even though the foliage is regularly mown down! Small bulbs always look better and more important if they are grouped by variety and not mixed up together. When planting, leave some space between the different varieties, for the little bulbs spread very fast both through multiplying underground and also by seed.

The fat green seedpods of the small bulbs should always be allowed to ripen, unlike those of the big bulbs, which should be picked off. The reason for this double standard is the fact that seed-making is an exhausting business. Big bulbs do not naturalize freely enough in this part of the country to make it worth taking the chance of exhausting the bulb, for the seed takes from three to six years to reach blossoming size. Small bulbs spread so easily that a few can always be allowed to overdo it by setting seed. And since the seed grows to flowering size in a couple of years, it is well worth having. After the heavy fat pods begin to drop down on the ground, I often pick them and allow them to finish ripening in a bare place where I want extra bulbs. This has worked extremely well, but the pods cannot be picked until they are huge and fat and changing color, otherwise the seed will not be sufficiently matured. This particular group of small bulbs does not need a great deal of sun to ripen the foliage or the pods; there must, however, be good light, for they will not flourish in deep shade.

Of all the small bulbs that lighten up the shady places, snowdrops are my favorites. From childhood I have always felt sad when they faded. Snowdrops grow unnoticed and unappreciated under the snow for so long and have so short a stay in which we can appreciate them. Also when their flowers die, it marks the end of that first anticipatory period, the longing for tangible evidence of spring, that is sometimes better in promise than reality. Everyone should grow snowdrops, if the climate makes it possible; their deceptive fragile appearance masks great sturdiness. They prefer a cool, damp place in the shade, but they are tolerant enough to stand almost any position except full sun. Snowdrops are available in the shops in the fall along with all the other small bulbs, but oddly enough they do not get off to a very good start that way. You will get a far better effect if you can dig up a clump just after the flowers are over and as the seedpods begin to form. Lift out the bulbs, which sometimes run quite deep, keeping as many roots intact as possible. Separate them into little groups of three and four bulbs with the leaves and seedpods still intact, then replant the separated groups in light shade and forget them. Next season you will have flowers from the divided bulbs, and the ground around them will be green with tiny spears which are the seedling plants. Snowdrops are the only bulbs I grow that

*Crocuses in
a single color.*

can be lifted and divided successfully while they are in active growth—this is such a useful characteristic that we should all make more of it.

For sunny areas the best of the small bulbs are crocus. These come in two varieties, both extremely useful in every yard. The earliest to flower, and the ones that spread the fastest, are the species crocus, which are unimproved small varieties. Species crocuses hug the ground when they bloom, so they should always be set near the house where they can be appreciated. If possible they should also be planted where there is space for them to spread, for spread they will into the path if there is nowhere more suitable! The more familiar Dutch crocus needs no description, but I have one reservation about them: to me they look far more effective planted in sweeps of a single color. Mixed plantings of crocus always seem muddled and ineffectual. All the crocus family make new corms each year, and they spread by additional little cormlets that form around the base of the new one. Crocus foliage has, of course, to be allowed to wither off, but it dies down in the North almost before the grass needs cutting, so if you are determined to have bulbs in your lawn, choose crocus!

The small species or unimproved tulips are also a delight in a sunny place with good, quick drainage. They too are lost in a flowerbed and look their best in little groups around steps or near an entrance. When happy, the species tulips flower for many years, but with me they do not increase in number.

Some of the small bulbs have an untidy habit of throwing up leaf growth in the fall and carrying this over the winter. I find this is a great nuisance. The rather stringy leaves get in the way of the fall clean-up and cannot be cut down. Also these same leaves are usually extremely battered by spring, and this detracts from the appearance of the flowers. The worst offenders in the suburban garden are the grapehyacinths and the triteleias, and in the country garden the ornithogalums or star-of-Bethlehem. If the star-of-Bethlehem once gets into a flowerbed you had better make up your mind to like it; once in, you will never eliminate it. It has sneaked into the main flowering area in the country garden and now seriously impedes all my efforts for a neat fall mulch. I take it out by the bushel basket, but to no effect—rather typically it is refusing to establish itself in a small naturalistic glade we are creating along the back boundary line in the suburban garden where I would appreciate it. I am never quite sure why the mule is considered the most ornery of all living things; plants in my opinion leave mules at the starting post!

When we took over the country garden we found the place full of an intrusive little bulb called squirrel-corn. This is a half-wild form of bleedingheart, with a lacy fernlike foliage. It has now followed us to town, presumably in some potting soil, and is making itself at home among the other small bulbs. This is very rarely offered in the catalogues but is an addition to a sunny or mildly shady spot, and the foliage dies off quickly. If you see a clump in a friend's garden, ask for it without shame. If they have it at all, they will have it in quantity and will be perfectly willing to start you off with it too!

I am not lucky with anemones or the bulbous iris. Our winters are too cold and also without a completely reliable snow cover, so these bulbs just visit for a year or two and then peter out. I happen to be particularly fond of the bright blue *anemone blanda* and the scent of the *iris reticulata*, so I plant some each year to be sure of a spring show. Treating a few fussy bulbs as annuals is well worth the slight extra work and price. The small hardy bulbs should be established in every yard. They quickly give a wonderful return in their flowering habits in a way that does not hold true for other bulbs. And being small in size, they often fit better into the design of modern, rather cramped yards. Spring should not have to be daffodils, lovely as these are—it can equally well be snowdrops or dark blue scillas. But it is one thing to talk this way, and another to feel it, and to the majority of gardeners a spring garden would be incomplete without the big three, daffodils, hyacinths, and tulips.

Daffodils or narcissus, which is the horticultural name, are now divided into innumerable categories, turning on the length, shape, and color of the trumpet and the surrounding petals. These categories also divide the varieties into types that can take hot sun, those that need damper than usual conditions, and those that are more weatherproof than others.

The best way to discover which type does best in which position is to buy daffodil bulbs through the catalogue offerings of the bulb specialists. These list the positions in which the various kinds of daffodils thrive, and it is a money-saving way to get them. Without this essential information, daffodil bulbs are often planted where there is almost no chance for long-term success.

Daffodils are not bulbs that look their best planted in a formal manner in rows anywhere. They always look more natural if they are set out in clumps or groups. If the only place in the garden where they can be grown is a flowerbed, plant them in groups at the very back where they will come into flower before anything else. Then the leaves can fade away unnoticed as the rest of the planting develops. I have just such a bed in the suburban garden for an early show of perennial flowers before we leave that house, and I have clumps of early daffodils at the very back. The bloom from the daffodils is fairly good and always attractive, but the later

Anemone blanda.

Daffodils originally forced in pots.

plants shade the foliage of the bulbs rather too much, and I have to add a few new bulbs each year. We have found the bays of the shrub borders and the little piece of semi-wild woodland that we call "the glade" the most successful place.

Unquestionably daffodils are a sight after the flowers are gone, but any attempt to hide or control the withering foliage is a grave mistake—and one of the reasons why this bulb does not settle into many gardens and naturalize as well as it should. These are hardy bulbs that don't mind cold. They are extremely tolerant of almost every soil—except very wet ground. Planted where they get half a day of sun and sufficient moisture, they should spread delightfully. The reason they do not is the tidiness syndrome, which is the enemy to successful cultivation of daffodils. Meticulous gardeners find the sloppy, long-lasting, yellowing foliage of all the members of the narcissus family a great irritation, particularly in flowerbeds or in the grass beside a lawn. What's more, they mind it far more in the spring than they would at any other time. Gardens in spring call for prim neatness. By midsummer most of us have given up this attitude and are a good deal more relaxed about a little untidiness. If daffodils did not bloom until midsummer, I am sure the foliage would be much less annoying and our bulbs would spread faster and bloom better!

For further bloom it also seems to be important to snap off the seedpod after the flower fades but leave the flower stalk itself to die down with the rest of the leaves. I used to cut off the whole stalk, but recent home experiments seem to show that the bulbs flower more freely the next year if the flower stalk is left to die naturally. The stalk itself appears to play an important part in the rejuvenation of exhausted bulbs. This makes the problem of the withering foliage even worse. Leaves at least droop slightly during this unattractive period, but not the flower stalk, which remains angularly upright. And there is nothing that can be done about this problem; all compromises that attempt to conceal the withering foliage do harm. If the leaves are pinned down, or folded into a neat bundle with an elastic band or braided, not enough light will fall on them to rebuild flower buds—you might as well have cut them off. What's more, that stalk won't braid; I have tried! Growing daffodils among tall ground covers won't solve the foliage problem. Recently we set out new clumps of a tall, strong-growing daffodil in a ground-cover bed of pachysandra. It was the King Alfred variety, of which there are none tougher. The pachysandra did conceal the worst of the decaying foliage, but overenthusiastically. It hid the leaves so much from the sun that now, four years later, there is no bloom. If you want daffodils to continue over the years, you must put up with the after-appearance of the foliage; there is no other way out.

Hyacinths are also bulbs that offend with long-lasting, extremely sloppy foliage. But even with the most dedicated aftercare, hyacinths do not naturalize well. After a few years they deteriorate, though that is not the way I happen to think of it, into much smaller flower trusses. To me, this is an improvement; I dislike the huge flower heads on newly planted hyacinth bulbs. In bloom they are often too heavy for the supporting stalk, and the monstrous head falls onto the ground. If you like these big-headed plants, you must replant each year, for you will never get a repeat performance from old bulbs. Hyacinths smell sweet while they are in bloom, but they offend the nose while they are decaying. For this reason, and because hyacinths flower better in subsequent years if the flower stalks are not cut, I strip off the individual bell-like flowers as soon as they fade. This is a messy, sticky job and one that takes a certain amount of dedication, but it does pay dividends in sustaining the bulb.

We grow some hyacinths in the glade, usually potfuls that are planted out in the spring after having been forced in the house. Hyacinths need less sun than daffodils to ripen the leaves, so ours are set in the shadier area. To make any sort of impression, hyacinths must be planted in very large groups, preferably massed in a single color. In this way, as the size of the flower decreases, there is still a strong effect. The old-fashioned way of growing hyacinths was massing or bedding them out to fill up a flowerbed. The bulbs were planted in stiff rows, like a football band at the halftime show, and lifted and thrown out when their time was over. This is the way I remember them being used in my childhood, and this is the way in which they are still planted in many European parks. But it calls for a great deal of work and for me is not worth the effort. I don't like short, stubby hyacinths all crowded together in a small area; there is nothing graceful about them. As you may gather, I am not very enthusiastic about big Dutch hyacinths as outdoor bulbs, much as I love them in pots in the house. I prefer the less ostentatious wood hyacinth, which in fact is a scilla and not a true hyacinth. In appearance, the scilla, which flowers in May, looks like a slightly larger version of the English bluebell or a smaller, more graceful hyacinth. Unfortunately the true bluebell will not thrive with us, and we depend on the Spanish bluebell instead. The colors are rather wishy-washy blue and pink, not the deep tone of the bluebell, and if you are going to use this large scilla, plant a lot or you will not have much of a show.

The last of the big three is, of course, the tulip. Tulips, like daffodils, exist in innumerable varieties, and they have a long drawn-out flowering period, for there are early varieties, others that bloom at mid-season, and spectacular tall late tulips. There are also some large species tulips that are reliable re-bloomers. Many of these, including the hybrids of *T. fosteriana,* come in such flaming colors that I don't use them in the yard, but there are delightful, scented varieties of *T. kaufmanniana* that I do use. Like all the other species tulips, mine continue to bloom successfully, but they do not increase.

Tulips look their best grouped together. They are impressive massed in stiff rows in a flowerbed, for they are very graceful plants in themselves and they can be bought in an immense variety of delightful colors. I like to mass the early single varieties, or the late Darwin tulips. Both of these have extremely sturdy stems and repay the work you will give them. As always, I prefer to mass tulips in a single color, and since the area where I now grow them has a crab apple that is a difficult pink and a great many azaleas in varying shades of orange and yellow alongside, I use white tulips as a relief to the eye.

Unlike daffodils and even hyacinths, I don't think tulips look well if they are naturalized. Used as a semi-wild plant, if you can get them to accept this treatment, which is a trick in itself, they seem to be ineffectual and mismanaged, like a trained actress in an amateur play. Anyone wanting to reuse old tulip bulbs would be well advised to replant them in big blocks in an area given over entirely to them and used for picking rather than for display. Unfortunately tulips cannot always be depended upon to bloom equally successfully a second year if they have been crowded together to make an extravagant display. For that reason if massed tulips are to be a planned feature, it is necessary to dig the bulbs after they have finished flowering and either throw them out or find somewhere else to plant them. And if you mean to use the

same place for tulips the following season, it is also necessary to dig out the old soil and put in a new supply of soil.
Tulips take a great deal out of the ground, and the trace elements they use up in a massed planting need renewing. We
use massed tulips in the small beds that are part of the new
patio in the suburban garden. This is not too large an undertaking, and the results are excellent.

Planting tulips each year is always a big undertaking and
the cost of the bulbs no small item; the show itself is sometimes a disappointment. In a matter of hours, the strong
winds of spring—my mother all too accurately used to call
them the tulip winds—or a sudden heat wave can ruin the
display over which the gardener toiled for weeks. As soon as
the flowers are over, the bulbs have to be dug. Tulips can be
lifted while the foliage is still green, but this is not a job that
can be delayed. If you are to succeed in moving tulips at such
a critical time, the work must be undertaken immediately
after the flowers fade. Since we leave that garden after the tulips are lifted, the little beds are heavily mulched with fir bark.

If you have neither taste nor place for elaborate massing
of tulips, they can be grown very satisfactorily in clumps of
seven to nine bulbs set at the back of a flowerbed, or, if you
are willing to lift them out afterward, in the foreground of a
bed. Tulips set out deeply in flowerbeds need not be crowded
together as closely as when they are massed. If they are provided with a planting hole that gives space for the bulbs to
be set about four inches apart, they need not be lifted so long
as the foliage gets good light as it dries off. Deep, comfortable planting of this sort gives the tulips sufficient food supply
to enable them to continue flowering regularly for many
successive years. If flowers stop coming, make sure that the
place where they are growing still has enough sun to ripen
the leaves. If a whole number of small, single-leaved tulips
with no bud appear, the bulbs may have split too much for
further flowering. In that case, dig them and replant new
bulbs in the fall. I have old clumps that reflower regularly
in flowerbeds in all our gardens. I don't know the varieties;
I wish I did, for some are much better at this than others.

If you can't bear to throw tulip bulbs out, you can try to reestablish them somewhere in the yard. We have a place in the third garden where old tulips have been successfully reestablished, in spite of the fact that they are growing in grass, which is not the way they like to be cultivated. The area is sunny and well drained, both essential requirements for tulips, but the main reason for their continued success is, I am sure, the fact that this is the place where potted chrysanthemums for the house are stood from mid-August onward. This means that the tulip bulbs in the grass below the pots get all the steady runoff of water and fertilizer from the chrysanthemum cultivation, and the fall roots of the tulips make full use of this moisture and extra nourishment to sustain the bulbs and set a new bud.

Tulip foliage is as important as any other bulb foliage—and twice as hideous, but it is essential that it be saved. These bulbs also subsequently flower better if only the seedpod is removed and the flower stalk remains intact.

In the days of plentiful labor and when there were large growing areas in gardens, tulips used to be lifted from the

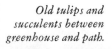

Old tulips and succulents between greenhouse and path.

beds where they had flowered and set out in deep trenches in the vegetable garden where they could be allowed to wither off in decent obscurity. When all the foliage was dead, the tulips were then re-dug and the bulbs cleaned and stored in open trays in a cool, dry place. This was the way it was done in my youth, and this is advice I still see regularly repeated in books on the cultivation of tulips in this country. I have not found that it works for me, and I have tried it a great many times. It is twice as much work, something which should be discouraged in these days when every man is his own gardener. What's more, dry, cool storage that is also airy is exceptionally difficult to provide, unless you are the fortunate possessor of an air-conditioned wine cellar. We do have a cellar in which I store a great many plants, but it is also damp. The tulips bulbs I stored there always rotted. I also tried storing them in the shed; that was too hot and the bulbs withered and desiccated. I now am against relifting bulbs. It is better to choose a place where tulips can be allowed to naturalize in a block, for, invariably, no matter how careful you have been, some will come up blind—that is, without a flower bud. If there are plenty of bulbs, there will always be enough flowers to give a good impression.

If you want to save tulips, replant them as deeply as before—the necessary six to eight inches. I open a narrow trench with a shovel, and drop the tulips in one by one with plenty of space between them. I then press the opened-up slit back with my foot and allow the foliage to wither away, leaning against the side of the trench. At this stage, it is not necessary that the bulbs stand upright alone. Tulips stand relifting and replanting when the foliage is still green almost as well as snowdrops.

After flowering, tulips split up unless they are planted deeply. They can split even when six inches below ground, but deep planting is something of a preventive against what otherwise is an inevitability. If a tulip bulb fragments into many little bulbs, it is not worth trying to save it. You can see whether this is going to happen as you dig them. Don't, however, decide that if a depth of six inches is good, twelve inches will be even better! Tulips planted too deeply exhaust themselves trying to reach the light and will also do poorly.

Occasionally there have been years when I planted no tulips. I was bored with all the fuss, but I have always regretted it when there have been no tulips in our gardens. Now I have decided that tulips are worth it for me in a limited quantity—for a small, dramatic show. And that I will also take the time and effort to set them out where eventually they will recover. I am no longer prepared to make a fetish out of huge beds of massed tulips, and my life has been simpler since we made that decision. This is something every gardener must judge for himself. My only aim is to make sure that all the pleasures as well as the drawbacks to growing tulips are frankly stated.

None of the spring bulbs are hard to plant; it is just a matter of taking the time. The simplest tools are a spade or a long-handled shovel. With either, it is possible to open a good-size strip of ground so that groups of bulbs can all be set at the same depth. They can also be planted singly by trowel. This is perfectly satisfactory if only a few are to go in. For a large operation, working a trowel can be hard on the knees as well as on the hands! Planting bulbs by trowel also has the disadvantage that they do not all go in at an identical depth; inevitably there is a difference in the amount of soil taken out each time. To get flowers at peak bloom simultaneously—always desirable for massed effect—bulbs must be at the same level underground. Planted at varying depths, the flowers will open at slightly different times.

Opening up wide strips of ground also makes it easier to incorporate additional food. Any fertilizer that goes into the ground at planting time makes no difference to the flowers the first year. With all·bulbs, the preset bud is not affected. But rich, fortified soil around and under a bulb planting can make a great difference to the subsequent performance of the bulbs. Don't rest the basal plates, that flat part from which the roots grow, on fertilizer. This will only injure young, tender roots. Spread a thin layer of fertilizer, well mixed with soil, where the bulbs are to be set, and cover that with a layer of compost. Put the bulbs on the compost. This gives the roots a chance to start out in unfortified soil, but as they grow stronger and thrust down more deeply, they will reach the richer material underneath and by then will be tough enough to make use of it. In the past, I used a mixture of bone meal and dried cow manure both in the planting soil and for that extra top-dressing mentioned earlier. But now we are told that bone meal is being "improved" out of all the beneficial elements that once made it so useful. In recent years, evidence has been accumulating that bulbs gain huge benefits from the use of sludge in the soil around them. I am going to run some rather simple tests with sludge and with the old bone meal and dry manure mixture on different groups of bulbs to see whether there is any vast difference for the amateur grower. I find this sort of simple testing great fun; it adds a new dimension to gardening, and more of us should try it. If the milorganite, or sludge, proves superior, I hope the price of it will come down or that other similar products will appear on the market.

Naturalizing bulbs, that is, planting them as they might grow in the wild, in an informal manner is excellent for those that can take this type of handling: daffodils and the small bulbs here in the North being the best. I often read advice that the best way to get a natural effect is to throw the bulbs casually around and plant them where they fall. If you want to do it this way, fine: they are your bulbs, and the effect is casual all right. The only trouble is finding them again after all that tossing about. Most of us naturalize bulbs under the drip line of shrubs or in light woodland. At planting time, the ground is often covered with leaves and there is a certain needle-in-a-haystack atmosphere about finding small brown bulbs that have been shot into the air! I have tried it; I always follow garden advice when I read it—at least once. But I thought the after-effect spotty. The bulbs were too thinly strung out.

I now open big planting holes with the shovel and set out groups of five to seven big, double-nosed daffodils in one place. With daffodils, buy the largest offered for sale, for these will throw up several flower stalks. Unlike "jumbo" hyacinths, the flowers are not too heavy for the stalks. I space these clumps unevenly: some close together, others a distance away, and I only use a single variety of daffodil in each. While I work, I save out a few of each variety of daffodil and these I do toss between the large open groups. I start by planting the tossed-out bulbs, which go in at varying depths. The big groups do not have the soil put back into the planting hole until the outriders are in the ground. This method has some advantages. The larger groups of bulbs planted at the same depth bloom simultaneously, and I try to have both early and late varieties set out to prolong the show. The scattered bulbs come into flower a little earlier or a little later, depending on the depth at which they were set. This gives a more uncontrived look to the area and links the groups. Shops often sell naturalizing mixtures of daffodils at bargain rates. Beware of these. Sometimes they are the culls of the crop, and the bulbs are small; often they are made up of uninteresting varieties. It is far better to choose your own bulbs. If you want to add a few bulbs each year, which is a sound policy, mark the main groups with an unobtrusive green stake while they are still visible. If you don't it is almost certain that you will dig into them the next year! The stake stays in all summer and is pulled out after the replanting in the fall.

Newly planted daffodils always carry the flowers on a very tall stalk no matter how deeply they have been planted. The height of the stalk is as much predetermined as the embryonic flower. For that reason, new bulbs are always rather obvious and never look naturalized, no matter how fine the flowers. Established bulbs flower on a much shorter stalk, and the blossoms will be smaller than those of the new bulbs. There is nothing much you can do about this. Those first big flowers are unnaturally large; they come from force-feeding in the growing fields. The slightly smaller flowers that will appear on naturalized bulbs are the normal size. If you become alarmed at this reversion and overfertilize the ground, the only result will be a lush growth of extra leaves;

the flowers will not get any bigger. If the flowers become very scarce, then fertilizer may be in order, but as was explained earlier, other factors may also be involved.

Trick tools for planting bulbs have a fearful fascination for manufacturers. They appear on the market as soon as the birds start to fly south. Most of them are a penance to use, and, as far as I can prove to myself, they don't do anything for the bulbs. One, which is sometimes offered for sale, is a pointed metal tool, with a blister-raising, all-metal handle. In appearance it is not unlike the monstrous sharpened point of a pencil with the stump very short and the end a little curved. The idea of this tool is to make it easier to produce a planting hole by using a pointed tool. For tiny bulbs, if you have only a very few to plant, it may be of some use. For big bulbs, it has almost every disadvantage. Being pointed, the hole it makes tapers, and any large bulb dropped into a tapered hole hangs helplessly, for the narrowing passage prevents it reaching the ground. Caught like this, the bulb will die; roots will not grow unless the basal plate can feel moisture. I hate to think of the number of expensive bulbs that have perished miserably, forever suspended in space, through the misguided use of this implement. The only way to be safe using this tool is to make the hole, drop the bulb in to see where it sticks, take the bulb out, refill the hole up to the sticking point with soil, and then put the bulb back. This is not my idea of a labor-saving method.

Recently it has been a little supplanted by another equally tiresome planting tool, allegedly perfect for bulbs. This is a circular object, like an open-ended can, sometimes lined with Teflon, with a longish handle with a cross bar at the top; there is also a small hand version. In new models the crossbar has plastic grips. You can use this tool standing up for part of the time during the planting operation, which is an advantage. The circular part is marked on the outside to show the various depths to which it should be driven into the ground for different-size bulbs. I have found it extremely difficult to get this open-ended can into the ground at all; it means putting a good deal of weight on the foot flanges that are on both sides of it. Once you have got it into the ground, you have to stoop down to see the depth, then twist the planter and pull it out of the ground with a plug of earth inside, the idea being that the bulb is dropped into the hole and the earth stuck in the planter is returned to fill the hole up. But things don't work out that way. The hole this planter makes is too small for the big double-nosed daffodils. It also means that to plant a large group you must struggle five or six times to make the necessary holes. And Teflon or not, the soil sticks in the circular part of the tool and has to be poked out with a stick, and extra soil is usually needed to fill up the depression. Bulb planting is an exhausting job under ideal conditions, and I cannot fathom why we are constantly offered expensive tools that make the job twice as hard.

A great deal of attention has been given so far to spring bulbs, mainly because they are the most familiar and the most used of all the bulbous plants. But there are also a great many summer bulbs that will give a sure show of color. We use only a limited number of them in the country garden, but I am well aware that we are not making use of anything like the number that are available.

Like everyone else we grow gladiola, even though I have rather mixed feelings about this flower due, no doubt, to associations with funerals and rather frightful commercial flower baskets. But this is a very useful flower for cutting for indoor use, and we use it for that purpose. I never plant it as a decorative plant in the flowerbeds, for I loathe the way it dies off with the bottom flowers fading, or even dead, before the top buds have opened. I also get bored with the long-lasting, dull foliage. But it is a useful plant for tubs to make a splash of color on the patio. For tub planting, use rich compost and put in as many corms as possible. Make sure they are all planted at the same depth and, in a tub, the deeper the better, for stakes in tubs look horrible. Deeply planted, the plants may not need support. All gladiola need full sun and they do better with moist soil. For patio or terrace use, the tubs should be mulched, and where they are to be prominently featured, use buckwheat hulls.

I enjoy watching tub plants develop. That is part of the pleasure of growing them. So I put our tubs straight onto the terrace or my flower porch. If you only want to see the plants when they are at peak perfection, grow them in full sunlight near a faucet, so that the tubs do not dry out, and move them onto the patio when the flower spikes show. Gladiola only face one way—and it is not possible to tell from the corms which way it is going to be. With tub planting, it is necessary to resign yourself to the fact that some of the flowers will look at you and others turn their backs. There is absolutely nothing you can do about it. If you have never grown gladiola in tubs, do try. You don't need too many corms, so you can splurge on the new expensive varieties and you will have a lot of pleasure from the results. Since they will be right under your eye, make it a stern rule to go around each evening razoring off the dead flowers. This way you will get a better effect and longer pleasure from the spikes. I am against using gladiola in heavy planter boxes that are a permanent feature of the terrace. This means digging them out when they are over and refilling the planters with something else. Tubs that can be taken right away are far less trouble.

For cutting for the house, we plant the corms in a furrow in the vegetable garden. The books always suggest a deep trench, but the shallow planting does not seem to harm ours. About a dozen gladiola are set out; when their shoots show above ground, another dozen go in. This staggered planting starts as soon as the ground is workable and continues until around the Fourth of July. Stakes are driven in deeply on both sides of the furrow and a long thin cage of string is made by tying twine between the stakes at the bottom, in the middle, and at the top. This way the plants grow up inside the string cage, which serves to support them instead of individual stakes. They don't look terribly neat grown this way, but they are far less trouble. The soil in the vegetable garden is tremendously rich, for a heavy top-dressing of compost is laid down each fall. For that reason we do not put any fertilizer around the gladiola or give them any while they are developing. The garden is also mulched so that the soil is always cool and moist. This cuts down on watering, though in very dry weather I do run the hose slowly along the rows for an hour or so, if the flower spikes are just showing, for this is a critical period.

After flowering, the plants grow on until the first hard frost kills the foliage. After that they are dug rather carefully, for the newly made corm often has dozens of little cormlets clinging to it. After digging, the plants are spread out in a warm dry place for a week. We use a garden shed, but anywhere that is not heated and where the corms can stay dry will do. After this, the foliage is cut off close to the corm, and they are then stored in wooden boxes packed very closely together with moth flakes. They remain in the shed until the weather turns cold; after that, the boxes are moved into the cold cellar of the suburban house, or the extremely cold but frost-free country house, to ride out the winter.

The para moth flakes are added to keep a disease known as "thrip" out of the corms. Thrip is a menace; it stunts the flowers and disfigures the leaves. If it appears among your gladiola, all will be infected. If you find thrip-ruined plants, you should pull them out and send them out with the rubbish. I don't attempt to cure this ailment; I merely get rid of the infected plants. Thrip-infested plants should not go into the compost pile.

Gladiola are hardier than is sometimes realized. Every so often a corm is "overlooked" and spends the winter unprotected outdoors. The next spring it reappears full of vigor and flowers sooner and with stronger color than those that have been stored. But this is a gamble with the better types, which are more delicate. New, hardy varieties of gladiolas are now appearing on the market, and for those who like these plants in a flowerbed they might be the answer. Except for the years with thrip, we have had great success reusing our corms season after season. In time, the better, rarer corms vanish, and you will find yourself left with a few old varieties. That is the moment to spend some money on new stock.

The cormlets are planted like peas in a row beside the

parents. These usually grow to flowering size in two years, but not unnaturally the corms that produce most of the cormlets are the least interesting varieties. Cormlets take far longer to sprout than mature corms. Don't get discouraged when nothing happens for over a month, and dig the row up in disgust. The outer casing of the cormlet is very hard, and it takes time for a root to break through. Eventually the grasslike sprout will appear.

A plant that looks a little like a much smaller, more delicate gladiola is the montbretia. This is also a corm that has been produced as a hybrid from two forms of crocus. It is hardy in our garden and, left alone, spreads into an unmanageable tangle with rather few flowers. I have better flowers digging up the montbretia each fall and treating them exactly like the gladiola. I am extremely fond of these little flowering wands. They come in rather autumnal colors, mainly yellows and oranges. However, the hybridizers are at work on them, and if better shades can be bred into the stock, they should become very popular. Montbretia are far less bother than gladiola. They need no staking, they are not nearly so overpowering in a flowerbed—in fact, for some years I used them in front of the herbaceous border. The only weakness is the late date at which they bloom; they come into flower at a time when I am beginning to think of cutting down the garden. If the hybridizers could also speed up the flowering date, I would use them even more. Montbretias are close cousins of another summer bulb, the tritonia, which I have not used much. I grew it for a couple of years, but I did not think the odd-shaped flowers worth the effort. This is a personal reaction and not sufficient reason for not trying them for yourself.

A summer bulb that we do grow in considerable quantity are lilies. Lilies are now being popularized as everyone's plant and something that anyone can grow. I cannot entirely agree even though lilies have come a very long way from the troublesome, disease-prone plants of my youth. Through the work of modern hybridizers, particularly Jan de Graaff, some lilies, his mid-century hybrids, for example, are now relatively easy to establish in a garden. But lilies still have rather fussy requirements, and as they are not yet very cheap, few gardeners are willing to treat them as annuals. Lilies will flourish in most gardens for a few years if properly planted. But they will not settle in and reproduce themselves unless some rather specific requirements are met—and it is sometimes extremely difficult to discover what it is about a garden that they dislike. I speak with some feeling. The country garden, particularly the third garden, is alive with half-wild tiger lilies. They come up everywhere and flower in impossible places. We also have natural stands of the rather rare wood lily in the little piece of woodland. This led me to the mistaken conclusion that cultivated lilies would be a snap to grow, for obviously the soil and the climate suited lilies of all sorts. This has not proved to be the case. I have planted a great many varieties of lilies, always following the instructions to the letter, for lily retailers are extremely good about attaching specific cultural notes. But success has been limited, except with the very easy de Graaff hybrids. Sometimes the difficulty has been solved by moving the bulbs a few feet from their initial position, though what specific difference this makes I don't know. Lilies have rather exact growing requirements, so there are not too many possible growing areas.

For the most part the lilies we grow give us pleasure for about three years; after that the stand begins to diminish, and a couple of seasons later there are none left. I would far rather grow them this way than not at all, but the cost of replacement is considerable and for new gardeners rather discouraging. Anyone reading this account should bear in mind that, though we do have fine lilies, most of them have not naturalized for me, so this will not be foolproof advice.

Lily bulbs should never be out of the ground for long; unlike other bulbs they never go completely dormant. It is now possible to hold them in good condition in cold storage so that the flowering period can be exactly timed. You can, for instance, have a deliberate show for a special occasion. I meant to have a fine display of lilies for one of our daughters' weddings, but apparently I gave the retailer the wrong date, or so he said. I had the best show of lily foliage you could possibly imagine at the wedding reception—the flowers appeared several months later!

Lilies packed in plastic bags with a little dry peat moss around them are not a good buy. There is no way to tell how long the bulb has been out of the ground and if the peat moss is dry; the chances are it has been far too long. Always buy your lilies from a lily specialist or a highly reliable catalogue dealer and have the place where they are to be planted ready before the bulbs are delivered; the less they have to wait around, the better their chances.

Lilies need a large, deep hole and a lot of rich soil put around the bulb. Fertilizer should never be scattered immedi-

DeGraff enchantment lilies.

ately around the bulb. Instead there should be a pad of sand or pebbles, about one-half inch deep on the floor of the planting hole. It is vital to success with lilies to have good drainage in the rather deep pits in which they are buried. Lily bulbs that stand in sodden soil invariably rot away. Some lilies throw roots only from the basal plate, others put out stem roots as the flowering stalk elongates. Most lilies, with the exception of the madonna lily, should be planted at a depth three times their overall size. This provides them with a big supply of nourishing soil into which the stem roots can spread, and it also keeps the bulbs safely below the baking heat of the sun. Lilies, like all bulbs, look better planted in groups. I like to open a very large hole and put in five at a time, with the bulbs at least four inches apart.

New lilies ought to have strong enough stems not to need staking, even though they carry a great many flowers. But it is a good idea to put a stake into the planting hole while you can still see what you are doing, before the hole is filled up. This serves as a marker in the spring, even if it is only a few inches above ground. Lily shoots can easily be broken during the spring clean-up. This means the end of the plant for that season and often forever.

One of the old problems about lily planting was the fact that the bulbs only went sufficiently dormant to be safely lifted and sold rather late in the year, and they sometimes reached the customer after the ground had frozen. Yet they had to be planted, for they could not wait. This meant special preparations had to be made to keep the planting area free from frost, which people found a nuisance. Today that difficulty has been solved by the new perfection of cold storage for lilies. The semi-dormant fall-lifted lily bulbs can now be kept in prime condition all through the frozen months and set out in the spring, when planting is easier. This is a great convenience and I have used cold-storage lilies with good results, particularly in tubs. But on the whole I think a lily bulb profits more from going into the ground in the fall, even if the weather is very cold. Lilies already planted deeply in good soil get started far sooner than those set out when the weather warms up. This means stronger roots and a longer season in which the foliage is sending nourishment back to replenish the bulbs. I now try and arrange to have all my lily bulbs sent to me when they are lifted. Keeping the planting area open is not too difficult. After the garden is cut down, we dig out the large deep hole where the lilies are to go, and put down the bottom layer of sand. The soil from the hole is mixed with compost and stored in a covered bin in a frost-free place. The hole itself is filled with leaves, and either evergreen branches or a sheet of black plastic is put over the leaf-filled hole. When the bulbs arrive, the ground is sometimes frozen hard, but the leaves lift out quite easily in a compact mass. The bulbs are put in and the reserve soil thrown quickly on top of them after the stake is in. If it is bitterly cold, a heavy layer of mulch is put over the top fill, usually buckwheat hulls, which do not freeze in the unheated shed where they are stored. If the ground has not frozen, we hold off mulching until cold weather comes. This may sound like a lot of trouble for some lilies, and in a way it is. It can also be a rather chilly job if the bulbs arrive very late. I only wish I could state flatly that my lilies do wonderfully well with this treatment. Sometimes they do and sometimes they do not, but I always have some and they do symbolize summer to me.

Lilies have other rather stiff requirements as to how they should be grown, even apart from all the planting fuss. They like morning sun, but not full sunlight, for that bleaches them out. With me they need full air circulation to thrive. I have seen wonderful lilies growing in other people's gardens against walls and fences. I have never had luck with lilies anywhere except in the open. Lilies like their heads in the sun and the lower part of the stem in the shade. This is the hardest trick of all, and I am not sure it is necessary with the de Graaff hybrids. I had these for many years in the big herbaceous bed, where they had no protection at the base of the stems. They did wonderfully well in that position and there was a constant increase of innumerable little plants. I now have de Graaff hybrids in a bed with ivy to shade their

ankles. This position produces good flowers on longer stalks, though not better in color or in the number of buds per stalk. But planted this way, the bulbs are not increasing; the ivy ground cover must be strangling them out.

Regal lilies no longer do well for me. Before the hurricane spoiled their growing area, I had two fine stands of these lilies, which were increasing fast. After I lost these, I was never able to reestablish them successfully. Something had changed, and I can't discover what. Nevertheless I still plant regals, for they are my favorite among the lilies, with their wonderful but not overpowering scent. But the present-day inhabitants of the country garden are a pathetic caricature of the lilies that once were there. The massive autumnal lilies, the auratums and rubellas, only visit with me. I consider myself fortunate if they flower well the first year, and since they are so expensive I soon shall give them up if I cannot solve their problem.

Part of the difficulty may be lack of aftercare. I do take a lot of trouble at planting time, I follow the instructions extremely carefully. But after that I get busy with other gardening chores and don't do anything very special for the lilies. Possibly if I were more attentive about watering, summer mulching, and even feeding, I would have better luck. But my lack of success should not deter other gardeners from trying lilies. Once established, lilies are extremely tough; it is getting them established that is the problem. I am strongly in favor of everyone trying at least the simple de Graaff hybrids. If you succeed with them, ambition will lead you to try others. And who knows, your regals may be the talk of the town!

After flowering, cut off the lily seedpods, leaving the stalks. If you have huge stands of lilies, it is worth allowing a few to set seed, for lilies come fast from seed, particularly the regals. Growing your own takes patience, and a rather large growing area, but it can be done. As with all bulbs, lily foliage must be left to wither, but the sturdy, dark foliage is an asset in a flowerbed.

Our most successful use of lilies has been to grow them in the bays of the freestanding shrub border in the third garden. Here most of their rather demanding conditions can be met, and we have planted a succession, from the early hybrids to the tiger lilies. Using tiger lilies is not good cultural practice where other lilies are concerned. The tiger lily carries a virus disease that does not particularly harm it but can be disastrous to the more delicate bulbs. Lilies do extremely well in pots and tubs. Here again, cold-storage lilies can be bought and the tubs planted in the spring. I prefer to plant mine in the fall and winter them over in a deep cold frame. This is a luxury that happens to be available in the suburban garden and does not exist for everyone.

The Easter lily that comes to us all prinked up in foil can have its dignity restored by being carried on in a cool, sunless window indoors until the weather warms up and then planted outside with all the usual qualifications about depth, shade, and so on. If you have to bury some of the lily stem getting it into the ground sufficiently deeply, never mind; this is one time when a change of growing level does not matter. After the foliage withers off, which will happen quite fast, mark the place with a stake. This lily sometimes sends up an additional flower in the fall, and in any case there is no point in digging by mistake into its planting area. Our replanted Easter lilies reappear quite satisfactorily; I don't think they are increasing, but at least they are still there. Do plant yours outdoors. It is hard to get bloom in a pot again, and since a great deal of effort has gone into getting the flower you enjoyed, why not give the bulb a chance to establish itself in your yard?

There are, of course, innumerable other summer bulbs—cannas, dahlias, tuberoses, caladiums, and the like—all of which can be planted out each spring and lifted and stored in the fall. I have tried a great many of them in a great many places. On the whole they have not been quite worth the trouble, and, with the exception of dahlias, I have not taken to them sufficiently to make a summer feature of them in the garden. Every gardener should try for himself and find out which of these summer bulbs, all of which call for a certain amount of time-consuming work, suits his taste the best.

One group of hardy bulbs that appeals to me strongly, and which I would recommend for every lot no matter how small, is the autumn crocus. These little bulbs are entirely self-sufficient and they make a delightful end to the flowering year. Every fall as the leaves turn scarlet, small colonies of mauve and purple chalices shine out suddenly in the wet grass. They reappear without fail just as we are getting ready to leave, and every year I am grateful to my predecessor who planned this delightful send-off. Considered individually, the autumn crocus looks unimportant and delicate. But grouped in little colonies, they are most effective and are, in fact, extremely tough bulbs.

In their time, they have ignored hurricanes and years of total neglect, just as they are now ignoring my changes in landscaping. They continue to grow imperturbably in what is now part of a lawn, and they also flower heavily in stretches of a shrub border that has replaced an old flowerbed. Clearly they have no intention of changing their established habits, into which they settled when they were planted around the turn of the century, to fit any new-fangled ideas of mine! I have no doubt that they will outlive all my attempted re-arrangements of the yard and will, in turn, delight my successor by appearing where they have always been.

The treatment for an autumn crocus is identical to that given the spring variety. They need good soil, a sunny, open area, and a chance for the foliage to wither off. The leaves appear in early spring, so if you will plant drifts of autumn crocus among your spring crocus, there will be no chance of the foliage getting cut prematurely.

I much prefer the autumn crocus to another fall-flowering bulb, the colchicum, the flower from which saffron is extracted. The colchicum is not strongly colored enough to suit my taste, for it is a watery purple. It also puts up thick, unattractive leaves in the spring, which must, of course, be left alone. Colchicums are easier to find in the shops and catalogues than the true autumn crocus. They are the unhappy little bulbs that are offered as "miracle plants that will flower without soil and water." And so they will—just once! The yellow autumn crocus (sternbergia) does not thrive in our climate. This bulb leafs out in the fall before the flowers appear. Here in the North there is not enough heat in the air at that season to ripen the foliage.

When we leave the country and go back to the suburban garden, we are welcomed by clumps of hardy cyclamen. This miniature cousin of the big pot cyclamen is perfectly hardy in a sunny, well-drained place even in New England, and it should be grown more. The tubers spread underground and grow into a large, flat plant that will sprout delightful dappled leaves and small, scented, pink flowers. The wild cyclamen comes in several varieties and should be planted where it will not be overwhelmed, for it is delicate and charming rather than spectacular. I have put our clumps in a bad position: they are at the top of the ground-cover bed beside the drive. This gives them the necessary drainage and enough sun, but the little flowers are hard to see. Wild cyclamen are best moved in the spring when the tubers are dormant. I am going to transfer ours to the little bed beside the greenhouse, which is equally suited to their tastes and where we can enjoy them more. I have never tried to establish cyclamen in the country garden, even though it would look well with the autumn crocus. Rather sentimentally I like to feel that since we return a little unwillingly to the suburban garden in the fall, there should be something rather special in it at that time. In recent years the suburban garden has been a little overshadowed. We get so much pleasure out of the country garden that we take rather more trouble over it. But the suburban garden came first; I learned most of my American horticultural skills in it, and I owe a great deal to it. I like to think that it enjoys the exclusivity of those cyclamen and that it flaunts them at us when we come back, secure in the knowledge that we have seen nothing like them in the country!

Flowers & Vegetables | XI

During the years that I have been aware of gardens, nothing has changed as radically as the attitude toward flowers and their place in a yard. When I was small, flowers in great variety were always the main attraction; their color combinations, scents, and the skill with which they had been grown made the garden. Everything else, with the possible exception of the grass, came second. Today, flowers are a small, incidental part of the design of most yards. This about-face comes from a combination of the familiar excuse, too little outside garden help, combined with a complete change in garden taste, for modern garden design turns on labor-saving ideas and functional suitability. This is understandable but a pity. To grow good plants, whether for show or eating, requires better and more exact horticulture than any other aspect of outdoor gardening. When we cease to bother with plants and vegetables, many of the fundamental horticultural skills that have been passed on from time immemorial are in danger of being lost.

There are innumerable excellent garden books that describe in illustrated, accurate detail every facet of the art of gardening. While reading may augment knowledge, it will not turn anyone into a gardener. The only way to learn to grow plants is to try for yourself. Where every garden is an easy-care area, with paving, professionally planted shrubs, a few container plants, and a small plot of grass, very little true horticulture can be practiced. The basic common-sense approach to learning about growing things is to kneel down and dig to discover what has happened to that row of beans planted three weeks ago, or why a thriving aster has suddenly wilted or turned yellow. It is not only flowers that have suffered this decline; vegetables have also vanished from almost every yard. A whole generation of so-called gardeners are living in houses surrounded by land in which beans never uncurl like croziers from the soil, when carrots are not pulled and eaten raw, or sprigs of fresh parsley taken to the kitchen. Lack of space may make it impossible to grow vegetables in quantity, but not impossible to have some. Those who really want the pleasure of vine-ripened tomatoes will always find a way of growing them, even if it has to be a windowbox or a deep tub. What is lacking today for many gardeners is the encouragement to try growing their own flowers and vegetables. By leaving these jobs entirely to professionals, we are depriving ourselves of some of the best fun that comes from owning a yard.

I no longer have the time or inclination to grow flowers and vegetables in the quantity I once did. But since I cannot imagine a garden that would be satisfying to me without them, simplified ways of raising some have been worked out that are not beyond the capacity of the newest gardener on a tiny lot. In this way, I have kept my hand in at a down-to-earth practical level. Like all compromises, ours have their weaknesses, but on the whole they work and, since they are designed to be as labor-saving as possible, they have their place in modern gardening. Someday taste will change, for garden design is as much a whim of fashion as anything else. Presumably, flowers eventually will regain their popularity as a functional part of garden design. I would like to be sure that, when that time comes, there are still gardeners around who have kept in practice during these lean years. Growing good flowering plants calls for rather different horticultural skills, and it is important that we realize this.

Before I explain our way of ensuring a reliable and relatively painless show of flowers, it is necessary to understand the more conventional methods of growing flowers from which our style evolved. The present simplified pattern of the country flower garden is a modification of established ways of producing a long season of successive bloom. It grew out of my familiarity and firsthand experience with more conventional practices and is not anything new or revolutionary. It can best be understood by explaining its ancestry.

Everything I originally knew about growing flowers was founded on English practice. As I mentioned earlier, my skills, such as they were, were based on a double tradition, one rather rigid and the other more adventurous—and neither in the least labor-saving! The older, more old-fashioned style of showing off flowering plants was called "bedding out." Flowers were displayed in long, narrow beds, sometimes called "ribbon beds," that were usually freestanding and therefore planted so that they looked good on both sides. In them, young plants that had been raised in quantity elsewhere were transferred twice a year into massed groups—or, to use the technical term, were bedded out. Most of the plants used this way were annuals, that is, plants that grow from seed, then flower and set fresh seed in a single season. Plants that could have flowered a second year, such as carnations, which were much used for bedding, were always treated as annuals and not left in place. The most popular plants for this work were either dwarf or low-growing varieties that flowered profusely over a long season and needed very little staking; they were set out as close to each other as was consistent with good foliage development so as to produce a huge splash of color.

The manner in which the color effects were produced was a matter of taste. Sometimes the colors were mixed; sometimes they were cleverly contrived in blocks of a single color that shaded into each other. Sometimes the effect was augmented by an ingenious use of many plants and sometimes by constantly repeated patterns of a few plants. When several plants and colors were combined without taste to produce a change of level and color, the effect could be frightful. A dreadful combination of red geraniums, yellow calceolaria, and dark blue lobelia represented this form of bedding out at its worst, and, unfortunately, that is how this method of showing off plants is best remembered. Properly managed, bedded plants could be both elegant and highly dramatic. I remember a border in which many different flowers in varying heights were used in blocks that started in the distance with a splash of dark purple and wove toward the viewer through the color spectrum of violet, mauve, and lavender down to a pure white. Nothing more delightful could ever be devised.

Bedding out was a big job that often took a couple of weeks. When the displays were changed, in the fall and again in the early summer, all the old plants were pulled out. The ground was then weeded and covered with a thick layer of manure which was dug deeply in. Often new soil had to be barrowed in to keep up the level. After digging, the beds were allowed to settle for a few days, then they were raked smooth and the pattern for the new succession of plants drawn on the smooth surface with a pointed stick. When I first remember these beds, the planting plan was carefully drawn out in advance in watercolors by my grandmother. The curves were then transferred onto the ground surface by the head gardener, while my grandmother, plan in hand, sat on a chair on the lawn supervising his activities. She wanted to be sure that her carefully thought-out arrangements were carried through at planting time. The color schemes had a curious way of changing as the plants went in. She had very strong horticultural views, but then so had the gardener. Her taste was impeccable, and his was dreadful. But he had the actual plants and their color labels under his control, which she did not, and since he was a man who liked his own way, this eagle-eyed supervision was considered essential. Even so, confrontations sometimes occurred, mainly over his efforts to incorporate tall and screamingly bright red geraniums, of which he appeared to have an unending supply, into my grandmother's delicate pastel color schemes. I recently saw that very same geranium offered in a trade paper as a delightful, sturdy novelty. It is always a pleasure to meet an old friend, but I am still on my grandmother's side: that plant is a fright! In my immediate family, with far less help available, my mother drew the curves straight out of her head; she also planned the color sequence. This was not her style of gardening, but since my father insisted upon having some flowerbeds laid out this way, she preferred to have a hand in the operation, for my father had no eye for color.

After all the trauma of planning and planting was over, the work on those beds had only begun. While the little plants were small, they had to be weeded, and the constant enrichment of the soil made the ground a weed heaven. Since the plants were set so closely together, hoeing was not practical, so all the weeding was done laboriously by hand. In dry weather the beds also needed regular watering, which was always done with a watering can and not the hose, so that no plant was overlooked. Later, when the flowers were out, watering cans were still used for fear of splashing and spoiling the blooms. To keep the display at peak as long as possible, the beds needed regular checking over and all the dead flowers and withered leaves removed.

Much reduced versions of this style of flower growing can still be seen in municipal parks, and many American flowerbeds are also treated in a manner that is a lineal descendant of this method of growing flowers. For that reason I have gone rather fully into the process. But as I grew up, these formal beds were increasingly criticized. Adventurous gardeners considered them dull because the variety of plants that could be used in them was so strictly limited. The unnatural manner in which they were planted was also loudly condemned, as was the need to raise dozens of young plants each season. These were all valid objections, yet bedding out had some concrete advantages. Using massed plants in this manner provided a long and reliable show of bloom without calling for much gardening expertise, as long as there was someone available to raise the necessary little plants. Once set out, the young plants gave a neat and good appearance from any angle during the entire time they were in the ground, whether they were in bloom or not. These are horticultural virtues that we can still find useful.

For those who disliked bedding out, the alternative method of producing a fine show of flowers was to construct what in England is called a herbaceous border, and here a perennial bed. These, unlike the ribbon beds, were not freestanding; they were against a wall, a fence, or a hedge. If possible, they faced south, and, since they were intended to accommodate much larger as well as many more plants, the layout was far wider than the ribbon beds. In them were planted a tremendous variety of growing material, with particular emphasis on perennials—that is, plants that flower year after year. Nothing was planted in rows or in a formal manner; instead the plants were set into the ground in huge, irregular drifts and sweeps that fingered into each other in a deliberately uncontrived fashion. It is, however, extremely difficult to produce an unbroken succession of bloom from perennial plants; there are often dull periods with no flowers—unless you are a superb horticulturist with nothing else to do except read up on new plants and work in that border. And since very few people, either amateur gardeners or those hired to look after the grounds, are willing to spend quite so much effort on one section of the garden, most perennial borders also have to take advantage of the lavish bloom provided by biennials—plants that grow nothing but leaves all one year, winter this greenery over safely outdoors, and then flower and die the next season—and annuals, but planted in large, irregular-shaped groups. In my youth, annuals were also grown in the herbaceous border from seed sown in open areas, which produced magnificent, sturdy plants, better than any that had been transplanted.

The main difference between the two styles of displaying flowers was the seemingly uncontrived manner in which a great diversity of plants was grown in the perennial beds. Well-managed herbaceous beds were a challenge, and by the time I had grown up they had almost completely routed the older style of bedding out, though I had a lurking affection for it. But this casual elegance concealed the fact that their upkeep was almost more than that required by the discredited ribbon beds, without the certainty of unending bloom, particularly in the hands of the inexperienced. It was necessary to understand exactly how tall and how wide various perennial plants would be at maturity so that they would neither be overwhelmed by their neighbors nor crowd others out themselves. Since a large number of specimens had to be included—for a perennial bed was not thought to be living up to its potential if only a few varieties of plants were in it—it was also important to understand and be able to adjust the soil requirements to any particular plant. The big plants at the back of such a bed also needed staking, one of the most difficult of the small horticultural skills to bring off successfully and unobtrusively.

Perennial plants also need regular pruning and pinching to do their best, and the informality of the layout, combined with the great width of most of these borders, made it hard to do this work. For since herbaceous borders could not be reached from both sides there always had to be a certain amount of tramping about in them, with invariable disasters to late-appearing or fragile plants. Weeding was another huge chore. As a perennial border did not have the twice-a-season going-over that was part of the growing system of bedded plants, perennial weeds, which are twice as destructive and twice as hard to eradicate as the annual weeds, got into them. The problem of keeping up the fertility of the land was also more difficult than the regular rejuvenation of the ribbon borders. After the perennial plants had been cut back in the fall, at the time the biennials went in, the whole bed was covered thickly with well-rotted manure. This was forked in lightly; the garden fork is far the safest way to dig carefully over an area that is full of established roots and yet do the least possible damage. After that the biennials were set out.

But this light forking was not nearly as effective as the deep digging of the ribbon beds, so about every third year in the fall the whole border was taken to pieces. Every perennial plant was dug out and laid to one side with the root ball covered with a wet sack. The bed was then completely dug over, this time with a spade, and massive amounts of new soil and fertilizer incorporated. After that, plants that needed dividing were broken up and the whole puzzle put back either exactly as before or in a new design based on the way the plants had grown previously. This, I believe, is still the way English borders are managed. Though the remaking of the perennial border took time and effort, it was done without any sense of pressure. Apart from planting bulbs and gathering up the leaves, fall is not a very exhausting season. It is a leisurely time when the weather makes work outdoors a delight, and, as a small additional bonus, an active gardener is by then usually in prime physical condition!

These two styles of growing plants combined to give the family garden a lively appearance for months on end. This feeling was carried into the house by the huge bowls of flowers that were in every room. Flowers were never cut for indoor use from the display beds, that would have been unheard of; these flowers were grown in rows among the vegetables in what the English call the kitchen garden. There, in a sunny place, a great many annuals were grown, and trenches of sweetpeas and many perennials were planted.

These, then, were the ways of growing flowers that I understood, and I complacently assumed I would be able to reproduce them in my own American suburban garden—on a reduced scale, since I was to be the gardener. After some wavering, ribbon beds were planned for each side of the lower back lawn, and a perennial border was laid out beside the house where the structural alterations had provided an excellent place. At first I had no intention of growing vegetables, for there was no room. But early in December, the first winter after we moved in, the Japanese attack on Pearl Harbor so changed the lives of everyone that it became a civic duty to grow vegetables. We therefore dug up the front lawn and used that for a Victory garden.

In very short order, the hard realities of translating English traditions to New England became obvious. The first disillusionment was the bedding out. The bitter winters and heavy snow made the spring show in these beds, which I set out in the fall, totally unreliable. Sometimes the sweet williams, Canterbury bells, foxgloves, and polyanthus came through unscathed. More frequently, when the snow melted, most of the plants proved to be dead. I also discovered that I had to grow all my own biennials if I intended to set them out in the fall. Biennials appear at the garden centers only in spring. Set out then, they grow into miserable little travesties of the plants they can be when planted successfully in the fall.

I also found it hard to time the summer show of bedded plants. Spring comes late in New England, and if the biennials had survived the winter, these were still in full flower in mid-June. If the first flowers are picked off Canterbury bells as they fade, the plant always produces a second show of bloom that lasts into July. In consequence, these beds were not ready to be dug and reset until after most of the better annuals that were available at the greenhouses had all been sold; it also gave them a very short time in which to form strong new roots before the withering blasts of the midsummer heat fell on them. To solve the shortage problem we tried buying annuals while they were still available, standing them in a sunny position, still in their flats, with regular watering and feeding. But this did not work. Full sun was too much for the crowded root systems, and in light shade the plants themselves became weak and spindly. When the time came to cut into the tangled root mass to set out the plants individually, the shock to the roots was so severe that often no new growth was made for several weeks. All this was not encouraging, and the work was not made easier by the effort of trying to refurbish those beds in the height of the summer.

For a few years we tried to hold to the traditional practice of a double season of bloom for bedded plants, but in the end the character of the beds was changed. We dug and replenished the soil in the fall as usual, but instead of being filled with biennials for the early spring the beds were then covered with a thick mulch. Around the end of May, when the annuals were on the market, we bought boxes of plants in single colors and set them out close together, using rows of white petunias in the front to quiet the show down. This worked, and, though the beds were not planted in loops and curves, the general effect was not unlike the ribbon beds, but with only one season of bloom instead of two.

This method of growing flowers is still the easiest for the new gardener. The beds will look better if they can be set in a little sunny patch of ground in the corner of a patio, against the wall of a garage or breezeway, or even at the base of a large evergreen shrub. To have it give the most pleasure, the place where these flowers are to grow should be passed, or looked at, daily. You will also make your life simpler if this little plot is dug over each fall, not in the spring, when, even if you are no gardener, you still have a thousand other things to do.

When the plot is dug, add compost. If you have no compost, buy a bag of milorganite or dry cow manure and dig that in deeply. Then cover the turned-over ground with a thick layer of leaves. Today, if I were still summering in the suburban garden, after those beds were dug in the fall I would fill them with tulips. These can be lifted out in late May, new compost added, and the summer annuals put in. In this manner it is possible to get a much fuller show from even a minute patch of ground. A couple of flats of the new F_1 petunias used this way can put up a fine show all summer, but steer clear of plants like salvia and celosia that come into

Dwarf veronica.

bloom late in the season. The aim in these tiny flowering patches is to have a steady, unbroken show of flowers all summer, not a final dramatic unfurling.

There's a pleasant little patch of just this sort in a nearby yard in the country. It consists entirely of marigolds, set against the silver, sea-weathered shingles of a garage. The back is planted with a few of the tall, yellow African varieties; these are fronted down with spreading yellow and brown varieties of French marigolds, and at the edge of the grass there are dwarf yellow marigolds. The whole border is about five feet by three feet and a couple of flats of each type of marigold must suffice. After the plants go in, the tall marigolds are staked, but, other than a little watering in dry periods and some very casual weeding, I don't believe the owners do anything more to it. And it gives not only them but every passerby a great deal of pleasure. This is not great horticulture, but it is an easy way to enjoy a few flowers. I am not fond of two or three marigolds, or any other plant for that matter, planted around a post. No matter how brightly they may shine, they do not have enough visual impact. To make a good effect, even with this very simple style of growing flowers, it is necessary to stick to the old bedding tradition of massing in sufficient quantity to provide a strong block of color from a distance.

Though our first entirely successful U.S. flowerbeds were along these lines, I wanted to be able to grow earlier and greater varieties of flowers. For that I turned to a perennial border beside the house. This started off extremely well. For the first few years there was an excellent succession of bloom from all the new stock I had bought and the additional annuals I added when I set out the other beds. By that time I was raising my own biennials in the Victory garden, and I found that, planted informally in the perennial beds, it was not nearly such a disaster when they failed to come through the winter. I also left open areas in which to try and grow annuals from seed. The variety of seeds that I found available in the catalogues had excited me very much. But in this climate, in order not to rot delicate seeds, it is necessary to wait to sow until the sun warms up the ground. This late seeding produced very poor results, for the heat of the sun by day combined with the hot winds of spring to kill most of the tiny seedlings as soon as they appeared above ground. Those that did survive these hazards were usually smothered out by the exuberant growth of weeds that appeared in the same open areas. So instead of being able to take advantage of all the exciting seeds offered in the seed catalogues, I had to rely on the far less interesting annuals I could find in the commercial outlets.

This, by the way, is a problem that has got steadily worse, not better, and one in which American gardening is far behind that of other countries. Today outdoor gardeners who want to be in the least adventurous with annual plants are in great difficulty unless they grow their own; it is almost impossible to find anything the least out of the ordinary, even at the most sophisticated garden center. And even more irritating, the familiar dull standbys are often offered only in mixed colors and a single boring variety.

Asters come in an enormous variety of shapes, and with a long succession of flowering dates, but all that is usually offered is the uninteresting mid-season type. Snapdragons have been vastly improved: there now exist huge rust-free giants, highly floriferous mid-season medium-size plants, and dwarf snapdragons that throw up dozens of blossoming stalks. But looking for snapdragons, you can count yourself lucky if you track down boxes of a single color rather than those horrid mixtures, and these are usually the unimproved old-fashioned varieties that flower late and rather feebly. It is almost impossible to work your way through all the various kinds of marigolds now available in catalogues as seeds. But a glance at the average roadside stand suggests that nothing exists except tall orange or yellow African types, the multicolored French varieties, and a particularly unfortunate new pigmy plant with a huge misshapen head on a very short stalk. Not the type, I may add, that is grown in that little marigold patch. Zinnias are also highly worthwhile plants in New England, for they have a long flowering season and can be cut heavily. These also exist in innumerable colors and shapes—but again, only in the seed catalogues. Some years the garden centers carry no zinnias; they are, we are told, a chancy crop for the retailer, for they often rot when set out, and the customers complain. This is because they are offered for sale too early. Zinnias are a hot-weather plant, but I can see no reason why we should be required to forgo them because it is deemed necessary by those who sell them to us that we should all buy our annuals, and get them into the ground, at exactly the same moment whether the season suits the plants or not. But if you refuse to set out zinnias at this date, because you may lose too many, there will be none around at the correct planting season.

Petunias, it is true, are available in every color and shape. Here the growers have taken advantage of the modern breakthrough in seed, even though petunias are tiresome plants to handle at the early stage and need a great deal of care. If the professional growers are willing to take so much trouble with petunias, surely it is not asking too much of them to suggest that they could extend some of the same care to providing us with better varieties of other annual plants, even perhaps at the option of paying a little more for them?

During the years in which we summered in the suburban garden, I never managed to grow any successful annuals from seed in the perennial bed, but I did produce excellent plants from those sown in rows in the Victory garden. Flower seed did well there because it was planted in identifiable furrows in which it was safe even in the heaviest downpour, instead of being irregularly scattered around in the perennial border, where the rain washed it out. Also being slightly lower than the soil surface, the emerging seedlings were safe from hot winds, and the little earthen ridges alongside each furrow provided some shade from the sun. But though we had fine biennials and good late-flowering annuals, I had no luck with the plants that need a long, cool period of growth in very early spring. When I looked up how to deal with these plants—it was larkspur I particularly wanted to grow—I found that American books advised the identical treatment that I had used in England: sow the seed very late in the fall where you want the plant to flower. I never had any luck with this method. Either there was an unexpected Indian summer after I thought the growing season was over, whereupon the little plants germinated and got killed off in the winter, or I waited too long and the ground froze too hard to get a furrow made. And if I got the seed in at the so-called right time I never saw any results. Somehow either the seed rotted or the seedlings were destroyed.

The main problem with the perennial bed was renewing the fertility of the ground, keeping out the worst of the weeds, and dividing overgrown plants. At first I again followed the ways of my youth (and, I might add, the advice given in almost all regional gardening books) and did this job in the lovely golden days of the New England fall, and I never doubted that I would be greeted by a tremendously improved display the following year. Instead, when the snow melted after the first big renewal, I found to my surprise that more than half the plants were dead. The first time this happened, I attributed the trouble to some natural freak of the weather or some gross mismanagement on my part. Perhaps something was wrong with the new soil from our first compost pile. But when I had the same dismal results in subsequent years, the grim answer made itself obvious. In cold climates most perennial plants, if they are lifted and particularly if they have been divided, cannot make enough strong new roots during what remains of the mild weather to carry them safely through the very deep frost penetration of the soil that occurs in this area. To be on the safe side, it is always better to do this work in the spring. This I think is still not made sufficiently clear to new gardeners.

In consequence, what used to be a leisurely fall job must in New England be crammed into the already overloaded schedule of spring garden jobs. This is a huge extra piece of work for the average home gardener and is, I am sure, why so few people grow really good perennials. Perennials also unfortunately are extremely heavy feeders; the long-lasting roots take a great deal of the mineral elements out of the soil. Any border full of these plants must therefore be kept regularly replenished by extra food, even if the plants themselves do not need dividing. This is a problem that most of us find very hard to manage, especially at that rushed period. Conventional perennial beds also must have regular spring and fall weeding—as well as a good deal during the course of the summer if the soil is left uncovered. This is not only for appearance's sake, but also to prevent

Self-seeded foxgloves.

the weeds from stealing much needed goodness out of the soil.

I made the changeover to spring dividing and renewal of the fertility of the land while I was still summering in town. And though the effort in the spring rush was exhausting, the results did at least keep the plants alive! And since I was around to look after the beds during the entire growing season the weeding never got beyond me.

Then we bought the country house—and our entire horticultural pattern of activity had to undergo a sea change.

Since we were no longer to be in town during the summer, and the war was over, the vegetable garden on the front lawn was abolished and the area reseeded to grass. The slow process of laying out the flowering shrub border described on pages 181–7 was begun. The small flowerbeds on each side of the lower lawn were also filled with flowering shrubs at the back, and self-seeding, long-lasting small bulbs and daffodils that would need no lifting and might naturalize were planted in front of them along with low ground cover. The perennial border against the house was abolished and eventually a lean-to greenhouse was built on the site. But since we expected to remain in town until around the middle of June, a new, narrow bed with early flowering perennials was opened up in front of the little

Oriental poppies.

hedge that divides the upper back lawn from the area below.
Into this we moved the peonies, Oriental poppies, colum-
bines, iris, and the like. This bed with most of the same
flowers still in it nearly stole the show many years later at a
daughter's wedding. A great many foxgloves had worked
their way into it, and for once a large number of Canterbury
bells had come safely through the winter, and their combined appearance entirely outshone the more formal decora-
tions that had gone into the tent that stretched over the bed.
These are the only flowering plants in that sense that have
been retained in the suburban garden; everything else that
was the least interesting, including those sunflowers that
made such a show along the raw new fence, were taken to
the country garden, where enormous problems faced us.

One highly urgent job was to bring some sort of order
back to two large perennial beds that had been laid out between the front door and the road, as one of the main
features of the place. In good condition and full of flowers,
these would be a delight and a very pleasant introduction to

the yard. But the first impression they gave me during the summer we rented that house was anything but pleasant, for they had been neglected and had become nothing but weed patches. Yet apart from an almost derelict rose garden, those big beds were all that remained of the flower garden; the rest had gone with the parcel of land we had not been able to buy. If, therefore, I wanted perennial beds, these had to be brought back.

Bringing order out of their chaos was not easy; the soil was depleted to starved sand, and the area was alive with every pest I had ever heard of—and many I had never known existed. The beds had also been underwater twice when the sea surged through the garden, so, though they had once been the pride and joy of a superb horticulturist, all the rare plants had been lost. With a huge effort we brought them back. We planted new, better perennials, replenished the soil, got rid of some of the worst of the weeds, and got a stranglehold on some of the pests, and for over twenty years those beds were again the main feature of the place.

But they did demand an immense amount of work, much more than had been needed to run the perennial bed in the suburban garden. Partly, of course, this was because there were two of them, but the main problem was the fact that I was now a part-time gardener, which made the close attention I had given my former bed quite impossible. We worked out a program that gave us a good show and kept the beds from getting out of hand, but it was hard labor. In the fall, before we had to go back for the opening of school, everything was cut down and all the annuals, even those still in bloom, pulled out. After as thorough a weeding as we could manage at a very rushed time, a thick top-dressing of compost was laid over the open areas and tucked carefully around the permanent plants. Into this we set the biennials that had been grown during the summer in the vegetable garden. After the first hard frost, we made a special trip to lay a thick wet mulch of leaves around the biennials, for these beds were raked by a cold east wind in winter. In early spring, long before we moved, and as an added inconvenience long before the water was turned on, periodic rushed visits had to be made to lift off the mulch, fork in the top-dressing, weed, and divide and plant out those blocks of summer annuals. We also had to plant a reserve store of those same annuals in rows in the vegetable garden, for the mortality rate of the bedded-out plants, when we were not there to look after them, was exceedingly high.

In mid-June, after we got down, the beds always needed weeding again. I have never seen weeds do as well as they did there! At this same time the perennials were staked. This was a job I loathed, for the beds did not look well for ages afterward; plants take time to reaccustom themselves to restraints. After that, a final summer mulch was put down to control the weeds and hold moisture. For this we used buckwheat hulls, partly for their appearance but largely because it was simpler to get this loose material which could be poured in among closely planted perennials.

All this took time and energy, but for over twenty years, where I was concerned, the results were worth the struggle. Then, in that curious way in which attitudes alter imperceptibly and vague feelings turn into a full-fledged desire, I had had enough. No one single factor produced this turnabout, though part of it was the fact that the beds were gradually growing too shady for some of the better plants. But it added up to the fact that I was bored with all that work and wanted out. It is one thing to realize this in your heart, and another to devise something to put in the place of such an old, well-established feature of a yard. It also took time to convince the rest of the family (who did none of the work in those beds) that such a revolutionary attitude had merit! A good many ideas were considered and rejected before the idea of transforming the area into the entrance court described in Chapter II was agreed upon. The problem was greater than just cutting out the flowerbeds; it ran deeper. We had also to decide whether we wanted to continue with flowers grown in flowerbeds as a visual feature of the yard. And, if the answer was yes, where were they to be grown, and was there a simpler, less exhausting method of handling them?

Of the three problems, the most important was the last. I had had my fill of conventional flowerbeds; that, after all, was the reason for getting rid of those already in existence. Unless some easier method could be worked out, I could see no point in starting up the whole laborious process again. Instead I would continue to grow flowers in a manner that had gone on all the years we occupied the country garden: in rows among the vegetables, to be cut for the house. Annuals and biennials would be used only as container plants for the summer porch. This upheaval coincided with the period when other labor-saving changes were also being made in the country garden: shifting the vegetable and cutting garden from its previous position to a smaller, more compact area beside the new cookout patio in the third garden. Removing the vegetables left a large, fertile, sunny enclosure protected by that venerable privet hedge, with no particular plan for making use of it.

The first intention was to grass it all down and use the enclosure as a protected playground for grandchildren. To give this better visual interest we decided to keep the flat cement blocks that had been laid down in a rectangle for mowing strips. The rose garden, for which the enclosure had been originally designed, had been centered on a large rock and we decided to add to the general decorative effect by surrounding it too with blocks. Then suddenly a possible solution to the problem of how and where to grow flowers came to me. Instead of grassing down the whole area, why not confine the new grass to the area behind the rock. The remaining front portion, which got the morning sun, and always grew the best flowers and vegetables, could then be divided by a double row of the same cement paving blocks. These would provide a path from the rock to the outer limits of the rectangular enclosure, thus making a focal point out of a necessity. And by dividing the remaining open area in this manner so that it could be reached and worked from both sides, we could reduce it to more manageable proportions in the old tradition of free-standing ribbon beds but on a much larger scale. These then could be planted in rows with bedding annuals, as well as annuals grown from seed. Better still, perennial plants could also be set out in rows as I remembered them in the family kitchen garden. All that was needed to take away the utilitarian effect was to give the rows a little more style, not lay them out in completely straight lines. To effect this, U-shaped lines were devised that spread over both growing areas with the center of the U passing across the path.

This scheme solved a great many problems. As a start, anything in a row is highly visible, so this arrangement of display flowers could be mulched and weeded by anyone, not just me. The simple style of planting out in rows would also make the spring work less overwhelming. I knew from my experience of growing cutting flowers among the vegetables, when plants are set out in obvious lines, the work goes faster.

To make the new plan workable, some strict ground rules were laid down. No plant that spread by underground runners would be included; the basic concept of plants in rows must always be kept firmly in mind. To cut down on the unending weeding, the rows also had to be far enough apart to allow a heavy weed-smothering layer of mulch to be put down and far enough apart for the worker to be able to get in to do this job without trampling on other plants. For a succession of bloom, each row of early flowering perennials should have a row of late summer annuals beside it, either in front or behind to take up the story when the early flowers were through. The late-flowering perennial plants would have biennials planted in front of them; when these were over they could be pulled out. The perennials could then spread into the opened-up area and develop their mature form, either billowing or tall, and this would break the rigidity of the planting style. The rows themselves would be graded in height, the taller plants being in the back on both sides and the dwarfs in the front of the bed, which now faced the entrance through the new pergola. As a sop to my particular dislike, the fewest possible plants that needed staking would be included! To soften this slightly austere set of regulations, plants that spread out over the summer, such as pinks, annual phlox, nasturtiums, and petunias would be grown on each side of the central path and along the outer edges of the growing area where they could spill onto the concrete blocks without ruining the grass.

Once the idea had burgeoned, it all seemed very obvious and the job went forward rapidly. The back was seeded, the open ground replenished, the path laid, and the U-shaped curves laid out, not with a pointed stick as in the past, but with bone meal so that they were highly visible. Once these curves were correct, in the right proportion to each other, and far enough apart, we marked them out with stakes hammered in very deeply so that the frost would not heave them. Since the work on the entrance court was also scheduled for that same fall, I had had my change of heart about continuing to grow flowers at a rather cliff-hanging stage. But it did make it possible to save anything I wanted to keep from the old bed, even though this meant lifting, dividing, and re-setting them into their new curved rows at what I now knew to be the wrong season. As usual, some died, but enough survived to give us a good idea the following spring of how many new plants had to be bought immediately to fill the gaps in these rows of perennials. When everything that could be done that first fall was finished, a heavy blanket of mulch, mainly half-made compost and leaves, was spread over the growing-area-to-be. The section where the grass seed was timidly germinating was left uncovered. This grew a fine mixture of weeds and grass early the following spring, but steady mowing soon eliminated the weeds, and this is now one of the better lawns! But by the end of the next summer we knew we had hit the jackpot. The curved rows, alternating with early and late flowers, proved an immediate success, and since everything was in those workable rows, a second, rich smothering of mulch was easily put down during the early months of the summer to lessen the daily chores. Furthermore, by keeping this steady thick layer of half-made mulch compost on the soil year in and year out, which we have done ever since, two other tedious former jobs have been cut out. The mulch, as it disintegrates, provides an un-

*New growing area
with path and
U-shaped curves
laid out.*

ending supply of fresh nourishment for the soil. Using it,
rather than the previous sterile buckwheat, there is no need
to dig the beds. As the compost breaks down, the goodness
from it runs into the earth beneath, and the coarse material
that remains keeps the soil structure in excellent condition.
By now, in fact, the soil in this area is so rich that plants that
need a lean diet to bloom, such as marguerites and nasturtiums, are no longer successful; they run all to leaves. The
mulch also keeps the soil cool and moist. Before it was put
down the earth in that enclosure baked iron-hard and cracked
in the summer. Since it has been covered with the mulch,
there is never any need to water even in the driest spells, except immediately after the bedding plants go in.

As an unexpected bonus, I at last have mastered the secret
of growing the hardy annuals that need to germinate very
early in the season. The method is to use those little pop-up
peat pots that are sold as compressed wafers. About three or
four dozen, depending on how many rows I mean to plant,
are allowed to rise up in warm water in a plastic bin. When
they are all up, they are drained for a day. These pots are
made of peat, and since they are enclosed in a nylon net, it
is difficult to squeeze the surplus water out of the peat before

using them. After some unfortunate experiences I discovered that the interior of these pots was too wet for seeds if they are used immediately after they have absorbed water. In April, usually in town, I sow a pinch of the seed I want to grow in each pot. My main candidates for these early flowers are annual delphinium, Icelandic and Shirley poppies, clarkia, and larkspur, but a different climate and soil will dictate a different choice.

Once the little pots have been sown, I keep them strictly segregated in old shoeboxes lined with plastic which can be thrown over the top to keep the moisture in. This is to make sure that I don't mix up the various plants, for it is much too much bother to label every pop-up pot! Once the pots are ready, an excursion is made to the country flower garden. Here the mulch is pulled back in front of rows of late-flowering perennials. These seeds are plants that will not take intense summer heat no matter how early you get them in,

The new growing area four years later.

so there should be other blossoming plants nearby to take over after they are pulled out. The pop-up pots are planted in the ground about four inches apart; seeded early this way, the plants grow unexpectedly large. It is very important to put the whole of the peat pot below ground level. Pull a thin layer of ground soil over the whole contraption. With any kind of peat pot, none of the peat sides should ever be allowed to show above ground. If they do, the peat will dry out and act as a wick, drawing moisture out of the ground and away from the roots and therefore inhibiting good growth. The mulch is left pulled back where these pots have gone in, so that the soil warms up, and the open area reminds me where they have been planted. I try to label and stake my rows; sometimes I even try to draw paper planting plans. But in spite of this care, it is extraordinary how easily one forgets what has been done; later in the planting season, when the bedding annuals are going in, there is nothing more exasperating than digging up a peat pot full of thriving roots, because you have forgotten the exact spot they went in.

When the seedlings appear above ground, each group should be reduced to fewer plants and at the same time the dozens of weeds that have also taken advantage of the open pot should be pulled out. At this stage the mulch can be drawn back around the emerging plants. If there seem to be slugs in the garden, don't reduce the seedlings to a single specimen in each pop-up pot the first time around; leave two or three and gradually eliminate them to a single specimen. If you have sown mixed colors, the smallest seedling will probably have the most interesting color. If you find seedlings cut off at the base, cutworms are the cause. Dig in the immediate area until you find the fat, white grubs.

This method gives us huge, long-lasting spectacular stands of relatively unusual, early-flowering plants for the longest display. Dead seed heads should be kept faithfully cut off. In spite of my efforts in this direction it now begins to look as though the Shirley poppies have established themselves all over that garden, so I am not going to bother with all these preliminaries with them. Icelandic poppies, however, which are in fact perennials but will flower the first year, will still have to have this special care.

At this same period, which should always be as soon as the ground can be worked (that is, when the soil is not so wet that it stays in a compact wet mass in your hand when you squeeze it together), the necessary dividing of perennials should be done. I no longer divide regularly; I only dig up the plants that clearly need attention, the signals being either a greatly overgrown plant, or else one that is spreading outward, leaving a dead center in the heart of the plant from which no new shoots are coming. Divide plants in the way described on pages 232–3.

For the rest of the growing season the care is minimal. Bedded annuals are set out at the end of May in this climate, and the seeds of the late-flowering annuals that need warm ground are sown in curved furrows instead of their previous straight rows at the same time. When we move down, a huge weeding is done. It's no good pretending that weeds don't move in, even with a mulch; they do, particularly into the hearts of the perennial plants. But with this style of planting, they do not come up much through the mulch, and they are extremely obvious when they do. They can be controlled for the rest of the growing season with two or three days of intensive work after all the planting is over, and after you can identify with complete certainty the special seedlings you have sown. This is the advantage of having the rows, for it makes it easier for the nongardener to help with the weeding if you point out the furrows. But there will also be weeds in those furrows, and before setting any helper loose, always make very sure that they have identified the leaves of the plants you want saved. Far too many domestic tragedies and subsequent loss of any further interest in helping with the garden will follow otherwise!

When this weeding is done, an extra summer mulch should be put down. For this we use grass clippings, and, contrary to all the usual warnings, I have never found that these heat up so much that they injure the plants. I would not pull newly cut grass close against the stems of growing plants; this might do some damage.

The next big effort with this bed does not come until after the first frost. Then it is cut down, leaving little stubs of the perennial plants above ground—this suits them better than shaving them to the ground. Leaving the withered foliage to be cleared away in the spring is a mistake. It gives the bed an untidy appearance all winter, pests lurk in the dead foliage for protection, and the clean-up job in the spring will be so horrendous that it is hard to face. Do the job while the weather still makes it pleasant to work outdoors, but don't cut the bed down so early that new perennial growth starts up again. When the frost kills this unseasonable growth, the heart of the plant is often seriously injured. The time to cut perennial plants down is when the leaves yellow.

After the area is cut, it is thoroughly weeded to get out summer intruders that have escaped notice. This may seem a redundant effort, for no matter how free of visible weeds the bed may be when winter comes, spring will produce a fine new growth. But the weed problem in the spring will be far

The new growing area in bitter cold, which has killed biennials.

worse if those of the previous season have been left to winter over. Not all weeds are annuals, and if you leave them in the flowerbed some will not die but will start growing far earlier than we can pull them out. The spring clean-up job is twice as ferocious in a bed that has been neglected the previous fall. So even though this job has to be done very thoroughly twice a year, the effort is worth it.

For the winter cover of mulch, we use half-made compost and leaves. If the soil looks in the least depleted by the end of the flowering year—and along the rows of greedy perennials like phlox and Michaelmas daisies this can happen—we add a thick layer of fresh-made compost beside the row of plants and cover that with the mulch.

Once this bed had proved a success, we decided to improve the winter appearance of the enclosure. For more interest after the flowers were done and the rather dreary mulch in place, we moved in a double half-moon of yews and chamaecyparis that I had grown from cuttings. These were planted in behind the central rock to make a more emphatic break with the grassed-over area and to provide winter height and color. As an additional feature a matched pair of golden rain trees (koelreuteria) were set out in stone circles on each side of that little back lawn. As a final touch, new flat blocks were cemented onto both rocks, and two of our hitherto inappropriate statues settled onto them as though the entire layout had been designed around them.

But it is not necessary to have statuary or a large area enclosed by an old hedge or any other elaborations to produce a fine show by growing plants in curves with a heavy layer of mulch between the rows. Basically this is an extension of those bright patches of flowers that I described earlier in this section. But this method makes it possible to fill a larger area and use a much greater variety of plants without undertaking much more work than goes into a tiny patch.

But there are some plants that cannot be used this way and it is important to be ruthless about excluding them. Those that should never be allowed in are plants that spread by underground runners. Some of the low-growing perennial asters are great offenders this way, the physostegia, sundrops, and monardas being others. Plants that spread fast by seed or bulb division below ground should also be avoided; for that reason the de Graaff lilies were excluded. Plants cannot be allowed to stray out of their allotted curves, for if these clear-cut definitions are lost, much of the ease of the planting style will go too. We had a good many of these unsuitable plants in the old beds, and I moved them into a rather ramshackle border beside the house about which I had never taken much trouble. Here they are now fighting it out with the original inhabitants—some highly aggressive lilies-of-the-valley—and what the outcome will be I don't know. Presumably one of these spreaders will ultimately overwhelm all the rest, but up to the present the battle is a draw and the bed has turned out to be unexpectedly attractive and long-lasting. Possibly this is a way to grow plants with takeover ambitions; concentrate them together, feed the area heavily with a thick layer of compost each fall after it has been cut down, and then stand back and let the best one win. Weeding is never much trouble in such a bed, the contending plants shade out the weeds!

One of the extra bonuses from growing flowers in rows is that as the early annuals finish and can be pulled out, space appears for extra plants that can bring a final touch of color to the scene. During the late summer and fall the roadsides are full of tempting signs: "Fall mums," which, on further investigation, turn out to be rows of well-budded plants waiting like eager puppies in a pet shop to be adopted. These have been field-grown, then lifted, and the roots encased in paper pots so that they can be planted out in the garden. Planting is simple: tear the paper sides and base off the root ball, make a good-size hole in the curve into which the plant can be set without crowding, and water it well. There will be a fine show of flowers, often as early as August, that will continue until frost. Do not expect to treat these plants as perennials. Anything put out so late in the season will not survive the winter in a cold climate. Occasionally a few may pull through, but in general consider them as annuals. I prefer a row of chrysanthemums to be in a single color, but this of course is a matter of taste.

An inexpensive trick is to grow your own. This can easily be done by buying sturdy cuttings of early-flowering varieties in the spring and growing them outdoors all summer in the cutting garden under a thick mulch. To get bushy plants, continue to pinch out the growing points of the stems after they are about four inches long until the middle of July. If you are growing chrysanthemums in poor soil that is not under mulch, they must be kept both fed and watered during the growing season. We lift ours after a thorough watering and plant them in the vacant curves in the flowerbed when the buds show color.

From the various casual references that have been made so far it must have become clear that our vegetable-cutting garden has to be a highly multipurpose area, for I am not prepared to take intensive care of too many places. Our patch contains not only vegetables but also the biennials, chrysanthemum cuttings, and all the flowers grown for the house. We stuff everything in it so thickly because we practice very intensive deep feeding and rotation of what grows where.

We have grown vegetables ever since the Victory garden, and at various times I have also grown raspberries, blueberries, and strawberries. But since as a family we consume more fruit and vegetables than I can possibly provide, I have cut this activity to a few luxury mouthfuls that can never be matched by store-bought goods. We raise our own early and late lettuce, miniature early and late cabbage, we have delicious tiny carrots in quantity, beets, early peas, and a great many too many green beans in spite of my efforts to stagger the crop. We also raise a few mouthfuls of midget corn, and we always have quarts of tomatoes. At one time I grew peppers and eggplant as well as New Zealand spinach. But no one liked the spinach and the eggplant, and peppers bore so late as to be hardly worth the effort. Now seed of an early small variety is available, and I may well try them again. In the fall, if the caterpillars have not been too bad, we have broccoli. We also grow parsley, mint, mustard, and cress.

This may seem a limited choice and I would not argue, but it is all I can undertake. To grow the various squash, melon, and cucumber, much more space would be needed, and I have no intention of taking on anything more. The soft fruit, while delicious, was not sufficient to satisfy our needs. Nor does its culture fit into my present style of growing vegetables, which I now confine almost completely to annuals. I do, however, still grow the *fraise du bois* as a decorative edging along the side of the garden.

Every family must make their own choice about what vegetables are worth the effort. I do think it important that some should always be grown. This is far the easiest way to teach children to understand the growing cycle, the necessity of good culture, and the dangers of casual sprays. It also links them to their heritage in a way that nothing else can do.

The methods we use in this plot are extremely simple and almost identical to those I have described for the flower-growing area. This particular garden, as was described on page 36, began as a piece of land beside the new cookout

The vegetable plot confined behind railway ties and edged with parsley.

area where the ground had become unusable. The soil was redeemed by piling a huge load of seaweed over the garden-to-be, leaving it there all one winter, and rototilling it in very deeply the following spring. Railway ties were then laid down to define the area for two beds and leave space for the path that runs between them. Next, a great deal of finished compost, which is still renewed annually, was piled into the bins produced by the railway ties, covered with a leaf mulch, and raked smooth. The reworked soil was left to lie fallow for the whole summer. The following spring we started a growing schedule that has been kept up ever since. When the ground is open, around mid-April, the heavy winter mulch is pulled to the side and rows of early peas are planted. I use dwarf varieties to cut down on the problems of setting out brush or nets for the vines. Peas should be planted as thickly as they grow in their pods. This is a short-season crop, and you need to get the most out of it. At this same time, we plant a short row of early lettuce. Early in May, we put in a second crop of more heat-resistant peas, more lettuce, beets, carrots, and parsley. They could all go in earlier, for they are very hardy, but, since April is also the time I am dividing plants, the vegetables wait.

All seed germinates better on a flat, even surface. Our method is to lay out a line with a string tied tightly between two sticks and open a furrow with a corner of a hoe. We then tread along the furrow heel to toe, to compact the soil and even it out. When the seed is down, the soil is pulled back lightly over it, leaving those useful ridges of earth on both sides. We thump the soil and the seeds into close contact with each other by going down the line with the back of the hoe. Other than peas, seeds should be sown rather far apart, other-wise you will have to waste time thinning plants out. Thinning means removing extra plants so that those left have space to develop. The distance you thin depends on the size of the plant at maturity; a cabbage obviously needs much more final space than a carrot. But just as it is foolish to plant too thickly in the first place, it is equally unwise to thin too enthusiastically the first time around. Give the little plants space to breathe, but don't isolate them in lonely splendor until you are sure that the slugs are under control.

Planting parsley and carrot seed has its own ritual. The cases of these seeds, which are closely related, are extremely hard, and germination is slow and also uneven. A solution which infuriates the scientific, but which works, is to take a kettle of boiling water and rush down the rows pouring it over the seed after it has been planted in the furrow but before the earth is pulled back over it. Then proceed as usual. This way you will get fast, even germination. But make sure the water is boiling, hot water alone won't crack the hard seed case.

In late May we plant bush beans, rows of miniature corn, and set out the tomatoes which I buy as small plants. This is also the time I sow the annuals for cutting, set out the gladiola, and bed out a reserve supply of annuals from flats. By the time the beans are up, so are the weeds. Once everything is planted and we are in residence, we weed and thin simultaneously, particularly among the perennial mints and *fraise du bois.* By mid-June a thick new mulch has been put down. In July biennial seeds are sown in the cold frame, together with the late cabbage and broccoli. When any crop is over, the ground on which it grew is replenished with a thick layer of finished compost and covered with mulch until the biennials and other plants are ready to be set out in their place. We try never to plant cabbage or any of the cabbage family twice in a season along the same row; this opens up the possibility of disease. It is as well to change the variety of plant that goes out along the rows not only during the double cropping of the current season but also from year to year.

We have had no trouble with rust or Mexican bean beetle, which once was a great nuisance, since we took to growing our vegetables under mulch. This may be pure chance, but I used to notice that the attacks always started at the ends of the rows where the growth was less strong, because there was lack of moisture. With the ground under mulch, this problem no longer arises. But as a general precaution against troubles with beans, don't work among them, or pick them, when the foliage is wet.

We do have a problem with the huge green tomato worm, a terrifying but harmless creature where people are concerned but one that ravages tomatoes. In recent years the white cabbage caterpillar has also been a nuisance on the late cabbage and broccoli. Finding the tomato caterpillars is extremely hard; considering their enormous size, they have brought camouflage to a fine art. When we spot them, they are hand-picked. Cabbage worms are controlled fairly successfully with a rotenone dust which can safely be used up to harvest time. I now use beer to attract slugs; a dribble left in an empty (and I trust returnable) bottle laid on its side along the rows lures them. Since they go inside the bottle for the orgy, it is easier to get rid of them in a bucket of boiling water. Earwigs can be partially controlled by hanging small, inverted flowerpots on low stakes along the rows. These pests cluster in the pots by day and can again be killed by dumping them into boiling water.

Tomatoes are the only plants we stake in this particular growing area. These are grown to a single stalk, and we rub the suckers out of the leaf axils whenever we notice them. The dahlias grown for cutting are all dwarf varieties. Sometimes rabbits are a problem, and in those years we surround the growing area with wire, and very untidy it looks. What's more, I am not sure it keeps out a determined rabbit, and I think I shall stop using it.

In the fall everything comes out, and a heavy top-dressing of the new compost is put on, which smothers the few weeds that are around. The perennial edgings along the railroad ties are then cut back heavily, and any adventurous root severed by driving a spade deeply into the ground alongside these plants. This is particularly important with the mint, which otherwise spreads wildly. Pull out all the severed sections or they will happily reroot, for these are not plants that are killed by fall division! The new compost is covered with a thick fresh mulch of grass and leaves which is steadily augmented as long as the lawns have to be cut and raked. Like the flowering area, this plot has never been dug after that first rototilling nor have additional fertilizers been used. The successful intensive use we make of it tells its own story of the continued fertility of the land.

The old rose garden that originally existed in the enclosure in the country garden behind the privet hedge has also been mentioned several times in this chapter, so this seems the proper place to discuss our experience with it, and with roses in general. In the suburban garden, we inherited a few rather uninteresting climbing roses growing against the south side of the house, and these are with us still. They give a pleasant flush of flowers in early June with no extra care from me, except an occasional cutting out of deadwood. They also look perfectly presentable when the flowers are over, for they do not suffer from the disfiguring disease, "black spot," that destroys rose leaves and is now such a general menace. This seems to be one of the few advantages of the air pollution of our cities. Controlled studies suggest that the sulfur content in the air in cities acts as an inhibiting factor against this disease.

The country garden and the third garden both possessed specialized rose-growing areas mainly given over to the rather delicate bush varieties known as hybrid teas. I was quite familiar with the culture of these and indeed of most roses, for the English are mad about this plant. But I have never been very enthusiastic about rose bushes. I always have considered them a great deal of work. Also there are long periods in which rose beds are dreary, open areas with nothing in them but leafless stumps. Nevertheless when I inherited the rose garden in the country, I was not prepared to destroy something that clearly had been a great feature without giving it a fair try, so we made a determined effort to bring it back. The job was not made easy by the manner in which the roses had been grown. The bushes were set out in a dozen or more small star- and crescent-shaped beds centered around the rock. These beds called for laborious, unending hand-trimming, for they were laid out too close together for a modern mower to get between them. When I started work, the soil was almost straight sand, and many of the gnarled, ancient bushes were dead. In other cases the under stock, on which the better roses had been grafted, had taken over and little of the original graft remained. The first job was to eliminate the little beds and concentrate the remaining usable roses into two large beds, adding new bushes and also modern, stronger, multiflora varieties. The survivors were reshaped by proper pruning. At this point, I discovered that in this climate roses cannot be pruned in the fall; it is necessary to wait until spring to see what canes have survived the winter.

The potential show of flowers that we built up with all this care, in the form of fat strong buds in the spring, was excellent, but this was the only satisfaction we got out of those bushes. As soon as the buds unfolded, rose chafers descended like biblical locusts and tore the flowers to shreds. When hot weather set in, black spots appeared and denuded the canes, and the second flush of flowers on the bare branches was devoured by Japanese beetles. The whole family used to walk around that rose garden every day in the hot afternoon sun when the beetles were drowsy, knocking them off by the hundreds into coffee cans with kerosene in the bottom.

Desperate, I went for advice to the professional growers, of whom there are several in our area. Here I learned that our many and varied rose problems could be partially controlled but not necessarily cured by a regular, intensive spray program that had to be started before the leaves unfurled and continued without let-up throughout the summer. There also had to be dual-purpose sprays, some directed against black spot and other fungous diseases, and some against the pests. Even before the present unpopularity of sprays, this was more than I was prepared to undertake, particularly since I did not admire the after-effects of all this care, for the foliage of roses grown under this program was perpetually covered with an unattractive residue of the spray material, which had been mixed from highly poisonous compounds. All this went so much against the grain that we decided to give up growing bush roses, a course we also followed later in the third gar-

Rambler rose climbing up dead juniper.

den. But this is a highly personal reaction and others may not feel the same way. If you love roses, there are many books devoted to their culture which can give you detailed instructions on how to handle them.

But though I considered rose gardens too demanding, it did not mean that the garden was deprived of roses. It is the type of rose and the way it is grown that can change them from a nuisance to a delight. The country garden is in rose country. There's a small, scented, white, multiclustered rose of Japanese origin that now grows wild everywhere, scrambling high into the trees, throwing itself around in the boundary hedges, and cropping up wherever the land is sunny and left in the rough. For that reason this is also an excellent part of the world for domesticated climbing roses and we use a lot of them. Grown in a simple manner, these profusely flowering varieties need very little care except the removal of dead canes and cutting off the flower heads if the appearance of the withering petals disturbs you. I clean up the petals but I leave the flower heads, for the red haws are a great bird delicacy in the fall. The climbing roses, including the old-fashioned rambler roses that bloom later in the season, that I enjoy the most are those that are the least controlled. Climbing roses were originally planted against the cedar posts that hold up the grape arbor in the third garden. This area overlooked the rose garden of that old house, and when we took it on, the climbers had been kept rigorously cut back and tied tightly to their posts. We grassed over the rose beds (no more of that), and gave the climbing roses their freedom, and they have since worked their way up among the grapes where they get pruned if they are too much in the way, but otherwise are left alone. Now they produce a magnificent uncontrived show of flowers poking up through the grape leaves, with wands of flowers that turn toward the sun. The roots are given a feeding of fish emulsion in early spring, but that is all the care they get—and to date there has been no black spot. And this is not because we spray the grapes, we gave that up years ago.

We also have roses scrambling over the stone wall that fronts on the road, and big stands of rugosa roses along the waterfront and in the flowering shrub border. In that same border a collection of old-fashioned shrub roses was planted. These have been the least successful of my rose efforts, for they were devastated by black spot. Nowadays we enjoy the roses among the cedars on the back boundary hedge. Roses first showed up in these bushes as escapees from some planted by a neighbor. And they looked so delightful poking their flowers out unexpectedly among the dark junipers that I deliberately set some more out on our side of the line, using the bottomless box method described on page 226, but with a much deeper box. Over the years, some of those first cedars died for lack of light or overcrowding, and when this happened we used to cut them out. Now we use the dead bushes as ladders up which the roses scramble, and if the effect is mildly untidy it is also delightful! Roses have also appeared among the swamp maples in a corner of the third garden where there is a dead tree. I had rather thought of trying clematis there, but the roses got in first, though I have no idea where from.

None of these naturalistically grown roses seems to suffer the plagues that afflict their more carefully nurtured relatives. I sometimes see rose chafers or Japanese beetles on the Rugosa roses, but never many, and the ramblers are free of the disfiguring mildew that makes them unpopular today. This perhaps tells us something about the overcultivation of garden plants that we would be well advised to think about more carefully. We get great pleasure out of our casual use of roses. We could use even better varieties, but here again it is a matter of balance and a question of how much emphasis and time are to be given to any one aspect of the yard.

This is a cursory account of how to handle roses; I lay no claim to giving anyone useful new cultural advice. And if I were asked, I would say that roses are not a particularly important feature of the yard. Yet when I go through all the pictures of the children and grandchildren over the years, there are frequently roses in full flower in the background. And when I think of that garden, in the months when I am winterbound in town, I remember the scent of the wild rose and the honeysuckle that greets us when we get down. This to me epitomizes all that is delightful and endearing about the old place.

XII | Work Areas

For many people, one of the hardest places to exhibit decent self-control is in a well-stocked hardware store. The urge to take home everything in sight is almost uncontrollable.

But in spite of these violent feelings, it is a mistake to rush too enthusiastically into a tool-buying spree the moment you own a garden. It is wiser to buy only what you need for the job at hand when the need arises. Don't stock up in advance with tools that you think you may want sometime. The time may never come for that particular tool; it will become one more piece of clutter—and clutter is the novice gardener's downfall. Don't allow yourself to be talked into buying dual- or even triple-purpose tools. They may be excellent, but until you have gained some practical experience you will not get your money's worth. At first it will be a nuisance to have to go to the store each time a fresh tool is needed. But this stage does not last long, and it does make certain that you do not load yourself down with implements you never use. Furthermore it will prevent you from pricing yourself out of any further interest in gardening.

There is no point in re-listing the most basic tools, they have already been mentioned in the appropriate context. But do buy the best you can afford; this is not the place to save money on "bargains." Unfortunately the very best of the nonmechanical garden tools are imports and correspondingly expensive. If you can afford them, the money is well spent. Good tools, properly cared for, save effort and do a far better job. There is, for example, no comparison between the exhaustion that follows cutting a hedge with poorly designed hedge clippers and how you feel doing the same job with a fine, well-balanced model. The feel, or balance, of a tool in your hand is very important: to judge, think of it in terms of a tennis racquet or golf club. A badly balanced tool is unnecessarily tiring. The analogy of the golf club or tennis racquet also holds good where the handle of a gardening tool is concerned. Garden work is hard on the hands, and badly designed handles produce blisters. Be very sure before you buy that the handle is smooth and well made. I much prefer them to be of wood, though plastic-handled tools are now available. If you value your hands, steer clear of any tools with metal handles, particularly trowels that are made all in one piece with holes in the metal handle to lighten it. In my experience, the holes mark the spot where frightful blisters will appear, but serve no other purpose!

Avoid thin flexible blades on any tools that are going to be used for turning over the earth or for planting. Flexibility of this sort is not an asset. No one wants to be burdened with cumbersome, overheavy tools, though for some jobs I still far prefer an iron-bladed wooden-handled trowel. But for all heavy jobs the blade must be entirely rigid or it will not be strong enough. Don't buy full-size rakes, brooms, and hoes if you are not tall or strong. The lightweight, small-size equipment, made presumably for lightweight, small-size female gardeners, is in fact also extremely useful to tall, male, heavyweight gardeners, as my husband can attest. Often more work will get done with the small-size bamboo rake, even though it collects fewer leaves at a sweep than with the full-scale version, for one will tire less rapidly. Human nature being what it is, it is wise to paint the handles of your expensive tools a highly distinctive color as soon as you get them home. Bright orange or wild purple stripes will mark those hedge clippers as yours even from a distance! A strong color on the handle also makes it less easy to overlook tools and leave them lying outdoors in all weather, a practice that is ruinous to fine, precision equipment.

Tools, however, are only a small part of the accumulation that builds up wherever gardeners are at work. Even the most conservative, economical gardeners soon find themselves the owners of coils of hose, sprinklers in varying sizes, bales of peat moss, and bags of mulch and fertilizer, lawn mowers, spreaders, stakes, rakes, twine, bamboo sticks, and the like.

Though the equipment that piles up seems rather alarming, if you have bought it only on the as-you-need-it basis, you can feel certain that everything that accumulated is, in fact, essential. Most tools do not have built-in obsolescence; once acquired they last a lifetime. Mechanical equipment does change—usually for the better. Such things as the new electric starters on mowers and tractors are worth every penny. Nevertheless, I would never buy an expensive new mechanical tool until I had either tested it myself at home or talked to someone who had used it successfully. This is not a matter on which to accept the word of the salesman.

As the tools and the gardening mishmash begin to accumulate, a highly urgent problem of storage arises. Basements, if the house is built with one, or garages are usually the first places taken for this purpose, but they are not a complete success, for they are not designed for such use. Most garages have very little spare space, and it is maddening to have to maneuver the car around lawn mowers and tractors.

Excessively tidy people sometimes produce space for garden equipment where none exists, by arranging things so that everything is hung from the walls. Tools stored this way are a nuisance. Big equipment is heavy to lift down and worse to hang up again, and it is a bore always to have to put everything away in one exact position. Once any part of a hobby or occupation becomes a bore, all the fun goes out of it. Much the same situation applies to keeping tools in the basement, particularly if it means passing through a bulkhead door to reach them.

There are innumerable inexpensive ready-made garden huts or sheds on the market that are the best solution for the garden storage problem. There are also elaborate ready-made wooden structures available, a little like the summer houses of my youth, that have space for sitting out as well as garden storage. If you like, and can afford them, decorative wooden toolhouses, which is the way they are usually described in the brochures, can fill the double purpose of serving as an interesting visual feature of the yard as well as providing functional storage. Swimming pools today often include a shed to house the pool machinery. Sometimes it is possible to buy a somewhat larger version than the pool itself requires, in order to use it in addition for garden storage purposes.

My own preference is to have an entirely separate structure somewhere in the yard, used only for garden storage and gardening jobs, so that it can serve as the nerve center or headquarters for all garden activities. I never think that dual-purpose areas work well. Overlapping functions call for considerate, tidy self-control on the part of those who use this place. It is also important, for reasons that will be gone into later in this section, to be able to lock up the garden storage area. This is not possible when the place also has to serve another function. There should always be space in any tool shed for a padlocked hanging cupboard for electrical tools and dangerous poisons.

These are not particularly expensive requirements if the gardener is prepared to settle for an inexpensive ready-made shed. Some of these come in wood with a finished floor, some are made of metal. There are less costly models that have no flooring at all. A small yard does not mean you cannot fit in a shed. If it looks too hideous, paint it a neutral shade; there is no need to settle for the original color. Some towns have zoning regulations that deal with how near to boundary lines or roads any building can be set; most sheds will serve the gardener best if they are put as near the driveway as possible.

We have an extremely primitive tool shed of just this type —we rescued it from the previous owner who was getting ready to send it to the town dump. We found ourselves short of storage space for garden furniture when we acquired the third garden; we did not want to spend money on a pretentious building, so the battered old shed was exactly what we needed. It was put up alongside the drive to the guest house, straddling an old drainage ditch. To keep the floor dry, it had to be perched up on concrete blocks. In theory, it should be an eyesore—don't forget that it missed the dump by a matter of days—but we painted it an unobtrusive gray, put a new lock on the door, and let the wild vines of the neighborhood take over; it soon sank into being a part of the scenery. The beach chairs are stored there, and it has become so inconspicuous that visitors have to have it pointed out to them as the place to find those chairs.

If there is a choice of positions, put the shed near a water outlet, and also within reach of the compost piles. But you can always carry water to a hut and store it in covered bins, just as compost and peat moss can also be stored. What you cannot bring in without a great deal of extra expense is a hard, paved path. If there is a choice between water and a position close to the drive, I would always opt for the drive.

Before you order a shed, measure the width of your heavy equipment. It is extremely important that the door be wide enough for everything to pass through. Some sheds are sold with sliding doors. These take up less room but have a tendency to freeze in snow. This can be tiresome when you are trying to get at the snow blower. If the only possible place the shed can be put is a little damp, perch it up like ours on concrete blocks. It is always possible to hide the mechanics with inexpensive latticework, the type that still can be seen at the base of a great many old wooden porches. If the shed is raised, a small wooden ramp should be built to allow easy access for mowers, tractors, and wheelbarrows. Wooden ramps get fearfully slippery in wet weather. Always nail wooden cleats across a ramp to solve that problem.

If you have no hedge into which you can set your shed, you can mask the sides by latticework painted the same color. Make sure to treat the legs of the lattice with a strong wood preservative before sinking them in the ground. Vines, both annual or perennial, or roses can be trained on the trellis. I am not too keen on vines being grown over the building itself. Had I been able to prevent it, I would have kept them off ours, for they have found their way into the woodwork and make it hard to paint. Vines do poorly on metal sheds, the reflected heat is too great. A shed can also be quickly hidden by planting fast-growing privet along the sides and letting this reach the height that affords the most effective screen. To hide a shed year-round, evergreen shrubs should be used. I do not think that all this vanishing act is necessary. A functional place, fulfilling its purpose, automatically looks well and blends into the landscape, and this becomes even more apparent if the area around it is used as a working place for all garden jobs. Work benches and cold frames make any shed look important and intentional, as well as filling a great garden need. It is, however, important to have a hard-surfaced path leading up to it, so that the heavy machinery will not ruin the ground in front of the shed in wet weather.

Paths always present a problem in a garden. Packed gravel is hard to keep weed-free and neat; loose gravel gets equally weedy and is a danger if rotary mowers are going to cross it. And with the present shortage of labor, all gravel paths look unkempt unless the owner-gardener gives them a disproportionate amount of attention. Stepping-stones of flagstone or concrete paving blocks are easy to put down and not very expensive. Set on a lawn they are, however, inclined to sink and get covered by the grass. This calls for steady trimming as well as lifting and putting fresh soil underneath them at regular intervals. A path made of concrete paving blocks butted together looks nice in a limited, enclosed area, but unnatural snaking across a lawn. To carry heavy garden machinery, paths made of concrete blocks also need a hard, firm surface underneath them. Brick paths are fragile. They look delightful as a feature in a small rose or herb garden but, again, all wrong as a long path in an open yard. Hard-top paths look institutional, cement paths uninteresting.

This list goes to show that I am not really in a position to give good advice, for I have not solved how best to handle the matter in our own yards. In the suburban garden we have hot-top paths. We were young when we bought the house, and this was the least expensive path we could put down. We also needed paths that could easily be shoveled clear of snow. In the country there were only two paths left after I redeemed the garden from the wilderness. Both were of hard gravel

Wood path with the unnatural curve in winter.

and had been well made with a high center that sheds the rain. One was abolished when the entrance court was made; the other still leads to the back entrance and needs constant weeding and edging. For the paths through the woods we use wood chips, but these areas are totally inaccessible during the winter, and in the summer, moss and wood wildings look delightful growing along and among the chips. We do not try to have those lovely wide grass paths that are such a feature of English gardens.

Probably the best paths today are those made of concrete with some extra textural interest added either by pebbles embedded before the concrete dries, or by wire brushing— the same treatment by which the appearance of concrete is improved in outdoor living areas. All paths look better if they are wide. Two people should be able to walk comfortably abreast along a path, and it must also be able to accommodate the wheels of the widest of the garden equipment. Paths are always more attractive if they are functional and take the direct route from place to place. A path should only curve if there is some immovable object in the way—unless you are deliberately creating a *trompe l'oeil*. Our stretch of woods is extremely narrow, the path runs through it only to our neighbor's garden. To create the impression of greater depths to the little stretch of woodland, we curve the wood-chip path so that the end is lost to sight. But this is not a functional path in the sense that it is a direct route to anything, so this piece of deception is permissible. A false curve of this sort would not work in a path that led from the street to the front door and was used every day for practical purposes. In that case, people make a shortcut across the unnatural curve. The same holds true for paths that have been laid out where the owners would like visitors to walk, rather than along the actual direct route. People will not follow a path that meanders just for the sake of meandering, particularly if this is the way to the front door. No matter how often the householder rushes out and begs visitors to keep to the path, a false route will be ignored, and a worn track will eventually appear along the direct route.

In a new development it is always wise to take your time projecting where the garden paths should go; wait until it becomes obvious. In old gardens, paths sometimes cease to be useful and should be abolished. Our present policy is to have close-cut grass tracks alongside the freestanding shrubbery in the third garden and on the routes we walk to get to the waterfront. Other than that we use stepping-stones so that I can reach the working areas with dry shoes. In town we still hot-top when the old asphalt cracks. While it is not very decorative, the material has proved far the most successful in our snowy climate—and since we now have that terrace in the same dark color, it would be absurd to change.

Paths do not look well with little plantings of petunias or marigolds beside them. These get trodden on and battered and look spotty. Reserve this type of softening effect for areas around steps. If you long for softening effects beside a path, try ground-cover beds set back a little on each side. These can be filled with plants for sunny or shady places and need very little upkeep. But don't let the ground covers spill over onto the path and narrow it down; this produces a mean appearance. It is also important to remember that any plants set out beside a path in a snowy climate are going to have heavy piles of snow thrown on them when the walks are shoveled. Make sure that anything planted in such a hazardous spot is extremely tough and resilient. If you can afford it, and need a lot of paths in your garden, professional advice from a landscape architect is well worth taking.

Having provided the yard with a shed and an attractive, wide, hard-surfaced path leading up to it, what more is needed? To begin with, the shed can serve as a storage space for more than just garden tools. With so much emphasis in modern gardens on constructional patios and decks, gardeners are turning increasingly to plants in containers to provide summer color and greenery in what otherwise would be rather barren acres. An unheated shed that can be used for safe winter storage of the large evergreen shrubs and small flowering trees that can be successfully container-grown is invaluable.

Yews, weigelas, vitex, crab apples, cherries, rhododendrons, and laburnums are some of the many hardy outdoor shrubs that have flowered in big redwood tubs on our porches. The care is simple. Healthy stock is bought, bagged, and burlapped from the garden center, and planted in a tub in rich soil with plenty of drainage material at the bottom. An inch of pebbles has suited our specimens the best. The first summer the tree or bush looks a little silly since there is often more tub than bush. After the leaves fall and frost comes, the tubs are rolled away on a dolly to the unheated garden shed, where they spend the winter months with very little light and absolutely no attention from me. At the most, they may have a trickle of water if there is an unexpectedly warm spell in January, but the aim is to keep all growth entirely dormant during the winter. The earth in the tubs will freeze hard, but under cover the roots will get just enough protection to prevent their destruction from cold. When you notice that the soil in the tubs has thawed out completely and that there are signs of leaf growth, start watering, for the roots are again active. In New England, bring the tubs outside into the shade in April. If there is an unexpected snow storm they will not be hurt. Move them into the sun on the patio in May, and water and feed them regularly.

Our tubbed shrubs are top-dressed with rich soil every second year. If the branches seem to be getting rather scraggly, the flowering specimens are pruned immediately after the blossoms finish. The evergreens are reshaped after the spring growth has fully developed. For food, we use a strong concentration of that rather smelly fish emulsion in water. Recently I have also used a sludge concentrate. In hot weather we water heavily and spray the foliage regularly with cold water. With tubbed plants, as with any plant in a container, we don't water unless the soil looks and feels dry to the touch.

This is an old-fashioned way of growing excellent plants for a porch or terrace. It has been part of the European gardening tradition for centuries. The "orangeries" that were so much the rage in England and France during the

Weigelas flowering in tubs after wintering over in an unheated shed.

seventeenth and eighteenth centuries were unheated. The orange and bay trees that were wintered over in them survived because they were allowed to go through the cold weather under shelter and nearly dormant. Modern gardeners have rather forgotten this easy way to have spectacular terrace plants and provide themselves with shade.

Unheated storage for tubbed plants should be tried by beginning gardeners only with material that survives outdoors in their particular climate. No one living in a cold climate can carry on tender plants, such as tree geraniums or fuchsias, in unheated storage. These need to be wintered over in a cool, frost-free place—something that is exceptionally hard to find in most modern houses, but does sometimes exist in enclosed breezeways. As a general rule, anything that cannot live through the winter outdoors in your climate will die equally decisively in an unheated shed. But this is no reason for not trying the hardy plants and astonishing the neighborhood with tubs of flowering trees in the spring!

A garden shed should also be the place where garden jobs are planned and carried out. Garden notebooks are invaluable for those who have the self-discipline to keep them up to date. In them you record what did well, whatever special treatment you gave it, also what failed miserably. This is a great help the following season—and makes delightful reading in later years. I kept a garden book for many years; recording my mistakes and the occasional lucky breaks was an important part of my garden education. If you can't keep a diary you still should keep some sort of record. You will be a far better horticulturalist and enjoy your garden more if you do.

Sheds get hot in the summer, so I prefer to work outside. The sheds in both gardens have benches along one of the outside walls where I do a lot of gardening odd jobs. Flowerpots are stacked underneath the bench, and I keep a huge old washtub of galvanized iron at hand to clean off dirty pots. Fortunately the sheds with the workbenches are near the compost piles, but before we got the third garden this was not the case in the country garden and I stored soil in large bins. I keep a broom beside the bench and I stand on a rough, homemade wooden floor that can be kept swept clean of accumulated debris. The small hand tools are kept in a box to the side, for it is a nuisance to have to go into the shed every time I want a knife or a trowel.

There are a good many garden jobs I prefer to do standing up at a workbench; planting the bulb pans for the house is one. Most outdoor gardeners grow house plants indoors in the winter—and a work area is invaluable not only as a convenient place to summer them outdoors, but also for all the various pruning and repotting jobs that may have to be done.

Cold frames that basically are nothing more than open boxes with a hinged lid are excellent in a work area. These do the best job in a cold climate if they face due south, something that may not be possible in every working area. They will be even more effective if they are set against the wall of the shed. They should also be built so that the back is higher off the ground than the front, to allow snow to slide off and let the low winter sun shine longer into the interior. Many gardeners are a little afraid of cold frames; they think of them as miniature greenhouses demanding regular daily attention. But there is no need to be scared of a cold frame; they need extraordinarily little attention for the amount of return they give, and they are worth having even if they are used only for bringing on bulbs for the house. The way to prove this is to start with a bottomless wooden box, a large apple box will do. Put it in a sunny place, if possible with the back to a wall or building. Pile earth around the other three sides as insulation. I keep the earth in place with small-mesh wire that is pegged down with those invaluable wire clothespins made from the long side of wire coat hangers. After Christmas, for further insulation, I cover this earth around the frames with cut-off boughs from the tree.

Plant some bulbs in the usual way in a bulb pan; it does not matter whether you use plastic or clay. Water the planted pan thoroughly; this is effectively done by setting it in a pan of water until the soil at the top becomes wet. Put the

Working area in suburban garden with cold frames and a bench.

pot, or, I trust, pots, on the ground inside the box and fill up the rest of the interior with wet leaves. Cover the box with a pane of glass, and do no more. Sometime after the New Year, take a look at the bulb pans. Unless you failed to water them properly at planting time the pots will be heavily rooted and there may well be strong top-growth. You can now bring the pots indoors to a cool, dim place for the first few days, and then into a sunny window. The chances are these cold-frame pots will be the best house bulbs you have ever grown. Later in the winter, during one of the spring thaws, fill the now-empty box to within four inches of the top with soil that has been stored under cover so that it is not frozen. Make some furrows and sow lettuce, radish and even early cabbage seed. Put back the pane of glass. The seed will germinate as soon as the weather warms up and get you well ahead in the matter of spring seedling plants.

If you find this rather fun, have a larger, better frame made by a local contractor—in cold climates those ready-made metal frames are too thin. If it is possible, have an electric outlet inside the frame. There are safe, inexpensive heating cables with a built-in thermostat that can safely be spread over the bottom of the frame. These provide just enough warmth to keep the soil from freezing once the worst of the winter is over. A frame with a heating cable can be used for raising annual and perennial plants from seed as well as many vegetables. The only problem with using a cable is that the frame then needs daily attention. In warm weather the glass must be propped open so that there is good air circulation, and it is necessary to see that the ground soil does not get dried out.

I use cold frames without heat for all the house bulbs. I also use them in the suburban garden as a wintering-over place for questionably hardy garden plants such as some of the better chrysanthemums. The mild protection and dryness provided by the enclosure will get these plants through the bitter winter with no further attention until the weather warms up again. The method that has worked for me is to lift the plants before the ground freezes hard. Cut off the dead top foliage and pack the roots tightly into boxes, covering them with soil that is not too wet. The boxes are set, without further watering, into the frames and the glass left slightly open. The aim is to let the plants feel the cold and fall dormant, but to keep out the rain. When the really cold weather sets in, the glass is shut down. It is only opened if I happen to notice it steaming in a spring thaw. About mid-March, if the frames are not snow-covered, watering of the boxed plants can be started. As soon as the weather and ground really warm up, the old plants are lifted, divided, and reset in the garden. In early summer I sow seeds of biennials in the cold frame in the country garden. For many people these plants are a lot of trouble for a short return; I happen to like them, for, as I explained in Chapter XI, they form a bridge that gives me flowers in the country garden in June. Biennials can be sown straight into the garden, but started in the cold frame, they are under my eye and are far safer from hungry slugs. I don't put down the glass at this stage; there is no need.

Cold frames are also invaluable for carrying cuttings of plants and shrubs through the first difficult winter. Growing your own long-lasting shrubs from cuttings is a satisfactory, if rather slow, experience and a great money-saver. More gardeners should learn the rather simple processes involved. Once they are mastered, all that is needed is a little patience while various shrubs grow to a reasonable size in the nursery beds. If you take a regular sequence of cuttings, say half a dozen each season, you will accumulate a magnificent store of material that can be used in the garden about four years from the time you begin.

For the beginner, the deciduous shrubs that bloom in the spring and early summer are the easiest. In the North, branches from bushes with long whippy growth, such as forsythia, weigelas, kolkwitzias, and even rhododendrons, can be turned into good new plants by the process called layering. Mid-July, when the new growth of the season is ripe, is the time to try. Test the suitability of the material by bending the end of a branch. If the new green growth snaps, it is ready; if it just bends, it is not ripe enough. Choose a long branch low down on the bush and make sure that it is long enough to have at least eight inches of the end lie on the ground. Make a deep nick with a knife in the part that touches the ground. The nick has to be on the underside of the stem so that it will rest on the earth. It must be deep enough to be able to be wedged open, but not so deep that it cuts right through the branch. This takes a little practice, but it is the only difficult thing about the whole job. When you have the right combination, force the cut to stay open. You can use a stone; I normally put in part of a kitchen match. Dust the wounded area with a rooting powder. Put a pad of compost mixed with damp peat moss on the ground immediately under the wounded branch and peg the branch into this pad. I use those wire pegs from coat hangers, and I peg down the branch just in front and just behind the wound. Cover the entire soil pad and the pinned-down section of the branch with heaped-up soil. The tip end of the branch, which should extend about six inches beyond the nick, should be free of soil, while the far end of the branch must remain attached to the parent bush. That's all there is to the process as far as you are concerned; nature and time do the rest.

Shrubs vary considerably in how long it takes for roots to form around the wounded area. During this wait, which can last for two years, it is important to prevent the soil pad from drying out. Nothing else you can do will speed up the process. About a year from the time you made the layer, pull some of the earth aside and take a look. If there is a thick mass of new roots around the cut, you are on your way to the next stage. If there are no roots, put the soil back; they'll come eventually. With good roots already made, cut the link to the parent plant as close to the wound as possible. This is the second tricky stage. The layer suddenly has to depend entirely on itself for nourishment, and it sometimes goes into shock and the leaves on the tip of the branch wilt. If this happens, I cover the layer with a plastic tent for a few days. Usually the layer will take severance from the parent plant without turning a hair. But don't try to move it. Let it grow on as an individual plant where it rooted until after Labor Day. Then water the ground well and dig it up carefully. You should try to take up the new ball with so much soil that there is no injury to the feeding roots. All that remains is to transfer the little plant to the nursery area, for it is now large enough and sturdy enough to grow on. When you replant, take care that you do not change the soil level. The mark where the earth lay on the stem is the part that should be underground. During the process of forming roots, the branch tip will probably have turned upward again. When you set out the layer, the main stem will therefore already be upright. Occasionally the layered stem remains on the ground throughout the root-forming period. In that case, plant the roots so that the stem slants a little upward. Push a stake in the ground beside it and slowly straighten the branch by tying it to the stake with soft rags. This may take a little time; don't try and rush the process or you may break the branch.

Layering produces sizable plants immediately. But not all shrubs make long whippy branches that can be pegged to the ground, and to get new plants from upright bushes, cuttings have to be made. Once again the proper time of year is when the new growth is ripe, and the test is exactly the same as the one used for layering. Choose the tip end of branches that have not flowered; the side branches of deciduous shrubs make the best cuttings. Clip them about five inches long. Bring the clipped material to the workbench and put the stem ends in water, but keep the foliage dry. Prepare a clear flat, one of those small boxes in which annual plants are sold, with a fifty-fifty mixture of sharp sand and damp peat moss. Put in about two inches of this mixture and pound it down hard in the bottom of the box. Round up a length of plain cheesecloth and a large plastic bag—not the kind with holes punched in it for ventilation but the solid sort. You also need a jar of the same rooting powder that works for the layering. Make two big loops of coat-hanger wire that fit over each end of the flat.

When everything is on hand, recut the stems of the cuttings with a razor blade at a node, the place where a leaf grows. Roots form the most easily there. The shortcut of clipping the material from the bushes at a node in the first place won't work. Clippers cut with a squeezing action that bruises plant tissue, and stem ends will not form a healing scar, called a callus, from which roots grow, if the plant tissue has been bruised. After retrimming, the cuttings should be about four inches long. Dip the trimmed end in water, then into the rooting powder. Shake off the excess powder and make a hole with something like a bamboo stake in the mixture of peat moss and sand. Put the cutting in the hole with the powdered base resting on the bottom of the hole. Don't use a sharpened pencil to make the hole. A

cutting will not callus and root if it is suspended in the sand
and peat moss; the rooting medium must be pressed against
the cut end. Firm the cutting into place so that it stands upright alone. Most people fill a flat with cuttings from the
same mother plant. This means rooting will take place at
the same time, and also allows for a considerable percentage
of failure. The rootless little sprigs also form a mutual aid
society by providing necessary atmospheric humidity. To
survive, their leaves have to take in and give out moisture,
and this close association enables them to live off each other.

Water the box carefully; it is important not to get the
foliage wet, for mold is a danger. Drape the length of cheesecloth over the wire loops so that the entire box is covered.
Then slip the whole contraption into a plastic bag and tie
the end with an elastic band. The plastic will allow air to
pass in and out, keeping the atmosphere buoyant, but it
will not let the moisture in the peat moss and sand escape.
The cheesecloth will catch this water as it is drawn up and
respired by the leaves of the cuttings, and in this moist air
the stems can stay full of water. The tied-up box needs to

*Chamaecyparis being
rooted and the first
transplanting.*

be put in a warm place with plenty of bright light but not hot sunshine. Under an artificial light unit is ideal. Failing that, somewhere on the north, bright side of the working area. Sun has to be kept off the box because it heats up the air inside the plastic, which kills the cuttings. The time taken to make roots varies immensely from plant to plant. Sometimes you can tell by looking—when roots form, there is a new air of perkiness about the inhabitants of the plastic iron lung. Sometimes the only way to tell is to open the plastic and give a slight tug to a cutting. If it resists, roots have formed. Once roots start, the bag should remain shut for at least another week. After that, open it slowly. The incubator atmosphere has enabled the cuttings to survive and turn into new plants, and if they are suddenly taken out of this close atmosphere, they collapse. It usually takes at least a week before the box can come completely out of the plastic bag. During the period it is open (don't forget that moisture now can evaporate), careful watering may be needed. Keep the cuttings growing on in the box in the bright shade for a week, and during that time give them a very mild dilution of water-soluble feed—less than a quarter strength of the suggested dose.

Once the cuttings are fully accustomed to outdoor living, they can be potted individually. For this I use plastic pots, usually the three-inch size with a good drainage layer of small, broken-up clay shards. The rooted cuttings are set into rich compost, and after one good watering, all the little potted plants are usually put into a plastic garment bag held up by four stakes in the shade. They stay in it until the shock of repotting is over, which may take several days. After that, grow them in the open, still in the shade for a couple of weeks, and then slowly accustom them to the full sun. If you take the cuttings in early July, there should be potsful of lusty little shrubs fully used to sunlight in fine health by late September.

All this takes time, though it is not nearly as much trouble as it sounds when written down. But there is nothing particularly difficult about it as long as the boxes do not get mold in them. If this happens, throw the whole thing out, including the rooting medium, and wish yourself better luck next season. Even if some of the cuttings have not succumbed to the miseries, these refugees from the plague never, in my estimation, turn into good plants.

The real problem comes when cold weather approaches. These plants are outdoor shrubs, they cannot be wintered over indoors. Nor are they large enough to take the cold-storage dormancy that big plants can survive. Many gardeners make dozens of successful shrub cuttings each year, only to lose them in the first winter, for the little roots are not ready for outdoor living. This is where a cold frame is invaluable. Our newly rooted shrubs are sunk, pot and all, into the soil of an unheated frame and a cover of something like an old windowscreen is put over the top. Outdoor shrubs don't need the full protection of glass until the weather turns bitterly cold, but they do need something to deflect drying wind. When deep winter comes, cover the frames with glass but leave an air chink. There is no need for alarm if the glass gets snowed under. Darkness will not hurt the little shrubs at all. During mild spells, the little pots sometimes need water. For the most part they need no attention. In the spring count your losses. Some will have died, but nothing like all of them. The survivors will be bursting to go, with roots thrusting out of the pots. Now they are ready for the growing-on area where they can be safely left unattended until you want to use them as feature shrubs.

Evergreen cuttings can be made in exactly the same way except that some conifers do better taken later in the season. My main experience has been with ilex, yews, arborvitae, and chamaecyparis. I take the yews in late September and handle them under lights. If you have no lights, keep your conifer cuttings in their plastic bag in a bright north window. The great difference between evergreen and deciduous cuttings is the way the stem is cut. Evergreen cuttings need what is called a "heel." The sprig is pulled, not cut, from the mother plant with a piece of bark from the original plant still attached. I do this by twisting the material I want backward up the stem, away from the growing point and toward the heart of the bush. This treatment tears it off with that vital strip of bark still attached. The strip should be trimmed with a razor—it should not be more than one-half inch in length—and then it too is powdered and buried in exactly the same way and given the identical treatment in the same rooting medium I have already described. My friends use perlite and peat moss to root their cuttings with seemingly successful results. I use perlite nowadays for most of my pot soil; I am getting over my dislike of the color, but I do not have very good luck mixing it with peat moss to root cuttings. I still prefer builder's sand for that job, and this now can be bought neatly packaged at some garden centers.

Evergreens can take forever to root; sometimes I despair. As long as the foliage remains green there is hope; sometimes roots won't appear until spring. But don't be lured by spring rooting into imagining that the first winter—which then is six months away—can be spent in the growing-on area. I tried that with some rather nice yews; after a long wait I finally got them to root in April. By July the little plants were bursting out of their pots, and I was sure they were ready for outdoor life. But they were not. The cold winter soil of the open ground was too much for the new root systems; they could not get established and after all that effort I ended up with a hundred percent loss.

Most of my unusual specimen shrubs have been grown by this method. Since I am not at all a patient person, the process clearly is not too long and drawn-out. It took a couple of failures before I got my first rooted cuttings, but the sense of achievement was like giving birth. Do try it. There is nothing like a shrub border which you made, as it were, from nothing. Other gardening triumphs pale in contrast!

Since I grow a great many house plants, the working areas in both gardens have always had some lightly shaded place where shade lovers in pots can rest comfortably during the hottest weather. The perfect position for most house plants in the summer is high, light shade, the kind produced by very tall trees. This is not possible for many homeowners, and an equivalent spot for plants like orchids, gloxinias, azaleas, and the rest must be provided. Very simple lath houses do this job the best, for, like tall trees, they produce a moving shadow and the plant gets sunlight without being overwhelmed by it. Lath houses are used a lot in hot climates as a summer shelter for plants, but are not sufficiently appreciated in the North, where they are equally useful. They can be extremely simple, consisting only of four posts

Home-raised junipers and chamaecyparis in 1964 and six years later.

set in a square, with a roof over them that filters light. The roof can be made of frames over which laths have been nailed about an inch apart. Since we live where heavy winter snow is a regular occurrence, our lath roofs are removable, otherwise the winter snow would break them. In milder climates they can be a fixture.

In the suburban garden, the vital high shade exists naturally beside the work area within close range of the cold frames, and for years I summered all my house plants successfully there. After we acquired the country garden and went there for the whole summer, the house plants were moved also. As my interest in them increased, their numbers multiplied enormously, and moving them turned into a dreadful job. I now leave plants that are perfectly happy with natural rainfall in the summer months in the old area to look after themselves. These include the Christmas and

orchid cactus, all of which are hooked onto the branches of some convenient trees. I also leave the bromeliads and the huge monsteras. The orchid cactus have done better left alone than they did in the country; swinging from a tree, they are safe from slugs, which are particularly partial to the wide blades.

On our rare summer visits to town, I check the pots to see if they are too dry; if there is some danger I dunk them in a bucket until the soil is saturated. After the soil is thoroughly wet, I feed them with a weak dose of fish emulsion. The big monsteras, which are tied to trees in deep shade, can go a long time without water, and I have never had any loss of these plants left alone outdoors.

But there are plants that cannot be treated in this way, azaleas and camellias, for example, and some kind of summer resting area had to be devised for them in the country garden. This was not particularly easy. The tool shed was blazingly hot in full sun. The compost piles were far away and also a long way from water. In the end, my long-time helper and I constructed our first lath house. This was a remarkable object. It had four posts nailed together out of odds and ends, a wooden floor, and a roof made of hideous green translucent plastic. It was no beauty spot and it was extremely hot under that plastic roof, but it worked, and I did a lot of propagating in it. The main drawback was the fact that the area was so small that every time I turned around something got knocked over.

When we acquired the third piece of land we tore down this first lath house and made a new one out of one end of the grape arbor. To do this, we cut out all the vines at the far end. and replaced them with frames on which laths had been nailed. Until the lath frames were finished I used snow fencing for the roof, which was just as effective but looked less tidy. The grapevines themselves had to go because they provided too dense a shade; what was needed was moving light and shade. To have dry ground underfoot, this end of the arbor was also paved with those square cement paving blocks. This simple makeshift structure blends

Plants under lath house constructed from old grape arbor.

well with the rest of the grapevine and is not nearly as noticeable as the old one with the plastic roof. It has provided a successful proving ground for work with house plants and a summer resting area.

But not everyone has an old grape arbor that can be converted in this way—and almost everyone would object to the appearance of my first work area. Today I could build a better one, for there are several books available on the construction of garden features of this type, full of good ideas and excellent pictures; those published on the West Coast by the Sunset Book Company are outstanding.

One of the few necessities is water nearby. The lath house should also be within easy reach of the workbench. If these two essentials are not just around the corner, it will not be used, for looking after it will be a chore. For that reason, I would suggest combining a lath house with the garden shed wherever possible. This can be done quite simply by using a wall for the area to be in the deepest shade and stretching some kind of light covering, laths, reed mats, or snow fencing from the roof of the shed to a pair of posts set six or eight feet out from the wall at each end.

In cold climates where snow is a regular feature, these lightweight roofs have to come down in the winter. In milder climates where snow is no worry, a lath-house roof can be a more permanent fixture. Decorative, custom-made lath houses can also be used to feature summer-blossoming pot plants that need shade. Tuberous begonias, for example, do beautifully in them. With so much emphasis on paved areas in modern gardens, a lath house full of flowers provides an unusual and highly decorative note.

Earlier in this chapter I spoke of the need for a padlocked cupboard in every shed for the many dangerous poisons that we accumulate in order to run our gardens. Anyone who reads detective stories is well aware of the fact that arsenic was common property in garden sheds in the past. Unfortunately the past is not sufficiently past in this matter; a great many highly poisonous compounds, both old and new, are still sold freely across the counter to any casual pur-

House chrysanthemums raised from cuttings and from plants grown-on in the cutting garden.

House plants summering outdoors in high shade.

chaser of a remedy for garden pests. And these poisons are bought in frighteningly large quantities by amateur gardeners. The old garden poisons, arsenic, strychnine, nicotine, and the like, are extremely lethal if mishandled, and the frightful effects are immediately visible. For that reason we are careful how we use them. But many people still seem unaware of the potential dangers from the new chemical controls, be they sprays, vapor strips, or fumigating devices. And the long chain of environmental destruction that their overuse can set off is also forgotten.

I prefer to play extremely safe and use as little poisonous

material in our gardens as possible. And since I prefer known to unknown dangers, when and if I feel something toxic must be used, I stick to the older remedies—though I treat them with great respect. I do, for example, put down an occasional concentrate of weed-killer, as I have mentioned elsewhere. But I buy the smallest possible amount so that no residue remains to be stored after the growing season is over. This is wise practice with any pest-control material. Much of it loses its potency in time.

I used to scatter arsenical bait among the seedlings to save them from slugs, but I am not doing that anymore. One year we had a terrible scare with a grandchild who dropped his pacifier into a row of lettuce where bait had been put down. The baited area had been covered with wire for safety, but the mesh was not small enough to keep out the pacifier or his fingers. We saw the episode from the arbor and hurried across the grass. But the child, seeing a group of adults rushing toward him, was alarmed. To reassure himself, he immediately popped the tainted pacifier in his mouth! All turned out well, but the episode taught me a lesson. There are simpler baits which are equally attractive to slugs and no danger to children or pets. I have already mentioned that beer and halves of squeezed oranges, placed squeezed-side-down on the ground between the rows, also attract these pests. The garden may look mildly squalid with this type of preventive strewn around, but a little squalor is far less hard on the nervous system than a hurry call to the poison center!

I do not plant anything that will survive only if it has numerous sprayings. If some heavy insect infestation breaks out among the plants, we wait for it to work itself out. If the same problem appears the following year, we give up those plants for the time being. This does not lead to a garden full of horticultural rarities, but we prefer it that way. Asters come and go in my flower garden for that reason. There are years when I can have them for successive seasons with no trouble. Then infestations of a virus called "aster yellows" sets in—or else the roots are attacked by aphids and the plants become stunted. I do not try to grow any more asters for two years after this has happened, to give the pests time to move on. I then plant again. If the diseases reappear I pull out the plants, and put them out with the rubbish. Plants attacked by a virus should be kept off the compost.

We have grown excellent gladiolus for years, but recently the plants have been attacked by thrip. In consequence, I do not plan to have any of these plants for a couple of years, by which time I hope the infestation will have gone. This is not a scientific method of coping with plant problems. But it is a highly practical way of handling the pest problem and one that calls for a minimum of deep study or overenthusiastic controls on my part.

Gardeners must take somewhat of a live-and-let-live attitude to both pests and plant diseases if they are to have any pleasure out of their yards. It is not in anyone's power to stop all problems. Disease can be spread through the air and by a combination of climatic factors. Good sanitation, that is, the cutting down and clearing out of decaying material, can keep plant disease to a minimum, but in a bad year you can no more banish it from your garden than you can prevent yourself from ever catching cold.

Nature is a matter of balance. Slugs, snails, aphids, mealybugs, and the like eat our plants, but at the same time they too are preyed upon by natural enemies for whom they serve as a tasty meal. One of the constructive ways to attack the pest problem in a garden is to encourage the natural enemies of the worst pests—always bearing in mind that those same natural enemies can have some disadvantages for us too. In the country garden there are innumerable ladybugs and praying mantis, both invaluable scavengers of pests. We also have thousands of spiders, which are another natural ally. The spiders congregate in such numbers because there is no casual spraying. Though I feel rather strongly about webs brushing across my face when I walk outdoors in the evening, the good done by the spiders far outweighs their disadvantages.

The proliferation of ladybugs and praying mantis is due to the efforts of one of my near neighbors. He is a superb horticulturist and a dedicated organic gardener; no sprays at all are allowed in his yard. Instead he buys natural predators which he releases in his yard. In early summer, when the rest of us are picking up mail at the post office marked "Resident" or "Box Holder," he is receiving small parcels from which faint scratchings can be heard. When this happens, I know that reinforcements are on their way in the neighborhood battle of the bugs! Organic gardeners are a brotherhood who pass on to each other the news of where to buy these treasures. You and I can get in on the secret by subscribing to one of the organic gardening magazines. My neighbor has followed this excellent practice for so many years that often the new purchases find the insect pickings rather slim in his yard. So some of them move over onto our land, where, unfortunately, there is a great deal for them to eat. But even ladybugs have territorial imperatives. Each piece of land can only support a fixed ration of the insect devourers, and when the quota is filled on one piece, no more venture in. If, therefore, you buy ladybugs or praying mantis egg sacs, don't expect subsequently to find one on every twig. The strong among them will seize territory, the rest move elsewhere.

There are also plants that can help control various pests and diseases. The list is long and is the subject of an excellent book (Beatrice Trum Hunter, *Gardening Without Poison*) which those of us who are serious about reversing the dangerous trend in the environment would do well to study. My practical experience has been limited to two plants, and I can vouch for their excellent effect.

When we first took over the country garden it was ravaged by the Japanese beetle. As soon as the really hot weather set in, they boiled out of the ground in horrid iridescent turmoil, and went promptly to work ruining every bright flower on the place. Then I read somewhere that white geraniums were poisonous to these menaces, and since nothing else was doing any good, there was nothing to lose by trying. The following summer, we set white geraniums out among other plants in the herbaceous border and also on the porch. It worked. The white flowers proved a tremendous lure to the beetles, which collected around them in thousands, and to my delight were destroyed in equal thousands. Japanese beetles are now not nearly such a bother. When they were new to the area, the local wildlife and birds did not appreciate them as a food supply. This situation has changed markedly, and the beetles have almost vanished. But I am glad to know that in an emergency I can always fall back on geraniums!

Marigolds control a pestilential nuisance called "root nematodes," which collect in several different varieties in the soil and stunt plants. Marigold roots exude a substance that kills nematodes not only in their immediate vicinity but also over a large area. Nematodes became an increasing problem in the country garden, while the third garden was infested with them. But since we have taken to planting a few marigolds wherever we grow flowers or vegetables this situation has cleared up completely—while simultaneously providing me with plenty of flowers for the house.

The principal natural allies against pests are birds, which should always be encouraged. Occasionally I suspect I shock some of my more ardently ornithological friends because I think birds can be a pest in themselves; the seagulls which strew the pier with sharp broken shells dropped from a height irritate me considerably! Nevertheless birds in general are a huge benefit in every garden, and the greater variety of birds that can be attracted to a yard and induced to winter over, the greater the variety of pests they will consume. Our Japanese beetle problem dwindled away to almost nothing when the starlings learned to appreciate the grubs which are an early stage of the development of this nuisance. Both the pest and this particular bird are aliens in this land, and it took a little time for them to find each other out!

Flocks of starlings wheeling against an evening sky can be a highly romantic sight. Flocks of starlings befouling the roof and deafening the neighborhood with their chatter can be a nuisance. If I had only these two images of those birds

I might find it hard to decide whether the romantic aspect was worth the more obvious disadvantages. But when I see those same noisy flocks quartering our land, heads cocked to look for juicy grubs, I condone their other sins, manifold though they be! This is what is meant by nature being a matter of balance; you never gain a reward without taking some kind of consequence; there is nothing for free in a garden. The starlings now have to share the grubs with skunks, which have also discovered their succulence and dig for them industriously in the lawns at night. Here again I have slightly ambivalent feelings. Our lawns are weak enough, heaven knows, without innumerable skunk holes adding to the disheveled look. It is also slightly hazardous going out after dark during early fall when the skunks are hard at work. But it is thanks to the industry of skunks and starlings that I now can again grow bright-colored flowers without having them torn to pieces.

Mosquitoes are devoured by the tens of thousands by swallows and also by purple martins. It is also important to work at mosquito control yourself. Standing rainwater should never be allowed to collect anywhere on the place. After rain, walk around and make sure that there are no saucers or pots harboring even a quarter inch of water. This is where the mosquito larvae flourish. The country garden has drainage ditches in the woods and along the side boundary. If it is a very wet summer, we put a little kerosene into them to kill the larvae. Those ditches used to be full of frogs, there were bullfrogs in them too. Early in the summer they used to keep us awake with their courting songs. The frogs and tadpoles did a good job of coping with mosquito larvae. Unfortunately, they have all been killed by the overhead sprays which our town utilized against mosquitoes for several years, so we have lost a natural ally—without eliminating the pest.

Around the cookout area and the compost piles, we use rotenone sprays if the bugs get too bad and we know that we are going to be outdoors in the evening. We also anoint ourselves with various bug repellents, which do an excellent job without killing off harmless insects at the same time.

As far as possible, we try to live and let live with everything in the garden. Hornet and wasp nests are left untouched as long as they are not in a place that would endanger us. I am extremely allergic to these insects, just as I am to bees. But it would not occur to me to destroy a hive of honey bees because it is dangerous for me to be stung. I use common sense and keep my distance. The same rule should apply to the hornets and wasps, which are very useful scavengers in a garden. If a nest has to be taken, it is best done at night when the insects are all in it. We use a modern selective killer on the nest.

I can take this slow and easy approach to pest control because I am not a professional grower, and I realize that the amateur is privileged in this respect. All amateur gardeners should be aware of this advantage—the fact that it does not really matter all that much if their garden is less than perfect. There are enough of us to make a considerable difference to the ecology of the country if we will only begin at home.

At the end of each growing season, I go through the locked cupboards in the tool sheds and throw away any poisonous compounds that are not used up. Getting rid of some of the hard phosphates is a job. They should not be poured out on the ground, for that is how the long-lasting damage occurs, nor should they be emptied down a sink. Most communities also prohibit taking them out with the rubbish. If we stop to think of the difficulties facing us in disposing of these materials, maybe we will also think twice before we buy them. If you are in a quandary about getting rid of old sprays or powders, contact your local agricultural field station for advice.

The discussion of a shed and work area has covered a very big segment of outdoor gardening and has taken in many aspects of outdoor work. Every potential gardener should have a specific area where all these activities can be centered. Don't put off making such a place for your yard. Having one is often the difference between unwilling lackluster care and enthusiasm!

Coda

A garden gives you back what you put into it, physically and emotionally. There is no warranty and no formula for instant success. To be a gardener, in the sense of some kind of real involvement, calls for realism and a great deal of patience. These are virtues well worth cultivating, and they will come to the gardener of even the smallest plot. Start in a small way and build up from there; there is no need to take on everything at once. What is important is to keep any work you undertake realistically in line with your own physical capacity. When you are younger, the time you can spare for the garden may slowly increase. As you grow a little less active, it may be sensible to cut down the area that calls for active labor. But by using common sense, you can continue to garden even after you have had to retire from other outdoor activities. A tennis victory is forgotten, a golf card torn up, and your past triumphs in those fields are remembered mainly by yourself. But a garden not only keeps you at work far longer, it also stands as a monument to what you have put into it as well as to your involvement with nature in an era of ever-increasing divorce from wild things. To save what is left of our heritage we have all got to understand natural forces, how they work, and how they can be disrupted. Where better to learn this than in your garden?

Plant List

Genus | *Common Name* | Species & Variety

Aegopodium | *Bishop's-weed, Goutweed, or Ground Elder* | podograria (plain), podograria variegatum (variegated)
Ageratum | *Floss Flower*
Ajuga | *Bugle* | reptans atropurpurea
Anemone | | blanda
Antirrhinum | *Snapdragon*
Arctostaphylos | *Bearberry* | uva-ursi
Aster (Perennial) | *Michaelmas Daisy* | novae-angliae, novi-belgi
Aubrieta | *Rock-cress*
Bellis | *Daisy, English* | perennis
Berberis | *Barberry* | vulgaris
Brassia | *Mustard* | nigra
Brodiaea | *Triteleia* | uniflora
Buddleia | *Butterflybush* | alternifolia, davidii
Caladium | |
Calceolaria | *Pouch Flower*
Callistephus | *China Aster (Annual)*
Calluna | *Heather*
Camellia | | japonica, sasanqua
Campanula | *Canterbury Bells* | medium
Campsis | *Trumpetvine* | radicans
Canna | |
Caryopteris | *Blue Spires* | incana
Celastrus | *Bittersweet* | scandens
Celosia | *Cockscomb* | cristata, plumosa
Cercidiphyllum | *Katsura-tree* | japonicum
Chaenomeles | *Quince* | lagenaria sanguinea plena
Chamaecyparis | *False Cypress* | nootkatensis Glauca
Chionanthus | Fringetree | virginicus
Chionodoxa | *Glory-of-the-snow* | luciliae
Chrysanthemum | *Marguerite or Boston Daisy* | frutescens | *Ox-eye*

Daisy | leucanthemum pinnatifidum | *Florists Chrysanthemum* | morifolium

Cichorium | *Chicory* | intybus

Clarkia | *Rocky Mountain Garland* | elegans

— **Clematis** | *Old Man's Beard or Traveler's Joy* | vitalba, hybrids

Clethra | *Sweet Pepperbush or Summersweet* | alnifolia

Colchicum | *Meadow Saffron* | autumnale

Convallaria | *Lily-of-the-Valley* | majalis

Convolvulus | *Bindweed* | arvensis

Cornus | *Flowering Dogwood* | florida | *Kousa or Japanese Dogwood* | chinensis

Coronilla | *Crown Vetch*

Cosmos | | bipinnatus

Cotinus | *Smokebush* | atropurpureas

Cotoneaster | | horizontalis, divaricata

Crocosmia | *Montbretia* | crocosmaeflora

Crocus | | aureus (Dutch), vernus (Dutch), chrysanthus (species)

Crocus (Autumn) | | nudiflorus, sativus, speciosus

Cyclamen (Hardy) | | neapolitanum

Cytisus | *Warminster Broom* | praecox

— **Dahlia** | | hybrids

Delphinium | *Larkspur* | ajacis (annual), grandiflorum (perennial)

Deutzia (Dwarf) | | lemoinei compacta

— **Dianthus** | *Sweet William* | barbatus | *Carnation* | caryophyllus | *Chinese Pink* | chinensis (annual) | *Maiden Pink* | deltoides (perennial) | *Cottage Pink* | plumarius (perennial)

Dicentra | *Squirrel-corn* | canadensis

Digitalis | *Foxglove* |

Eranthis | *Winter Aconite* | hyemalis

Erica | *Heath* |

Erythronium | *Trout-lily* | americanum

Euonymus | | fortunei

Fagus sylvatica | *Copper Beech* | Atropunicea

Fern | *Hay-scented* | Dennstaedtia punctilobula | *Royal* | Osmunda regalis

Forsythia | *Golden Bells* | hybrids

Fragaria | *Strawberry (Fraise du Bois)* | virginiana

Galanthus | *Snowdrop* | nivalis

Gladiolus | | hybrids

Hedera | *English Ivy* | helix

Helianthus | *Sunflower* | annuus

Hemerocallis | *Daylily* | flava (lemon), fulva (tawny)

Hibiscus | *Rose of Sharon, Althea* | syriacus

Hieracium | *Hawkweed*

Hosta | *Funkia or Plantain-lily*
Hyacinthus | *Hyacinth* |
Hydrangea | | paniculata grandiflora
Iberis | *Candytuft* | sempervirens
Iris (Bulbous) | *Netted* | reticulata | *Siberian* | sibirica
Juniperus | *Chinese* | chinensis Pfitzeriana (spreading) | *Creeping* | horizontalis | *Eastern Red-cedar* | virginiana (tree)
Kalmia | *Sheep-laurel* | augustifolia | *Mountain-laurel* | latifolia
Koelreuteria | *Golden-rain-tree* | paniculata
Kolkwitzia | *Beautybush* | amabilis
Laburnum | *Golden-chain tree* | watereri (or vossii)
Lathyrus | *Sweet Pea* | odoratus
Lepidium | *Cress* | sativum
Leucothoe | | fontanesiana
Ligustrum | *Privet* | amurense (evergreen), vulgare (common)
Lilium | *Goldband Lily* | auratum | *Madonna Lily* | candidum |
    Easter Lily | longiflorum | *Wood Lily* | philadelphicum |
    Regal Lily | regale | *Rubellum* | rubellum | *Tiger* | tigrinum,
    hybrids
Lonicera | *Honeysuckle (Japanese)* | japonica 'Halliana'
Malus | *Crab apple* | floribunda
Mentha | *Mint*
Monarda | *Bee-balm or Oswego Tea* | didyma
Monstera | | deliciosa
Muscari | *Grape-hyacinth*
Narcissus | *Daffodils*
Oenothera | *Sundrop* | fruticosa
Ornithogalum | *Star-of-Bethlehem* | umbellatum
Pachistima | *Paxistima* | canbyi
Pachysandra | *Japanese Spurge* | terminalis (plain), terminalis
    variegata (variegated)
Papaver | *Iceland* | nudicaule | *Oriental* | orientale | *Shirley* |
    rhoe
Parthenocissus | *Virginia creeper* | quinquefolia
Petunia | | hybrids
Philadelphus | *Mock-orange* | lemoinei
Phlox | *Blue* | divaricata | *Annual* | drummondii | *Summer or Garden* | paniculata | *Creeping* | subulata
Physostegia | *False Dragonhead* | virginana
Picea | *White Spruce (Dwarf)* | glauca conica Albertiana
Pinus | *Japanese Red* | densiflora | *Mugho* | mugo (dwarf) |
    White | strobus | *Japanese Black* | thunbergii
Pittosporum | | tobira
Plantago | *Plantain* | lanceolata
Polianthes | *Tuberose* | tuberosa

Prunus | *Beach Plum* | maritima
Pyracantha | *Firethorn* | coccinea
Ranunculus | *Buttercup* | acris
Rhododendron | | catawbiense, hybrids
Rhus | *Poison-ivy* | radicans
Rosa | *Hybrid Tea* | dilecta | *Father Hugo* | hugonis | *Rambler* |
    multiflora | *Rugosa* | rugosa | *Climbing* | wichuraiana
Rubus | *Bramble (wild)* | occidentalis | *Raspberry* | idaeus
Rumex | *Dock* | acetosa
Salvia | *Scarlet Sage* | splendens
Scilla |*Wood Hyacinth* | hispanica | *Bluebell* | nutans (nonscripta)
    | *Squill* | sibirica
Sedum | *Stonecrop* | sieboldii stoloniferum
Sempervivum | *Hen-and-chickens* | tectorum
Sternbergia | | lutea
Syringa | *Lilac* | vulgaris
Tagetes | *African Marigold* | erecta | *French Marigold* | patula,
    hybrids
Taraxacum | *Dandelion* | officinale
Taxus | *English Yew* | baccata | *Japanese Upright Yew* | cuspidata
    | *Spreading Yew* | horizontalis
Thuja | *Arborvitae* | occidentalis
Thymus | *Thyme* | citriodorus (lemon), serpyllum albus
Tropaeolum | *Nasturtium* |
Tulipa | *Tulip* | clusiana (species), dasystemon (species),
    gesneriana (garden), greigii (species), kaufmanniana (species)
Vaccinium | *Blueberry* | corymbosum
Vinca | *Periwinkle or Myrtle* | minor
Viola | *Sweet White Violet* | blanda
Vitex | *Chaste-tree* | agnus-castus
Vitis | *Wild Grape* | labrusca
Weigela | | Hybrids
Zinnia | | elegans
Zygocactus | *Christmas Cactus* | truncatus

Index

sheds: tub plantings, 321–3; tools
and equipment, 314–18; work,
323
shredders, 103
shrubs, 14–16; bare-rooted, 166–7;
birds, 159, 170, 171, 203; borders
(*see also* hedges), *illus. 6,* 145 ff.;
buying, 147–8, 152–3; cabling,
158–9; cuttings, *illus. 331,* 329–
33; dormancy, 152; espaliered,
72–4; evergreen (*see* evergreens); exposure, 154–5; fences
with, 145 ff.; fertilizing, 79–80;
ground covers, 205, 206, 208 ff.,
213, 228, 234; guarantees, 151;
layering, 327–9; mulching, 156–
7; nursery area, 162–5, *illus. 163;*
overgrown, 14–15; planting,
150 ff., *illus. 155,* 166–8; planting, professional, 151–2; planting
time, 152; preplanting care, 153;
pruning, 158, 165–6; root balls,
152, 153 ff.; snow and storm
damage, 158–9, 189–90; snow
barriers, 145; soil, 59–75, 151,
153 ff., 166–7, 184; spacing and
growth, 150–1, 160–1; tub plantings, 321–3; watering, 157–8;
windbreaks for, 188–90; *see also*
shrubs, flowering; specific names
shrubs, flowering: berries, 175, 203;
borders, *illus. 6,* 175 ff., *illus.
177, 180, 183, 186, 200, 201,
270;* buying, 179–80; evergreens
with, 175, 177–9, 188; laying
out, 180 ff.; planting, 187 ff.;
pruning, 191–4; soil, 184; spacing and growth, 179 ff.; 187;
underplanting, 199; *see also*
shrubs; specific names
sludge, 258
slugs, 306, 307, 340
smokebush, 70, *illus. 71*
snapdragon, 285
snow, 13, 16, 145; on bulbs, 239,
248; ground covers and, 210–11;
mold, 112–13; on shrubs, 158–9,
189–90
snowdrop, 238, 239, 245–7
sod lawns, 99–101; *see also* lawns
soil: acidity/alkalinity (pH factor),
93–5; air supply, 66, 75; color,
67; compacted, 66, 74–5; condition, 8, 66; debris, construction,
48; debris, natural, 79–80, 82 ff.;
fertility and improvement (*see*
fertilizer, chemical; fertilizer, organic; compost, composting), 8–

9, 65, 67 ff., 138, 143; fill level,
68–9; loam, commercial, 85–6;
moisture, 64–6; poor, 69–75; subsoil, 67–8; testing, 93; texture
(tilth), 67, 75–6; top dressing,
89; topsoil, 3, 67, 68; waterlogged, 66
spiders, 341
spreaders, 106, 110–11
squirrel-corn, 248
star-of-Bethlehem, 247–8
statuary, 61–3
stepping-stones, 33, 320
stones, as mulch, 142–3
strawberries, 134
styles, casual vs. formal, 11–12
suburban house and garden, 3 ff.,
*illus. 5, 13–16, 18, illus. 59, 60,
146, 149, 172, 177, 183,
189, 192; see also* specific subjects
succulents, *illus. 255*
sugarcane, as mulch, 141
sundials, 63
sundrop, 302
sunflower, 161–2, *illus. 161,* 202
sunlight, 13–14, 64–5; *see also*
specific plant names
sweet william, 281–2
swimming pools, 9, 37, 49

terraces, *see* patios and terraces
thatching, lawns, 113
thrip, 263, 341
thyme, 133, 211, 215
tip borer, 195
tomatoes, 306, 307
tomato worm, 307
tools, *see* equipment and tools;
specific names
topsoil, 3, 67, 68; *see also* soil
trees, 14–16; fertilizing, 79; fill
around, 68–9; flowering, and
shrub border, 188, 196 ff.; fruit,
38–9; ground cover under, 224–
6, 231; ivy in, 218–20; mowing
around, 120; opening up, 197;
planting, 154, 188; pruning, 196–
200; root-pruning, 198–9; shade,
15, 38–9, 61; soil, 69–75, *illus.
71;* spacing, 151; staking, 188;
tub plantings, 321–3; underplant-
ings, 199; weeping, 200; windbreaks for, 188–90; *see also*
specific tree names
trench planting, 37, 166, *illus. 167*
triteleia, *illus. 240,* 245
tritonia, 264
trumpetvine, 4–6

A Note About the Author

Thalassa Cruso was born in 1909 and spent most of her childhood in Guildford, Surrey. She was trained in archaeology and anthropology at the London School of Economics, where she took an honors diploma in 1931. After apprenticing under Sir Mortimer Wheeler at Verulamium (St. Albans) and Professor Christopher Hawkes at Colchester, she excavated and published a report on the Iron Age Fort at Bredon Hill in Worcestershire. From 1931 to 1935 she was an Assistant Keeper at the London Museum in charge of the Costume and Nineteenth-Century Collections and the author of a book on costume. During World War II she worked for the British Consulate in Boston, where she has lived since her marriage in 1935. Throughout her varied career she has maintained an active interest in horticulture. In the fall of 1967 she launched a very successful television career with "Making Things Grow" on WGBH-TV and five affiliated New England educational stations. She is a Fellow of the Society of Antiquaries of London, a member of the Royal Archaeological Institute, the Royal Horticultural Society, the Garden Club of America, the Garden Club Federation of Massachusetts, Inc., and the Massachusetts Horticultural Society, and is a horticultural judge and the winner of many gardening and greenhouse awards. In 1969 she was awarded the Garden Club of America's Medal of Merit by the Chestnut Hill Garden Club. In 1970 she was the recipient of the Horticultural Society of New York's citation for distinguished horticultural service and the Garden Club of America's Distinguished Service Medal.

A Note on the Type

The text of this book was set in Garamond, a modern rendering of the type first cut in the sixteenth century by Claude Garamond (1510–1561). He was a pupil of Geoffroy Tory and is believed to have based his letters on the Venetian models, although he introduced a number of important differences, and it is to him we owe the type which we know as Old Style. He gave to his letters a certain elegance and a feeling of movement which won for their creator an immediate reputation and the patronage of the French King Francis I.